FRENCH HUM

fond regards
for the
humoriste extraordinair

J.

Cover drawing
Seward Green

FAUX TITRE

Etudes
de langue et littérature françaises
publiées

sous la direction de Keith Busby,
M.J. Freeman, Sjef Houppermans,
Paul Pelckmans et Co Vet

No. 164

Amsterdam - Atlanta, GA 1999

FRENCH HUMOUR

Papers based on a Colloquium held in the
French Department of the University of Bristol,
November 30th 1996

Edited by

John Parkin

♾ Le papier sur lequel le présent ouvrage est imprimé remplit les prescriptions de "ISO 9706:1994, Information et documentation - Papier pour
documents - Prescriptions pour la permanence".

ISBN: 90-420-0586-6
©Editions Rodopi B.V., Amsterdam - Atlanta, GA 1999
Printed in The Netherlands

List of contributors

Keith Cameron is Professor of French and Renaissance Studies at the University of Exeter. He has published widely in the field of Renaissance literature, history and thought, as well as on Computer Assisted Language Learning, the French language, and in the area of European studies. In 1993 he edited a collection of essays on "Humour & History" (Intellect, Oxford).

Caroline Cooper is sometime lecturer in film studies at the University of North London. Her publications range from German literature to European art cinema and film studies, with a particular emphasis on filming fiction.

Keith Foley is senior lecturer in French at the University of Strathclyde. He has published extensively in the field of French lexicology and lexicography including major contributions to the Collins Robert Comprehensive French-English English-French Dictionary (1995). His book *A Dictionary of Cricketing Terminology* was published in 1998.

Michael Freeman is Professor of French Language and Literature at the University of Bristol. He has published widely on early modern authors in French, particularly Guillaume Coquillart, Pierre de Larivey, Etienne Jodelle, Rabelais and Villon.

William Howarth is Emeritus Professor of French at the University of Bristol. He is best known for his work on French theatre and theatre history which includes books on Molière, Beaumarchais, French Romantic drama and Anouilh.

John Parkin is senior lecturer in French at the University of Bristol. He has published on a variety of themes relevant to humour, including books on Rabelais, his influence, and theories of humour in the twentieth century.

Walter Redfern is Professor of French at the University of Reading. He is renowned for his books on twentieth-century French writers including Nizan, Sartre, Queneau, Vallès, Giono and Tournier, and has also written theoretical works concerning pun and cliché.

Alison Williams is lecturer in French at the University of Wales Swansea. In 1998 she was awarded a doctorate by the University of Bristol for her thesis entitled "Tricksters and Pranksters in Medieval and Renaissance French and German literature".

Contents

The wiles and woes of marriage as depicted in this famous text
are re-examined with special reference to female language and
female sexuality. These areas of self-expression are prime among
the means whereby its shrewish women defeat their male
opponents to the consternation of the narrator – if not in fact of
the reader or author – as they turn what are traditionally held to be
flaws in womankind to their own comic advantage. The moral
implications of this process provide an interesting lesson in satiric
practice: are we (as women or men) eager to defend the hapless
victim, or are we indifferent to him; and by what considerations
are we motivated in taking up either option? Do we despise the
cuckold in the tradition of Latin societies? Do we protect him by
counter-attacking in his name on the viragos who are outsmarting
him? Do we regard each participant in the text as equally
unfortunate, marriage itself being the problem? Do we see the
stories as so distant from reality that no serious comment is
relevant to them? Or is there a further choice available to those
who feel an instinctive affinity with the victim figure, however
low he may fall in the eyes of a hostile society and readership?

It is perhaps inevitable, given the enduring popularity of Johan
Huizinga's classic *The Waning of the Middle Ages*, that those who
do not specialise in fifteenth-century France should continue to
think of it as a period of decline and decadence. But a closer
inspection of the literature of the time reveals that there is also
much laughter. It was for the most part of a raucous and vulgar
kind, however, which did not appeal to the tastes of nineteenth-
century scholars when they "rediscovered" the period. For this
reason the abundant literary output which indulges in jokes and
playfulness has been generally misrepresented. By looking in
particular at the work of François Villon and Guillaume
Coquillart, it is possible to investigate the nature of contemporary

humour and see how it depended on a form of complicity with its audience. The overriding characteristic would appear to be a certain knowingness (which suggests a level of sophistication) and a celebration – often with tongue in cheek – of materialism (which suggests a level of prosperity). It reflects an urban, educated culture. It was also centred on Paris, at a time when the city was enjoying its post-Hundred Years War boom. Puns, innuendo, verbal humour relying on shared knowledge and assumptions, these are the typical devices of comic writing both in satirical poetry and in farce theatre. What becomes clear is that the humour of the fifteenth century in France is a natural prelude to that of the sixteenth. It also helps to explain the background to Rabelais' style, tastes and technique. The object of this chapter is to show that it is an over-simplification to see the waning of the Middle Ages in an entirely negative light.

Rabelais was France's greatest comic genius. Bergson was France's most famous theorist of humour. Yet *Le Rire* uses Rabelais only once for illustrative purposes, the main reason being that Bergsonian theory cannot accommodate the kind of humour which Rabelais was attempting most frequently to generate, one whose ambiguities defy the coercive and conformist tendencies which Bergson attempts to impose on his subject-matter, often, to be fair, with considerable success. However, those whose humour, or sense of humour, resists conformity and coercion will be less persuaded by the Bergsonian approach, and more attracted to Bakhtinian theories of liberation, whereby Rabelaisian laughter is grounded in a cyclic temporality in which a community renews itself irrespective of the social values it sustains in terms of serious living. Against the temporality of responsible life, whose humour is value-based and corrective, and the temporality of festive revelry, whose humour negates values and celebrates anti-heroes, one can also, moreover, set the temporality of the individual moment, as sustained via the imagination rather than the conscience or the collective spirit. The humour of this third kind depends on the spontaneous enrichment of the circumstances in which it is generated, creating a famous comic instance – of which there are many in *Gargantua* and

Pantagruel – out of a set of themes and elements which, though recognisable in themselves, are but the raw materials rather than the defining principles of great humour.

Defied by much of Rabelais, Bergsonian techniques are highly relevant to a more representative and value-based satirist such as La Bruyère, whose negative comments concerning Rabelais are famous. In arguing for the social utility of satire, moreover, La Bruyère is begging the question, for to insist that satire is a punitive mode is not the same thing as to demand that the punishment it implies be socially useful or desirable. The punishment in the alternative mode of clan-based satire relates not to values (whereby one mocks what is wrong), but to identities (whereby one mocks what is different), and much of the humour within closed societies (La Bruyère's Versailles in particular) has traditionally been of this kind. The satirist aims at least in part to encourage his readers to join the clan whose comic self-expression his satire represents, whilst also claiming, via his narrator, that the values his satire purports to uphold are worth supporting, whether or not he or his reader in fact believe this. Skilful technique will enhance the success of both procedures, and it is instructive to examine how La Bruyère's satire is more effective in manipulating his readers' loyalties and convictions, than are his moral pronouncements convincing in the way they seek to impose conclusions on his readers' responses.

French humour can be seen as particularly favourable to satire and caricature, and this in periods as far apart as the Religious Wars and the reign of Napoleon III. These humorous modes intend to amuse an audience while discrediting a target, and, as unashamedly partisan, they are applied vigorously to the illicit and semi-licit campaigns of opposition during the Second Empire, often employing and exploiting scurrilous and unfounded accusations in their attacks on the Emperor and several members of his family. Such satiric techniques can be traced back at least to the Roman period, and they are theorised in treatises of classical rhetoric. What they create is a humour which stimulates political awareness via a campaign of systematic and witty defamation and deformation. In the process humour is overtaken by ridicule, and ridicule by unremitting hostility, the skilled caricaturist and satirist having a potential influence on opinion which is quite as dangerous as it has been felt to be by the authorities who have so often persecuted and condemned them.

Bergson's *Le Rire* focuses on a more limited subject than its title suggests: the subtitle *"Essai sur la signification du comique"* is a better guide to its real subject, which is an analysis of the nature of French comic drama. This chapter considers the originality of Bergson's formula "du mécanique plaqué sur du vivant" against a background of the long-standing debate between the intellectualist and the moralist explanations of laughter, arguing that *Le Rire* stands on that side of the debate which sees laughter as essentially a spontaneous phenomenon, not morally motivated, and supports the view (not advanced by Bergson) that corrective elements in comic drama properly belong not to the element of *le comique* (laughter) but to *la comédie* (plot, characterisation, etc.). Looking ahead to some of the more important theorists of the twentieth century, and extending his survey beyond the central thesis of *Le Rire*, the author examines contrasts between concepts such as ludic and mimetic comedy, laughing at and laughing with, and *le comique (français)* and *l'humour (britannique)*. His conclusion is that while many leading theorists since Bergson have chosen to reject certain aspects of the latter's argument, very few have been able to disregard it.

This text seeks to analyse an area of humour often under-examined: bad jokes. It is not merely a knocking-job, for a necessary counterpart and criterion is the good joke. It makes a comparison with Proust's Dr Cottard, expert in misplaced, mistimed witticisms. Throughout it looks for metajokes: the internal commentary of the very self-aware author on the comic business being enacted. Joking is linked up with the various *modi vivendi* (and *moriendi*) displayed in Beckett's writings; life itself is seen as a bad joke, perpetrated by a Creator with a peculiar sense of humour. Where relevant, Beckett's French or English versions of his texts written in the other language are conned for cross-evaluation, as is the effect of his recurrent pedantry on his style of joke-creation. Other humour traditions under consideration are: the "Joe Miller" (or chestnut), dirty jokes, talking parrots. Other theorists or comparable practitioners of humour adduced include (ineluctably) Bergson, Michel Tournier, Céline and Queneau. Various kinds of punning relevant to Beckett are considered: puns as bargains (two meanings for the price of one word or phrase, an economy attractive to so laconic a writer as Beckett); inadvertent puns; macaronic play between languages; and recycled, literalised idioms.

The detective fiction of Frédéric Dard, writing under the pseudonym of San-Antonio, enjoys a wide readership and has done so for nearly five decades. The enduring popularity of this prolific author may be attributed at least as much to his ludic style as to the intricacies and interest of his plots, for Dard is a master of the art of verbal humour. The vicissitudes of the supersleuth *commissaire* San-Antonio, and of his various sidekicks and paramours, provide a convenient framework for the author to display his verbal gymnastics. In a jubilatory celebration of language, Dard exploits its humorous potential to the full, as puns, malapropisms, neologisms, reconfigured clichés and literary allusions jostle for room on the page. Dard has a particular predilection for comparisons, but rarely employs stock similes without embellishing them in some way. This chapter describes the stylistic mechanisms by which Dard seeks to enhance the impact of his similes.

Questions about humour, gender and cinematic comedy are taken as a theoretical framework for exploration of some early films by Truffaut, Chabrol and Godard. Bearing marks of art cinema (laconic narratives, characters with existential anxieties, low-budget cinematography) and of a certain self-conscious Frenchness (*l'amour*, Paris in springtime), films such as *Jules et Jim*, *Tirez sur le pianiste*, or *Pierrot le fou* usually play to laughs. They also have certain superficial similarities to romantic comedy, particularly in their humorous play with conventional gender roles. But their basic narratives, lacking conventional happy endings, and their underlying theme of the impossibility of communication between the sexes relate these films surprisingly closely to the potential tragedy of Hollywood melodrama.

Introduction

On comprend pourquoi les Anglais n'aiment guère disserter sur l'humour

R. Escarpit

French humour: the very title of our 1996 colloquium was problematic. Why is it that the French need an anglicism to designate a phenomenon whose history dates back way beyond the earliest *points de repère* here represented, namely the marital and sexual humour of the *Quinze Joies de Mariage* (see Parkin and Williams) and those other laughing matters evident in the waning Middle Ages (see Freeman)? Though to some extent the French are still laughing at the same things, and in the same ways, such traditions are older than the term which we here use to describe them.

Perhaps no other term is broad enough. At one remote time a humour was something you were – a comic type, as portrayed for our comic delectation by authors like Theophrastus, Ben Jonson or La Bruyère, and as theorised in moral terms by Aristotle's *Ethics* 2.7 concerning the braggart, the buffoon, the flatterer, the cross-patch, etc. But this sense, once general, only survived in England, whilst the French root *humeur* grew in a separate direction. Humour then became something you possessed if you were English, having, for instance, a sense of humour, which was in part the ability to laugh at oneself when recognising a particular comic quirkiness (an English humour) in one's own behaviour. Thereupon the English term, now specialised in this way, found itself readmitted to eighteenth-century French as *l'humour*, a noun designating some type of humour which developed within one's taste for matters English, witness the Anglophile Voltaire, who yet insisted that comedy did not travel:

> nos voisins les Anglais ... ont un terme pour signifier cette plaisanterie, ce vrai comique, cette gaieté, cette urbanité, ces saillies qui échappent à un homme sans qu'il s'en doute; & ils rendent cette idée par le mot *humeur, humour* qu'ils prononcent *yumor*; ils croient qu'ils ont seuls cette humeur, & que les autres nations n'ont point de terme pour exprimer ce caractère d'esprit.[1]

However the meanings assigned to *l'humour*, by Voltaire and others, were ill-defined and even contradictory – to my mind they still are – and, accordingly, could not be limited to English culture alone, a point Voltaire was quick to make in the same letter. Not merely some-

thing sought out, heard and enjoyed in the company of Pope or the
coffee-houses of Samuel Johnson's London, humour has become and has
remained, and in both French and English, something one may create,
generate or perpetuate wherever one goes, in varied forms and genres,
and to no small degree on one's own terms. Accordingly we now find
humorists (first attested 1596) and *humoristes* (first attested 1842) operating within a vast range of contexts and media, and inspiring a vast
range of comic effects and traditions, among them *l'humour noir, le rire
jaune* (see Redfern), *l'humour anglais*, and... French humour. Some
might consider the term to be overloaded, see Gifford on "Humour and
the French mind", for whom "the entire semantic field of the laughable"
is now threatened by *humour*;[2] however in particular terms it is hard to
be hard in one's distinctions, see the opening speaker at a Paris
colloquium of 1988:

> L'humour français lui-même est spécifique; il se différencie assez nettement de
> l'humour anglais ou anglo-saxon, même s'il convient de nuancer en fonction des
> époques, des genres, des milieux, des auteurs, et s'il convient de ne pas trop
> enfermer les choses dans des stéréotypes nationaux figés;[3]

– perhaps a reservation the French tend to observe less than fully.

So it remains an open, though far from nugatory, question whether
humour is best used as a broad term designating risible incongruity (certainly my own preference), or rather as a specific pattern within that area,
and one to be set alongside *le comique, l'esprit*, irony, satire, badinage,
mockery, burlesque, and any other terms within its semantic field
(clearly Howarth's preference, if not that of others whose theoretical
approach is less defined). Are these latter patterns merely subsets within
the global category of humour, or does humour by definition differ from
the bawdy of Rabelais, satire in Molière, Voltairean wit, Stendhalian
irony, the absurdities of Jarry, or the comical clown who was Coluche?

We made no attempt to resolve this open question, but asked only
of our contributors that they accept our general title, and then ride their
own hobby-horse wearing its somewhat bland colours. What emerged
was a rich set of contributions, none of which lacked its own theoretical
emphasis, but none of which managed, or indeed sought, to refute any of
its fellows. To this extent our endeavours were strongly practical, nay
empirical in the best English sense, moreover it would be a poor student
of humour who took himself, his approach (or his editor) too seriously.
As editor, moreover, my predilection, if not my job, is still to set the
terms of reference as broadly as possible, so letting French humour be
the humour of the French, to wit that set of incongruous situations and

behaviour-patterns which have consistently made French people laugh, and have accordingly left an ineffaceable mark on their culture.

I repeat: the phenomenon of French humour, however broadly or closely defined, existed centuries before the term *l'humour français* was coined. The *fabliaux* are proof enough: though their stock themes and comic victims appealed immensely, via Boccaccio, Chaucer, nay ultimately Cervantes, to non-French readerships, there must be reasons, social if not also psychological, why it was in France and within a relatively limited time-span that they were produced so abundantly, along with a strong tradition of medieval comedy in Latin, where the depiction of female wiles and the accompanying *hominis confusio* topos were as rich as they would be centuries later in Molière.[4] In between came abundant treatments of comic folly, a massive exploitation of the humour of the grotesque – on stage, in representative art, and in living spectacle – a varied set of parodies which guyed serious genres, serious thought and serious patterns of behaviour, plus such enduring masterpieces as the *Roman de la rose* and the *Roman de Renard*, whose humour was no less influential throughout Europe than the said *fabliaux* on which they also draw.

To seek a specifically French spirit within all this material is as hazardous as to claim that the *gaulois* spirit itself is uniquely Gallic:

> A ne considérer même que la littérature européenne du Moyen Age, il est évident que les pays scandinaves avec leurs *sagas*, que l'Allemagne avec des *Carmina Burana* et des contes courtois, que l'Angleterre de Gautier Map et de Chaucer, que l'Espagne du Romancero ou le l'archiprêtre de Hita, que l'Italie des *Rime giullaresche* ou des conteurs florentins en offrent bien des exemples. Voir dans l'esprit gaulois un trait proprement national, c'est, semble-t-il, prêter foi à un mythe.[5]

Hence, ultimately, Coquillart, Villon, Marot and Rabelais – archetypal exponents of *la gauloiserie* – did but trade in a common European market-place of themes and tropes where, for example, the cuckolded husband, the crafty trickster and the bawdy or shrewish wife, humours in the original sense, had long been laughable, and to many other cultures than their own. At the same time, their choice of material is significant. As great French humorists they are capitalising on a response and appetite for that kind of clever but irreverent, witty and individualistic mockery which perpetually reappears in French culture even if France has never enjoyed its monopoly: Villon and Renaud, or at worst their personae, would have got on like a house on fire, and Marot could have written verse for the *Canard Enchaîné*.

To this extent the *Quinze Joies de Mariage* is an interesting staging-post between a vast number of Medieval humorists who happened to be French, and the patriotic Humanists of the sixteenth century who were self-consciously French and anxious to establish an emancipated culture in which comedy too should flourish. It adopts stock medieval themes and can, via its harshness and its misogyny, be read into a context of French humour arguably different from the (English?) spirit of Chaucer with his "consistent overall sense of life, one of attained optimism fostered by a genial and tranquil spirit".[6] Unlike, perhaps, *The Wife of Bath's Tale* the *Quinze Joies* scarcely incite optimism: in reading them one enters a world where negative values predominate, and the "Comedy ... is a representation of inferior people ... a species of the base or ugly."[7]

But must one's reading be so linear? If the comedy depends on ridicule, is the humour (if that distinction be accepted) found not merely in the comical incongruity implicit in any marriage (see Cooper's treatment of Truffaut and Godard), nor in the cheap but deep laughs associated with the unblocking of the sexual taboo (see Foley on the *grivois* puns of San-Antonio, the dirtier the better), but also in the fact that with part of one's mind one is egging the wife on to ever more outrageous feats and exploits, while with another part one is somehow reassured by the fact that the husband's failure to control her is so abject? To do so is not necessarily to diminish the "roughness, satire, and unsympathetic sanity, of medieval comic tales"[8] by reading pathos and sympathy into their comic modes. Our contribution intended to problematise the satire by recognising its ambiguity, and so explain its appeal, which again was international: an English edition was printed in 1509 to be followed by German and Italian versions. At the same time this may be but a specifically English reading (nay misreading) of an archetypally French text in which one mocks the failed spouses as pitilessly and unremittingly as one did the ailing Charlemagne in the later Chansons de Geste, or the mad hero in *La Folie Tristan*.

Need I emphasise, gentle reader, that there is nothing which limits this pattern to the Middle Ages, or indeed to its waning? Read Marcel Aymé for proof. Read Thurber for additional proof, recalling that "French critics often picked up elements of humor in American writers such as Poe ... that serious American critics had missed."[9] The author, narrator and hapless cuckold of the *Quinze Joies* are but momentary encounters on a journey which will lead us through the Renaissance, where its traditional themes reappeared in Marguerite de Navarre's

Heptaméron, and on into the company of Georges Brassens – an emblematic figure of French unorthodoxy, too little known outside his country, but now revered in eponymous squares, streets and Metro stations; greater love hath no French *municipalité*: "Une chanson de Georges Brassens, c'est ... une force de la nature qui bouscule les conventions et qui vous fouette le sang."[10] But can one not say as much of many a chapter of Rabelais, an epistle of Marot, a strophe of Villon? The gentle bawdy and the saucy language are the same, enlivening the depiction of a similar range of comic types drawn from humble village and urban life, and all centred on the (comic?) inevitability of emotional and sexual disasters befalling the characters, most particularly the males. Such humour is coloured by wistful melancholy and a wry smile: "il finira misérablement ses jours", for "il n'y a pas d'amour heureux."

Looking more positively, we would also see the *Quinze Joies* as an uncompromising expression of female solidarity on its own terms, inverting male supremacy in a carnivalesque pattern which again requires little illustration. *Toutes conventions bousculées*, women come out on top, whether or not they in fact deserve to, and the text thus inverts another standard pattern whereby, traditionally, female humour (like *l'humour anglais*?) is coloured by self-criticism rather than self-assertion: see Cooper once more in her comments on the comic patterns in modern cinema. The man who laughs in recognition of his fellow-man's hapless disgrace is running against the aggressive mood often associated with male, macho, Latin wit. Meanwhile the woman who uses derisive humour to defend her sex may be defying the pattern of feminine self-deprecation, but in doing so she is fitting into a pattern of feminist counter-attack by now decades old, whether or not it was French in origin. Her negative side is sketched by Baudelaire's depiction of "cette garce dangereuse et fascinante dont toute la puissance vient du défi qu'elle ose lancer à l'univers tout entier";[11] her positive side is elaborated in Hélène Cixous' (endless?) series of novels through which echoes the *rire de la Méduse*.

Sexual stereotypes may vary through the ages, but a society upholding monogamy will always enjoy comic treatments of adultery, moreover a Catholic society will always enjoy licentious humour, being less outraged than pleased to catch its bigwigs *en flagrant du lit*: Marguerite tells stories against her own brother Francis I, while Clinton would have fared better in the Elysée than in the White House. Accordingly, *l'érotisme* having oft been seen as a defining element in French culture, it is interesting to read Freeman, and his quoted authorities, building the patterns of sexual banter and verbal inventiveness into what we may now see as positive and healthy trends in the Zeitgeist of an epoch once wrongly depicted as a *néant* where "l'âme ... a la nausée d'elle-même".[12] In contrast to this trend, the ludic hilarity of the latter decades of the fifteenth century becomes a sign of a social optimism concomitant with boom economies and post-war expansion, and those who saw the "vieille gaieté française" as having died at this time were missing the point in quite interesting ways.[13] Freeman shows how that same *gaieté* survived, but what interests him (and me) as much as that fact itself, is the reason why it was once so airily dismissed. It is both curious and instructive to see Michelet argue that Medieval farce is un-funny ("trop malheureux pour faire rire"),[14] and that even Pathelin is a symbol of "la misère irrémédiable du temps".[15] In his wake a consensus grew in the late nineteenth century which chose to ignore the bawdy revelry of Coquillart and Villon, seed-bed of Rabelaisian humour, and to insist that the comic culture of late Medieval France was coloured by malevolence, filth and bad taste.

One factor stimulating this consensus is a predisposition to look for moral lessons within humour, and, when they are not to be found, to denounce the humorist or humorous tradition concerned as cynical, vulgar or empty. And a key figure who emerges at this juncture is the most famous French humour theorist (*hélas*!?), Henri Bergson, named by six of our contributors, and a main subject for two of them. Bergson, to be fair, does not argue that humour must be morally edifying; indeed the psychological roots of laughter remain for him a slightly worrying mystery:

> Le rire ne peut pas être absolument juste ... il ne doit pas non plus être bon. Il a pour fonction d'intimider en humiliant ... Peut-être vaudra-t-il mieux que nous n'approfondissions pas trop ce point ... Nous verrions ... bien vite un peu d'égoïsme, et, derrière l'égoïsme lui-même ... je ne sais quel pessimisme naissant qui s'affirme de plus en plus.[16]

What he does argue, however, is that laughter must be derisive and corrective in its function, scorning and punishing the aberrant comic figure, and that is a presupposition that I have sought to refute, here using Rabelais, and elsewhere in more general terms.[17] Where I agree entirely with Freeman is in the notion that humour can be used as a means of establishing complicity (see the feminist conspiracy which can be seen lurking behind the comedy of the *Quinze Joies*), and hence his use of such phrases as "amused admiration", "affectionate satire" and "a collective sense of happy foolishness": all of these qualities presuppose shared enjoyment, and rather more readily than they do spite, venom or acrimony.

Where I should like to see a further advance is in the re-examination of my own sense of comic temporalities. Insofar as laughter is punitive (and it can be), so it seeks to achieve an end or goal, which is to use time in a linear sense whereby things are done so as to realise an effective and definitive purpose. Against this temporality one can, however, set that whereby events move cyclically, returning to the same patterns, or, for our purposes, to the same stock comic scenes and scenarios, without any goal being sought or intended: the motive is to re-create a mood even in defiance of value-based aims. Thirdly one can see the comic event as discrete: a moment independent of both cyclic and linear patterns, existing in an imaginative stasis wherein Villon is forever writing out his *Testament*, Panurge forever raving in panic through the *Quart livre* storm, or Renaud forever singing the comic praises of that ludicrous menagerie which inhabits – and will forever inhabit – his HLM.

In the particular context of Freeman's chosen period, it is intriguing to note how those theorists to whom he is opposed sought to read a sense of destructive malice (and hence linear temporality) into a humour which he would read into the cyclic temporality of a period and a society which were laughing with joy; for happy times were here again. Rabelais, for my money France's if not Europe's greatest comic genius, exudes this sense of joy in a context where religious division and persecution threaten it, and, moreover, the principles, beliefs and lives of himself, his fellows and sympathisers. Between the end of the Hundred Years War and the death of Henry II (which came not long after Rabelais' own) a century of political and administrative effort had created a recognisable nation-state on which its intellectuals and artists were, by the 1550s, imposing a sense of cultural identity which only gained full self-confidence in Bourbon France after the political survival of that state had been finally guaranteed. But this came over sixty years later. Meanwhile Rabelais' work owes its barely imaginable richness in part to a number of contradictions implicit in his period: the textual gaiety set against the sombre crisis which led to open war, the co-existence of popular humour and deep philosophical awareness, the fulfilment of a great comic talent in a work which is unfinished, in-harmonious, and barbarously unclassical despite its intense reverence for ancient authors. Rabelais belongs to a European culture by which again he was very swiftly adopted, but his reflection of the compromises and ambiguities of the flawed glories of Renaissance France makes him a uniquely fascinating object of study.

Extending this ego-trip into my chapter on La Bruyère enables me to reset the balance of modes and temporalities, moreover, and see how seventeenth-century satire, perhaps unlike fifteenth-century gaiety, Renaissance merriment or the humour of Augustan England, was value-based and corrective in a way which predetermined Bergsonian theory and rejected Rabelaisian practice. A culture which had regained political and institutional confidence, sanitised its taste, and produced a series of works by authors, Molière included, who were justly revered as great in their own time, preconditions La Bruyère's laughter as targeted, derisive and, by intention, corrective, an object lesson in how "La société se venge par lui des libertés qu'on a prises avec elle";[18] and accordingly the combination he achieves wherein biting sarcasm is delivered in light refined language has been seen as peculiar to, if not definitive of, French wit.[19] La Bruyère's very satires of snobbery and court élitism may be taken as signs of the social stability he and that court enjoyed: was he not in part the guilty conscience of his own era?

It is important, however, to respect the complexities of satire, even while limiting it in this way. To stimulate a value-based response to a comical incongruity is what a satirist like La Bruyère intends, however within that response there can be many competing and even conflicting elements, all dependent on our mood, personality or individual decisions: be we French, aristocratic, or whatever, if we set our faces against a particular satirist's approach, there may well be little he can do about it. These elements I would seek to class into two groups, hopefully a flexible enough approach to be applied to as wide a variety of humorists as we here consider, if not even more widely.

The first group are the value-systems intrinsic in satiric positions, these being at the primary level very obvious and superficial. A *caractère* may be pompous, fat, ugly, inept, rustic, loutish, etc., and, to catch the eye, the caricature outlines at least one such quality immed-iately. Behind this primary value-system lie others, moreover, some of which will reinforce the comic effect, and compound the satiric felony: a courtier may not merely be fat and ugly, but vain and envious with it, like the Baron de Guéret in Patrice Leconte's film *Ridicule* (1996), which is an interesting modern portrait of the very environment which La Bruyère studied first hand. Meanwhile still other value-systems may mitigate the punitive effect, rendering the victim not contemptible, so much as endearing, naïve or pitiable, as when Guéret is outsmarted by a cleverer man, but reveals at that moment a human weakness which leads him to immediate suicide.

So much for values: they can reinforce one another, as they do in Tartuffe, or conflict with one another, as they do in Alceste, and they have varying degrees of depth and power. But satire can also be clan-based, a point we have already made concerning the *Quinze Joies*. Yes, the husband is wimpish, stupid, gullible, spineless and all the things we mock him for: but to what extent is the satire we direct at him not in fact determined by his belonging to a certain clan, be it the clan of cuckolds, the clan of married men, nay even the clan of men in general; and is it not this identity (rather than any value-judgements which we make beyond the primary ones) which makes our comic response to him so powerful?

Ditto Villon's targets, to move on through our volume. We perceive qualities which we deride in Jehan Cotart (perhaps), in Franc Gontier (perhaps) and certainly in the arch-enemy Thibaut d'Aussigny. But clearly we are relatively indifferent to them as figures in themselves, and what produces the vigour in our response is the fact that they are set in the clan of Villon's enemies, while we ourselves join the clan of his friends, all in the spirit of Freeman's comic complicity and for the duration of our enjoyment of the text. With Panurge the problem is more complicated still. Rabelais satirises him in a number of ways, using visual effects (his dress), linguistic effects (his verbiage), and moral effects (his behaviour), all to compound our hostility in different forms and degrees. However the clan-loyalty of the Pantagruelistes mitigates this same reaction to the same extent as can a positive value-response nuance value-based satire: one forgives one's team-mate a stupid mistake much more readily than one does the clumsy tackle of an opponent. Moreover, to the extent that we too are Pantagruelistes, so we are drawn, by degrees which vary depending on our own choices and our own capacity for indulgence, towards the same group response. If we are not quite ready to defend Panurge *contra mundum*, we are certainly not required by Rabelais to bully him scornfully out of the text, or back into conformity with the norm of moderation which Rabelais, in serious mode, tends to uphold.

The term "serious mode" is, however, vitally significant, for it is just not true that all humour aims to reimpose those norms which society requires for its effective continuance, and which satirists such as La Bruyère (and philosophers such as Bergson) use as the basis of their comic practice and theory: Breton declared in his *Anthologie de l'humour noir* that "il ne peut être question d'expliciter l'humour et de le faire servir à des fins didactiques",[20] moreover to find a humour of "transgression" one does not need seek out Rimbaud, Jarry and Céline: La Fontaine supplies it.[21] So too does the greatest comic talent of his age, Molière, at least insofar as he perpetually supports the young (ever the triumphant clan in comedy) against the old (whose role, as often as not, is to shut their traps or be cast out). Again this pattern has very little in it that is archetypally French, for it dates back to Aristophanes and the origins of ritual drama;[22] however the adaptation which Molière applied to it, juxtaposing the clan loyalties structuring his comic plots with the value-systems implied by their development and articulated by the figures enacting them, helps create that fruitful ambiguity which is the whole essence of live comedy in whatever language and tradition. Hence even when examining "Social Structures in Molière's Theater", and fitting them into an intricate defence of the social patterns of the *Ancien Régime*, Gaines still sees the playwright as "refusing to construct his plays according to a single rigid behavioral standard."[23]

By Molière the voice of reason was set against unreason (a value-based position), while the sexual and mythic power of youth stood opposed to the social and material power of age (a clan-based dichotomy). When, as in the eighteenth century, these oppositions are given a political dimension, as for instance, in Voltaire's polemical *contes* or Beaumarchais' Figaro, the satiric pattern shifts further towards the node of values and away from the node of clans, but never to the point of exclusion. Speaking generally, one might argue that the irreverence patterning so much French humour, a pattern transgressive rather than conformist, is in the *Philosophes*' case legitimised by their critical perspective on the status quo: they can afford the luxury of the libertine insofar as their enemies are guilty of much greater crimes, hypocrisy among them. However this suggestion does not exhaust the issue, for in part the *ingénus* of Montesquieu, Voltaire and Diderot serve not to catalyse but to negate serious living, in which sense we admire less the way in which their comic feats reveal the follies of a society in need of transformation, than the way in which those same feats remain indifferent to sane standards and adult values, nay indeed invert those very standards and qualities. Who is to say that we should not love our comic hero, be he Panurge, Harpagon, Candide or the neveu de Rameau, not in spite of his weaknesses, but because of them?

To this extent French humour is a cultural conspiracy to defend certain anti-heroes (from Reynard the Fox to Pierrot le Fou, via Pierre

Faifeu, Sganarelle, Jacques le Fataliste and Bouvard et Pécuchet) and in defiance of the incomprehension of outsider clans, and of the norms governing serious life. Thus may a culture totemise a figure of fun (Astérix, for example) not because he is in some way admirable, but simply in order to assert a cultural identity of which in reality it is less than certain, meanwhile the fun enjoyed may simply discard the values and norms which structure serious social behaviour. Such humour, celebrating a comic hero, is not satiric in any definable way, however its obverse, whereby a culture may scapegoat a comic villain simply because he is foreign ("étrangler l'étranger" as Marcel Duchamp had it) is close to the essence of clan-based satire, and indeed with Cameron's study of the humour of caricature and propaganda in the Second Empire (plus glances at the Valois Monarchy) we are resolutely back in satiric phase. The series of *vignettes* he examines, comprising written sketches and graphic illustrations, confront us with a humour seemingly uncontaminated by love of the *ingénu* or the rebel, and which he analyses less in terms of a theory of humour than in terms of technique, topicality and effect.

What emerges is a trend of satire considerably less restrained than La Bruyère's and far less ambiguous than that of the great humorists of the Enlightenment, though bearing rich analogy with France in the sixteenth century, and some with Imperial Rome. The satirists concerned, who were applying satiric value-systems while addressing a clan of humorous co-conspirators, develop a kind of humour of obloquy by whose conventions very few limits are set around the permissible grounds for attack. In a society as radically divided as France in the 1860s (nay France in the 1580s) it is an easy option to superimpose the nodes of clan-based and value-based satire and give one's satiric target no reprieve. Physical appearance, private behaviour, official acts, family connexions, all are used as sources of ammunition against him, as he is seen failing on every value-scale that the caricaturist feels ready to apply, and the pattern is so one-sided that it could be seen as not humour at all, but instead polemical indictment: Cameron makes that very point in his conclusion.

Incongruity, the *sine qua non* of humour, is there in the "departure from the norm" to which he refers,[24] and it is identical to the primary value-system defined above. However incongruity alone is not enough to guarantee a humorous effect, otherwise life's little ironies (and their victims, be they paraplegics, quadriplegics or mutants) would be far funnier than they truly are. The question which Cameron raises via his distinctions between polemic and humour, and between humour, ridicule and indictment, is therefore an important one. What element is lost when a humorous incongruity becomes an incongruity of one of these other, less pleasurable kinds? Or, to reverse the equation, what element must be added to a primary incongruity (a boy with grotesquely fat lips, a woman naked on a billiard-table, three severed heads dripping blood) in order to make it risible? Furthermore, emphasising the context of French satire, might we not ask if these patterns, as examined by Cameron in his chosen area, while pre-empting comic sympathy and comic celebration, and bridging two epochs which are hundreds of years apart, do not again reveal a particularly Gallic form of aggressive comedy, apparent in Villon's assaults on his enemies, as much as in the violent pugnacity of today's alternative press. I have before me a June 1998 number of *Charly Hebdo* which, prior to the unexpected French victory at the Mondial, denounced all football fans as morons, and the entire tournament as a commercial conspiracy of which the supporters – especially the foreign ones – were witless victims: "L'immigration footballistique. Le seuil de crétinisme est dépassé ... Le pays de Victor Hugo accueille 500000 Quasimodos."[25] By contrast some would certainly see the ability to "chuckle at our own follies through another"[26] as characteristic of *l'humour anglais*.

The satire of obloquy is thus both value-based and clan-based. Just as Villon's satires will not work unless, for the duration of the gag, one joins the clan of his comic henchmen, so the satire attacking Louis Napoleon is so one-sided that it presupposes in those who respond to it an unremitting hostility, in fact a hostility which has lost all reasonable sense of proportion. As a sermon to the converted, so it is scripted for a clan who are united in their opposition to the satiric victim, and woe betide that clan member who tries to invoke the ultimate value-system of loving-kindness towards that victim, or who sees that there is an ultimate clan of humankind beyond the divisions which separate the Bonapartist from his enemy (or the French fan from the foreigner). He will be shouted down, if the humour survives his intrusion. Otherwise he will stifle the humour: but does this make him a kill-joy, or instead a significant spokesman for the muzzled voice of conscience?

Bergson, as we have seen, was not insensitive to the moral ambiguities of humour. Essentially a student of satire, he certainly never reduced his subject to a straightforward moral didactics, indeed the function of "intimider en humiliant" belongs more clearly to satire in its clan-based than in its value-based mode. At the same time, Bergson never appreciated or integrated fully the notion of a *rire-détente*, which he certainly raises in his book, and which is exhibited by so many of the patterns of humour displayed in our studies: it is because we need not take them and their implications fully seriously that the comic scenes and figures in Coquillart, Rabelais and the figures in the *Quinze Joies* are so enjoyable, while the broadening of our cultural tolerance necessitated by a reading of Villon, nay even by the indulgence of obloquies drawn from a bygone age, may be a way of dissolving *égoïsme* rather than affirming it. However the fact that Bergson narrowed the range of his enquiry so greatly that he missed such points, does not mean that *Le Rire* is a worthless text. As Howarth says, a whole wealth of theorists would argue for its fundamental importance; moreover, given that our volume coincides virtually with its centenary, it is appropriate that at least one chapter be devoted to his positive reappraisal.

Howarth concentrates on Bergson's relevance to comic drama, a not inappropriate restriction given their shared preference for Molière, meanwhile the notion of comic catharsis to which he refers in his apparatus and his chapter has considerable philosophical and psychological importance. Has laughter a corrective function (which, for me, is true, in part at least, of the satiric mode), or is it merely an intuitive response to incongruity, as is argued by Pascal, Kant, Schopenhauer and, in certain sections of his text, by Bergson as well, given that he does not at first present the perceived clash of *le mécanique* and *le vivant*, source of all comic laughter, as implying a value judgement?

This is the implication which Howarth then seeks to deepen, using in his support an impressive range of authorities and examples. The essence of his argument is that the incongruity giving rise to laughter (*le comique*) only gains a moral, corrective or didactic dimension as a result of subsidiary factors which a dramatist (dare one say humorist?) may add into his comic scenes, thus creating *la comédie*. I must say that I entirely agree, though I wonder if Bergson would. However whilst Howarth pursues his point by rehearsing a number of binary oppositions applied by others (ludic/mimetic, the absolute comic/the significative comic, laughing at/laughing with, *le comique/l'humour*, etc.), I would find common ground with him to the extent that incongruity lies at the basis of all comic effects (and thus of all humour), but whilst that incongruity can imply the imposition of value-judgements, as in value-based satire, it can also reflect the release from those value-judgements, as in what I have elsewhere called parody.[27]

This is why Villon, Coquillart and Rabelais stand aside from Molière as interpreted by Bergson: because they are parodists, that is exponents of the humour of release, rather more than are they satirists, that is exponents of the humour of correction: I wonder to what extent Redfern would in fact read Beckett into the same comic mode. The problem is, of course, that there are rich satirical elements within them as well (how could it be otherwise in the work of great writers?), hence the Screechian reading of Rabelais (which is entirely valid on its own terms), plus the traditional misreadings of Freeman's favoured authors: they were reviled in the nineteenth century as being third-rate satirists because the scholars of that period could not accept the spirit of parody which they embodied, specifically in the way in which they released those taboos on bawdy and scatology which pervaded the era of Michelet, if not that of Lanson, Huizinga and Bergson himself.

What is more, Howarth then goes on to show how a parodic reading of Molière has developed, under the specific aegis of Bakhtin, though once again with only partial success, for it negates (I would say) the satire on which the Bergsonian reading capitalises. There is a mixture of both satiric and parodic patterns in Molière, and the individual director, actor and reader make their choices accordingly. Howarth's final binary distinction operates between *l'humour* and *le comique*, the latter being Bergson's home ground, the former being something "quintessentially English". Once again, moreover, he remains laudably unconvinced by absolute distinctions – for indeed is anything quintessentially anything? – noting, by implication, how comic raillery is to be found in English humour, just as Voltaire in no small measure appreciated the urbane wit which he discovered outre-Manche, but only because it was already a part of his own sense of humour.

What is more, is Beckett a Frenchman? Or, in studying him, are we not examining humour *in* French rather than humour *of* the French? Putting it yet another way, *Watt* does it matter in which language he drafted and crafted his works? Beckett certainly commanded his adoptive language to an impressive extent, but at the same time was able, as humorist, to exploit the incongruity whereby he used it in the first place. After all, as a member of that perpetually scapegoated clan of Irishmen, he was also a natural, even willing, victim of his (step-)mother tongue, meanwhile drawing, like Joyce, Wilde and Synge, on several of its richest veins of humour – Irish wit, Irish blarney, Irish folklore. For all that, as Redfern shows, some of his jokes, bad as well as good, defy translation and are thus best dropped from the second version of a work, be this the French or the English reading.

It all goes to show that no-one is true master of his own vernacular, as Redfern, Beckett and Austin severally observe, but there are many points raised by our chapter seven which have little to do with language per se. Redfern once again sees the shortcomings of Bergson, and of the nineteenth-century consensus which influenced him even as he reacted against it. Surely Beckett would have laughed himself silly had anyone suggested that his humour must, by definition, exert a corrective social pressure on a target, moreover that assumption was simply one of the "inhibitions of morality and didacticism" which French humour had been struggling against since Flaubert,[28] to the end that a detectable complacency within French philosophical thinking in the nineteenth century (Comte's if not Bergson's, for example) was exploded, as Camus implied: "Cette raison universelle, pratique ou morale, ce déterminisme, ces catégories qui expliquent tout, ont de quoi faire rire l'homme honnête."[29] By contrast, the *humour noir* which Beckett can most easily be seen to enshrine was first identified within our own century, and its nihilistic derivatives are resolutely post-Bergsonian, if not post-war.

Redfern drives their implications even deeper, however, while never losing touch with French analogues such as Queneau, Céline, nay even Proust and Descartes. The absurd perspective which radical nihilism looks out on makes a mockery of humanity itself, and life becomes just a big joke at our own expense, a joke the more perplexing for there having been no-one who cracked it in the first place. For Homeric laughter, in the sense of laughter of the Gods, presupposes that someone – like Molière's Jupiter (in *Amphitryon*), or Voltaire's Micromégas – is mocking us from on high, satirising us on the basis of his own superior values, or from the security of the clan of the immortals. But albeit as mere metaphors for the values they invoke, those gods do at least exist for their authors, whereas if they ain't even there, then the joke is even better (or worse), for the value-basis or clan-basis of the satire is revealed as non-existent: in fact even Molière can in places be read as dissolving "all established truths and values into illusions",[30] meanwhile is Camus' Sisyphus not in the end just a bloody fool?[31]

This in turn, however, helps question the supremacy of satire as a mode of humour, something I am anxious to do in my own chapter on La Bruyère. Once humour no longer bears the sanction of seriously held values (or sincerely respected clans, such as the reasonable and devout *honnêtes hommes* of the seventeenth century, the enlightened *lumières* of the eighteenth century, or the bourgeois positivists of the nineteenth century), is it not free to negate or invert those values via the parodic mode, even up to the level of the "risus purus" of which Beckett writes in *Watt*? In Beckett such parody involves the inversion of the writer's deference towards his reader, the undermining of his own self-respect, the kind of textual self-destruction threatening both absurdist theatre and fiction, and, perhaps, the inane giggles, rather than anguished hysteria, with which children, relatively untouched by adult values, react to a world which they do not comprehend and never asked to belong to. It is a moot point whether such effects are therapeutic, as releasing emotional pressure, rather than punitive, as enforcing emotional pressure (Bergson again). Redfern's final suggestion whereby humour, and particularly humour at this advanced level, in fact confronts one with reality, rather than allowing one to escape from reality, is one I have met before,[32] but not one I find easy to theorise away.

With Foley's author San-Antonio we are faced with bilingualism of a different kind. This is a Frenchman masquerading as an American thriller writer, but using his own language – or at least three hundred words of it – to compose his books. Again there are rich analogues to this novelist within French literature – among others, Céline, Queneau and Rabelais reappear – and in general the aim is to challenge conventional patterns of fiction, of language and of author/reader relations: one could say exactly the same of Céline, Queneau, Rabelais and Beckett. Obviously San-Antonio, or his persona, aims slightly lower than them in terms of genre, though Rabelais' works were in part a burlesque of the popular reading of his day. At the same time, Foley makes the point that Dard has a sneaking desire to be taken seriously: a trait not uncommon among French mockers of the Establishment.

Seen seriously, San-Antonio is struggling, like all European writers, to maintain a cultural identity independent of the universalising trend of popular American culture and its version of the English language. Hence his puns are at once a celebration of the French tongue – Guiraud's *Les Jeux de mots* is strewn with references to him – and at the same time cock a snook at *le sabir atlantique*:[33] "il crée ainsi un féminin insolite à musul*man* sous forme de musul*woman*, et transforme water*loo* en water*leau*."[34] Besides this pattern one finds in him a concern with sex, food and drink, themes which recur in French humour not always to the delight of those encountering it, while the *humour noir* is also there, see the Sing-Sing joke,[35] plus the semi-political jibes at the police and the Church, again traditional out-groups subjected to the clan-based satire of generations of French wise-crackers: after all a "romancier poli ne vaut pas un roman policier".[36] Alternatively, his preoccupation with health and *médicaments* is something we might build into our own satire of our Gallic neighbours: would we English be as amused by the simile "She was as pleased as if she were having a spleen op. without anaesthetic"?[37] Perhaps it depends on who tells it.

In fact, quite apart from all the verbal quips which Foley takes as his particular subject, the self-conscious travesty of the *policier* genre, with its hard-bitten protagonist and numskull side-kick, plus the deliberate over-sophistication of the narratorial and authorial voices, set incongruously among all the stock themes I have mentioned, are enough to generate our interest in an author who not only writes wittily, but also generates humour around this process, having his narrator tell us how hard it is proving to keep us amused. For me, however, and yet again, this is humour of a non-satiric kind. Despite serious inferences we can enjoy the jokes partly because they express no serious issues. We more than likely do not care who the targets are, they being, as often as not, merely the standard butts for ridicule we have seen before (more cuck-olds, more sexual inadequates), while such clan solidarity as guarantees a good part of the satire in Villon, La Bruyère and Cameron's various propagandists, is here sent up. Comic complicity is a theme in the meta-text: it is a moot point whether it operates genuinely within the humour.

Equally sophisticated is the humour of the New Wave *cinéastes*, who capitalise, like San-Antonio's burlesques of the *série noire*, on a fund of stock themes and tropes which are so standardised as to be funny enough in themselves. This too is an important part of France's struggle for cultural autonomy, for is not a Cary Grant comedy very close to *du mécanique plaqué sur du vivant*, and a George Raft *film noir* even closer? Yet the market remains the market – a resolutely internationalised threat to minority groups and movements – and what Cooper argues is that the French directors of her choice sought to exploit an attitude towards commercial cinema which was already incongruous – mocking and yet reverent at the same time – while overlaying its patterns with a highly self-conscious Frenchness, itself partly generated by commercialism and cultural stereotyping. Their French humour was thus at once a product of their own satiric wit and parodic lack of inhibition, and a concession to what foreigners might expect of the very genre they were bent on founding: sexual titillation, urban settings, racy dialogue, stock Parisian character-types.

The incongruity lies variously in the inconsequentiality with which these patterns are asserted, assorted and then put in question, challenging realism, but often with comic intent and result, and, to import once more my own approaches, I see the different temporal patterns as here of vital interest. To what extent are films like *Pierrot le fou* or *Tirez sur le pianiste* merely a series of comic sketches (pertaining to the temporality of the chronon), to what extent are they mocking the linear temporality of melodrama (see the way *Jules et Jim* and *Pierrot le fou* end in violent death), and to what extent do they belong to the cyclic temporality of comedy as defined by Northrop Frye (quoted by Cooper), for whom it is a mode which is always integrative, ending in marriage and thus emphasising human time in the cycle of generations?

Insofar as a New Wave film imposes preposterous tragedy on a comic paradigm, so it is inverting norms in a way which, for me, is characteristic of parody rather than satire, and indeed I feel that the spirit of New Wave cinema is not to aim at particular targets – Cooper makes the point that the directors were only superficially political – other than in adopting the same old Aunt Sallies we have met before: the cuckold, the ageing booby, the would-be Don Juan who is yet totally dependent on the women he affects to despise. To a great extent these figures are arraigned in the spirit of carnival, and it is a moot point to what extent the cinema, even the art-house cinema, is one of the surviving chronotopes of modern-day carnivalesque, in France or elsewhere: Cooper is right to quote Bakhtin in this regard. Additional carnival elements are the sexual ambiguity, the arbitrary violence, the seemingly pointless travesty and laughter, and the celebration of folly, which is quite clearly articulated by Chabrol.[38] Moreover at the same time as perpetuating the carnival spirit, these same films set it in question by using grotesque and ugly mask effects, showing us group entertainments which are manifestly failing, and presenting bawdy in a spirit which renders it depressing and sick rather than invigorating and healthy.

This is a very important cultural issue for France and her humour and for the rest of Europe: to what extent have the disappearance or narrowing of traditional folkloric modes and the carnival seasons in which they functioned been compensated by the appearance of new comic modes, sites and media such as the comedy club, the *café-théâtre*, the televised sitcom, graffiti, chat-lines and websites? Such developments have not resolved, but simply problematised the point of parodic humour and the meaning and transformation of carnival, and I am far from convinced that they aim at "celebrating and reinforcing the norms which are supposedly being mocked".[39] However this is a bigger issue than I have the time (nay the wit) to resolve. Easier to decide on is Cooper's reading of feminist elements into the complex comic patterning of her material – especially in the celebration of womanhood by Truffaut, and the satire of bourgeoisified sexual relations and discourse apparent in Godard and Chabrol. However, like Redfern on Beckett, she is reluctant to see these comic themes as unambiguously positive in their development, and how could it be otherwise when the *cinéastes* concerned are men, who, while raising great laughs, are also sounding the death-knell of that cultural supremacy which has given them (as men) their voice in the first place?

For all its archetypal patterns (including that of women on top) their humour will not fit easily with the mythos of spring. Is theirs not a hollow laughter rather than a rich laughter, issuing from individual disquiet as much as from collective security? Maybe so, but at least its mocking of the victim husband (*Tirez sur le pianiste*), its subversion of male alliances by a feisty jade (*Jules et Jim*), and its debunking of romantic love (*Les Bonnes Femmes*), allow our own volume to come full circle. These are but some of the *trente-six chagrins du mariage* which have always made French people laugh. Now why is that?

---

[1] Letter to d'Olivet, 20th August 1761. Cf. *Lettres Philosophiques*, 19: "On ne rit point dans une traduction. Si vous voulez connaître la comédie anglaise, il n'y a d'autre moyen pour cela, que d'aller à Londres, d'y rester trois ans, d'apprendre bien l'anglais et de voir la comédie tous les jours."

[2] P. Gifford, *art. cit.*, *Modern Language Review*, 76 (1981), 534-548 (p. 538).

[3] S. Faranjus, "Allocution d'ouverture", published in *Humoresques*, vol. 1 (Nice, 1990), 16-22 (p. 19).

[4] I. Thomson, "Latin 'Elegiac Comedy' of the Twelfth Century" (in P. G. Ruggiers, ed., *Versions of Medieval Comedy* (U. of Oklahoma Press, 1977)) notes the existence of some twenty such texts, all probably by Frenchmen, and all probably by clerics.

[5] P. Ménard, *Le Rire et le sourire dans le roman courtois en France au moyen âge* (Geneva, 1969), p. 15.

[6] T. J. Garbaty, "Chaucer and Comedy", in Ruggiers, 1977, pp. 173-190 (p. 190).

[7] Aristotle, *Poetics*, 5.1 (Loeb, 1927).

[8] cf. D. Brewer, "Notes toward a theory of medieval comedy", in *Medieval Comic Tales* (Cambridge, 1973), p. 141, concerning Romantic readings of early humorists.

[9] J. C. Austin, *American Humor in France* (Iowa State UP., 1978), p. 7.

[10] P. Benhamou, "L'Humour de Georges Brassens", *Thalia* 3.1 (1980), 17-20, p. 17.

[11] A.-M. Soucy, "Le Rire dans l'oeuvre de Baudelaire", *Thalia* 9.2 (1987), 32-39, p. 34.

[12] J. Michelet, *La Renaissance* (Paris, 1899), p. 31.

[13] cf. *infra*, p. 41.

[14] Michelet, *op. cit.*, p. 29.

[15] *Ibid.*, p. 37.

[16] *Le Rire* (Paris, 1947), pp. 151-2.

[17] q.v. J. Parkin, *Humour Theorists of the Twentieth Century* (Lewiston, 1997), c. 1.

[18] *Le Rire*, p. 150.

[19] q.v. H. Baudin *et al.*, "Humor in France", in *National Styles of Humor*, ed. A. Ziv (New York, 1988), p. 54.

[20] A. Breton, *op. cit.* (Paris, 1972), p. 11.

[21] q.v. F. Fabre, "La Fontaine s'amuse", *Thalia* 4.1 (1981), 33-39 (p. 38).

[22] See the treatment in F. L. Lawrence, *Molière: the Comedy of Unreason* (Tulane UP., 1968).

[23] J. F. Gaines, *op. cit.* (Ohio State UP, 1984), p. 82.

[24] q.v. *infra*, p. 135.

[25] *Charly Hebdo*, no. 311, pp. 2-3.

[26] cf. *infra*, p. 135.

[27] q.v. *Humour Theorists of the Twentieth Century*, c. 2.

[28] q.v. R. B. Henkle, "Beckett and the Comedy of Bourgeois Experience", *Thalia* 3.1 (1980), 35-39 (p. 37).

[29] A. Camus, *Le Mythe de Sisyphe* (Paris, 1942), p. 36.

[30] R. McBride, *The Sceptical Vision of Molière* (London, 1977), p. 166.

[31] cf. "La conquête ou le jeu, l'amour innombrable, la révolte absurde, ce sont des hommages que l'homme rend à sa dignité dans une campagne où il est déjà vaincu": *op. cit.*, p. 127.

[32] e.g. in H. Halkin's Introduction to Sholem Aleichem's *Tevye the Dairyman* (New York, 1987), p. xi: "It was consistently his method ... to confront the reader with reality in its full harshness, laughter being for him the explosive with which he systematically mined all escape routes away from the truth."

[33] q.v. R. Etiemble's *Parlez-vous franglais* (Paris, 1964), an early satire of a trend forever preoccupying French literati.

[34] P. Guiraud, *op. cit.* (Paris, 1976), p. 15.

[35] q.v. *infra*, p. 183.

[36] Guiraud, *op. cit.*, p. 50.

[37] q.v. *infra*, p. 188.

[38] q.v. *infra*, p. 214.

[39] *Ibid.*

1. Feminine wiles and masculine woes: sexual dynamics in *Les Quinze Joies de Mariage*

Alison Williams and John Parkin

The family and the marital relationship which created it were the basic social unit in medieval society. It must follow that the dynamics of action and discourse operating between husband and wife would exert an influence not only on patterns of personal power and control, but also on the gender roles effective in the wider contexts of extended family, neighbourhood and town, and finally, for our purposes, on the humorous portrayals to which these social patterns gave rise. Taking account of these factors, our consideration of sexual dynamics in *Les Quinze Joies de Mariage* will take as its focus the ambivalent function of feminine wiles and their use in enticing and manipulating the husband, and in ultimately eroding his male identity as traditionally represented, the wife or wives seeking throughout the text to subvert the power-structures of the domestic environment. Secondly it will consider the implications of this fundamentally comic process for the male archetype as portrayed in the *Quinze Joies*, he being in virtually every way an inversion of the various hero figures of medieval culture, and never once a master in his own home.

Feminine wiles in *Les Quinze Joies de Mariage* may be divided into two broad categories, these being the exploitation of language, and the granting or withholding of sexual favours. It is immediately apparent that these are two areas of female behaviour which established medieval opinion sought to limit. A variety of authorities and literary sources called both for restrictions on female movement and self-expression outside the domestic sphere on the basis that such freedom would lead to attacks on the already weakly defended chastity of women, and for restrictions on female speech which was popularly represented as being an incoherent, overwhelming mass of sound. St Paul gives the lead for this when demanding that "no woman ... have authority over man; she is to keep silent",[1] an attack which the misogynic clerics extend throughout the Middle Ages,[2] while, in the late Renaissance, the models of Cordelia, with a voice "ever soft, gentle, and low", and the shrew Katherina with her "loud alarums" provide lessons too obvious to require illustration. Meanwhile a Classical precedent for the approach can be found in Juvenal's sixth *Satire* where the author treats the problems of articulate learning, and portrays the linguistic consequences of women acquiring too much education:

> The grammarians make way before her; the rhetoricians give in; the whole crowd is silenced; no lawyer, no auctioneer will get a word in, no, nor any other woman. So torrential is her speech that you would think that all the pots and bells were being clashed together. Let no one more blow a trumpet or clash a cymbal: one woman will be able to bring succour to the labouring moon.[3]

Feminine language, satirised in these terms, is an example of a pattern standard in the *Quinze Joies* whereby, for comic purposes, the most effective weapons in the repertoire of feminine wiles are those characteristics that were most frequently regarded as flaws in women's nature. Rather than satirising women straightforwardly, it is a key strategy in the text to convert these female flaws into a variety of skills, using which the wives achieve dominance in the various scenes depicted from married life. The implication of this pattern for the analysis of humour within the text is more than significant, for the process is not a challenge to the popular conception of female nature, but instead supports it, appropriating the faults traditionally ascribed to woman and turning them into effective tools for the subversion of male authority, in fact that very male authority which supported, nay created the medieval consensus opposing women, plus Juvenal's satiric archetype, not to say Paul's and Shakespeare's lessons. However, though the text can be read as anti-feminist satire, this reading is not one demanded by the author, to the extent that, unlike Katherina, the rebel wife or wives in the *Quinze Joies* are never brought to their knees, or indeed anywhere near them.

In a behaviour-pattern as standard in modern Europe as in medieval, if the wife is to suffer confinement to the domestic sphere, she will appropriate it for herself and re-write its terms of reference to suit her wishes. The comic results of this process are illustrated as much by the television sitcoms of today as by the *fabliaux* of the 12th century, for in that process the wife effectively destabilises the home, forming alliances with servants, children and neighbours to challenge the position of the husband as head of the household, meanwhile the wives of the *Quinze Joies* both possess and wield the power to bestow or withhold the comforts and favours which a husband might expect to enjoy on returning home. Thus we see various scenes of him sitting furthest away from the fire (*4e Joye*) or having to satisfy his hunger by eating the scraps of meat left on the plates of the wife's friends who throughout the day have enjoyed hospitality at his expense (*3e Joye*). The home, far from being a place of refuge after the toils of the working day, becomes a battlefield for supremacy in a game of wit – a game in which he clearly loses every round – or else a trap into which the ever-devoted suitor or the ever-docile husband will fall, accepting thenceforth a passive role much like that of a domestic animal: he becomes an ass or a horse, so well inured to the goad or spur that he no longer feels them, see the *4e Joye*:

> Mes y est adurcy come ung veil asne, qui, par acoustumance, endure l'aguillon, pour lequel il ne haste gueres son pas qu'il a acoustumé d'aller. (27) [4]

Hence as the wives seek to establish new terms of reference for the sexual dynamics of the home, so the husbands are assigned new roles in the comic distortion of the home that these same dynamics affect. It make take two or three years (*14e Joye*), it make take thirty years (*9e Joye*), but in the end they are forcibly domesticated in a process rather like a taming of the shrew in reverse, and immediate evidence of this reversal is provided by the repeated use of the verb *dompter*: in the *3e Joye* a reputedly tyrannical spouse has been *dompté* to the point where he would dread nothing more than to cross his wife in word or deed (20), in the *12e Joye* he defers to her on all matters and decisions, being as *dompté* as an ox at the plough (90). The wife has expected all along to have a monopoly of the *autorité* and *seigneurie* of the household, hence her partner is reduced to a role which recalls that of the ideal wife: silent, acquiescent, consoling the children when she beats them, and ever trying to fulfil the wishes of the spouse, particularly by cooking her favourite dishes (22). The new man of our generation would be hard to find anywhere in the fifteenth century, let alone in this text, hence the language used to describe the husband's plight reflects not a wish to equalise the spouses' status, but rather a desire to relegate the man to a subordinate role which is comical in being so incongruous: the phrase *wearing the breeches* ("porter les braies") is actually used in the *10e Joye* (80), and woe betide the husband who commits adultery himself, and so lays himself open to his wife's revenge (83). Furthermore such subordination is even to be seen as unnatural, hence the animal metaphors repeatedly likening the husband to passive and stupid beasts fit only for slaughter, burden, or exploitation; and still more demeaning is the pattern of metaphor whereby he is deprived even of the dignity of the animal kingdom, and likened to a gutter through which passes the water of female chatter, as in this description from the *8e Joye*:

Le bon homme les escoute et passe temps, quar il est ainxin acoustumé a noise et a travail come goutieres a pluye. (69)

The humble and local quality of the image is significant. It reflects the domestic terrain on which the sexual war is being fought. However the challenges to male authority made by the wives move rapidly beyond this sphere and into the outside world. For the husbands, that world might be a place of useful toil, business, advancement or even warfare, all depending on the social class whose point of view is being reflected. For the wives, moreover, the same world represents an opportunity for gossip and for the building up of networks of female complicity whose function will be discussed later. It is a world of fairs, with their inbuilt tolerance of unorthodox behaviour, of ceremonials, including the ritual of church attendance where serious devotions are traditionally set against talent-spotting and self-display, and the attractive but in the end wasteful and even destructive ritual of pilgrimages as described in Matheolus' *Lamentations*, Eustache Deschamps' *Miroir de Mariage*, and the *Roman de la Rose*,[5] and which Erasmus was ultimately to savage in his satiric *Colloquies*.

All of these sorties beyond the home offer the wife occasions for pleasure which lead to her dissatisfaction with the limits of the domestic environment. Meanwhile, for the husband, the outside world is an unpleasurable place of labour and anxiety, with particular worries arising from financial matters specifically aggravated by the wife's excesses. Nor is he allowed solace within the home from these self-same worries. On the few occasions in *Les Quinze Joies* where a husband is allowed to bring his male world into the domestic space, via his business associates or his men-friends, the wives, instead of busying about so as to make the traditional good impression, maintain sulky silences and withhold hospitality. The effect of this, another standard comic inversion, is not only to cause possible financial damage to the household, as when the modern wife might fail to come up with a good meal for the boss, but also to disrupt the husband's homosocial bonds, alienate his friends, lose him useful contacts, and so fix him more firmly than ever into his subordinate domestic position. The technique is well illustrated in the *7e Joye* where the wife causes a rift between her husband and his closest friend in order to discredit that friend's allegations of her sexual misconduct, or in the *9e Joye* where wife and eldest son form an alliance and convince the husband's friends that he is suffering from senility, and that, consequently, his actions and words are not worthy of consideration. The consequence of such a humbling is that husbands become isolated from that outside world in which they might find self-expression and fulfilment, and are bound even more firmly under female dominion.

Having seen some of the social consequences of the use of feminine wiles we shall now turn to a closer examination of the ways in which language and sexuality are manipulated by the wives in *Les Quinze Joies*, for this purpose making particular reference to *Joies* 1, 11 and 15.

Such wiles are used to entice and seduce the male partner (whether husband or lover) until he is in a position where his reactions can be easily controlled. The wives usually have very definite objectives, these being principally centred on the sins of greed, lust and adultery: they want material goods, and they want sexual satisfaction outside marriage – motives which are, by tradition, much more easily forgiven in male characters, nay in real men. In furthering their desires they may use language in subtle ways which entangle the husband in a pattern of emotional responses from which they profit. They may equally use it as part of the game of seduction – again a highly traditional male behaviour-pattern set in the rituals of wooing. As a yet further possibility, language may become a chorus of critical female voices too strident and persistent for a husband to withstand.

The first pattern, whereby feminine wiles take the form of complex argumentation, is best illustrated in the conversations between husband and wife in the *1ere Joye*. In order to advance her campaign of getting and spending, the wife makes a calculated choice of the moment at which to entrap her husband in the subtleties of discourse:

> Et voulentiers elles devroient parler de leurs choses especialles la ou leurs mariz sont plus subgitz et doivent estre plus enclins pour octrier, c'est ou lit. (7)

If the marital home is the most fundamental area of social relations, then the marital bed is the most fundamental area of personal relations. It is in that very place, where, again traditionally, the wife submits and does her connubial duty, that in repeated passages she at once deploys words to strengthen her case, and rejects her husband's sexual overtures in order to exploit her advantage. The linguistic pattern is designed to set responsibility for the outcome of their debate on the husband, who remains unaware that his reactions and speech are being transformed into support for the wife's subversive plan, and such behaviour gives the impression of a husband who is an unwitting actor in a drama written and directed by an enemy who yet should be his strongest ally and indeed his

obedient servant, a technique which will become more explicit still in
the *11e Joye*.

Having rejected her husband's attentions, the wife will not define
her worries to her concerned spouse, but instead waits for him positively
to insist that she unburden herself. By then giving in to this insistence,
she feigns submission to his will and tells all: what is wrong is that she
is deeply concerned at being so poorly dressed. Of course her anxiety at
not keeping up with fashion is not the result of vanity, but more of
worries about the effect her dowdiness will have on public opinion: what
will people think of their status and their household? When the husband
responds by referring to their financial difficulties, her appeals to honour
turn into manipulations of sexuality with the addition of a good dose of
histrionics. She reminisces about previous suitors, yet protests her great
love for her husband, saying how she would rather die than marry
another man. The tactic exploits, with a degree of subtlety, her husband's
jealousy, meanwhile she assures him that she is frigid – a quality to be
admired since it must surely prove that she is chaste. Nevertheless, and
with clear comic inevitability, next evening the husband agrees to provide her with new clothes. Having won this round of the battle, the wife
is careful not to show immoderate joy, and she assures her husband that
she is only accepting the clothes because this is what he wishes.
Following this, the conflict of interests in the marital bed is further
illustrated by the husband's spending a sleepless night consumed by
financial concerns, worries which the latest expenditure has merely
increased, all in contrast to the wife who laughs in secret at her success:

> Et aucuneffois avient que la dame est si rusee que elle cognoist bien son fait et
> s'en rit tout par elle soubz les draps. (11)

Thus is the husband of the *1ere Joye* out-gunned in the linguistic
battle by his wife's sniper fire deployed in an intimate context. However
he fares no better in the *15e Joye* under the cumulative verbal broadsides
from a collection of women in the neighbourhood who intrude into the
privacy of the home to defend his wife's reputation. Language is here
shown to be a much more effective weapon for women than physical
violence would be, an apt reflection of the traditional playground roles
whereby boys rag each other physically, while girls needle each other
using spite. The aim is always to seek safety in numbers, so, having been
surprised by her husband whilst enjoying the attentions of her lover, the
wife takes refuge with her mother, and also benefits from the advice and
support of female servants, friends and relatives who automatically

sanction her actions and vouch for her mendacious excuses, despite knowing full well what and how much wrong she is doing. If the husband resembles the stooge or unwitting victim in a play, the neighbourhood women are all very conscious of their roles in outmanoeuvring him by dissimulation, and of the importance of presenting a performance which, even if not entirely convincing – and certainly not to the reader – will at least be powerful enough to overwhelm the wronged husband, and that, like as not, with the reader's complicity.

Dissimulation in language begins with the wife's tale to her mother which exploits the idea of female vulnerability and describes how she was forcibly seduced, "et vous savez que ce n'est rien que d'une pouvre femme seulle" (106). Rather than dwelling on the moral prize of virginity, or necessarily believing anything her daughter says, the mother stresses practical matters and assembles a convivial council of women whose advice to the young wife is a thinly disguised celebration of their own successes in having already achieved sovereignty over their own husbands. Enacting the plot they have hatched, their visit to her husband succeeds in coercing him into admitting that he has misinterpreted his wife's behaviour, and one of the most amusing if least convincing tactics used to overwhelm his objections is the assembled women's reference to their own moral integrity: surely this would not allow them to defend a woman who had been guilty of such a moral transgression!

> Et cuidés vous, fait l'autre, que nous soions si sotes que, si elle estoit telle come vous dictes, que nous la souffrissons en nostre compaignie? Par ma foy, fait elle, nanil! Nous ne suymes pas si sotes que nous daignasson parler a elle ne ne souffrerion pas que elle demourast en nostre rue ne environ nous. (112)

Again this pattern is most significant for the type of humour which the *Quinze Joies* contains. Less a satire which relies on shared values, in the way the humiliation of Shakespeare's shrew depends on the audience sharing the value-system of male superiority, the text becomes at such points an expression of female solidarity irrespective of traditionally held values, as naughty girls (or boys) gang up on a weakling simply because he (or she) is a weakling. The comic pattern may not be morally admirable, but nor is it intended to be, and can any of us say we have never enjoyed, nay incited it?

The success of the feminine wiles in the *15e Joye* lies in their forcefulness. For an illustration of feminine wiles incorporating more recognisably female subtlety and combining language, gesture and sexuality, we should turn to the *11e Joye*. The principal players in this scene are not a married couple, but rather a pregnant teenage girl, the mistress of the house in which she lives, a young and innocent bachelor, and a supporting cast of women who will be important extras in the seduction scenes.

In order to ensnare the innocent bachelor of the *11e Joye* the mistress of the house gives the pregnant girl lessons in the art of using feminine wiles. The first set of instructions covers the use of modest yet alluring gestures:

> Gete tousjours les yeulx sur lui bien doulcement de bonne maniere et fay ainxin (lors elle lui monstre comment elle fera). (84)

She also receives guidance on how to manipulate the conversation to show modesty and innocence in matters of the heart. Much emphasis is placed on theatricality, again illustrating how the suitor is seduced into unwittingly playing a role in a well-rehearsed drama. Operating once more as a sexually dynamic clan, the older women scrutinise the girl's performance and, as this quotation illustrates, prompt her if she seems to be acting badly: "Et a l'aventure la dame lui a fait signe que elle se taise, pour ce que elle a paour que elle ne joue pas bien son personnage" (86). Then, having used this role and its constituent script to trap the bachelor into marriage, the girl receives final instructions on how to feign virginity on her wedding night, and on this occasion her performance is, as the narrator tells us, flawless:

> Ainxin le fait et joue tres bien son personnage, quar il n'est rien si sachant come est femme en ce qu'elle vieult faire touchant la matiere secrete. (89)

The sexual dynamics of the *Joye* are again determined by gender difference in that sex is less something shared between partners than a means by which female clans, groups or individuals achieve power over men who are most effectively excluded from the sexual terms of reference imposed by the clan opposing them. Among other tactics women deliberately maintain a mystique around female sexuality, the better to mystify and perplex him, to hide their earlier moral transgressions, and to save themselves for their illicit lovers with whom, in intimacy, they share their *secrets d'amour*. Isolated in an outgroup of one, the husband is disadvantaged by his innate if unspoken fear of female criticism and mockery and by his ignorance about female sex, an ignorance illustrated by the narrator's use of the term *matiere secrete* to refer to it.

Such are the various ways in which the women of *Les Quinze Joies de Mariage* exploit the potential for manipulation in language. They use it to form labyrinthine entanglements, to force a retreat before massed ranks, to express alluring modesty, or to conceal their sinful natures. We also hope to have illustrated how, by excluding men from the discourse surrounding female sex, wives are able to subjugate their husbands, either as part of a strategy for material gain, or as a way of avoiding unwelcome attentions. Feminine wiles, specifically as connected with language and sexuality, are effective tools for subverting male authority within the household: they help to place the husband in the type of silent, acquiescent role recommended for women, and, albeit via a parodic distortion of reality, they form part of the folklore, traditions and comic self-expression of womanhood at large.

In such a comic process, whereby norms are parodically inverted rather than satirically reinforced, the wives of *Les Quinze Joies* do not achieve sovereignty over their husbands by challenging traditional male views of women, but instead exaggerate, exploit and enjoy those negative characteristics traditionally assigned them: what is bad becomes good, what is lamentable becomes desirable and women come out on top. The pattern has its modern analogue in writers like Hélène Cixous, who would revalue hysteria and make of it too an important principle of modern sexual dynamics, moreover the political implications of this re-interpretation of clichéd characteristics have not gone unnoticed in our times. For example Toril Moi in 1985 considered Mary Ellmann's earlier work *Thinking about Women* (1968), commenting that "as part of her deconstructive project, Ellmann ... recommends exploiting the sexual stereotypes for all they are worth for our own political purposes".[6] However, despite superficial resemblances, the political purposes of the Middle Ages were regrettably different from ours, and we would not suggest that the author of *Les Quinze Joies de Mariage* is presenting us with women engaged in a philosophically or socially reasoned struggle intended to improve their position in a patriarchy. Though the effect of their subversion of traditional sexual dynamics within the household is not confined solely to the domestic environment, the wives are motivated by personal desires rather than any wish to bring about social change, and the humour remains more a nightmarish travesty of real life than a seriously constructed template for the future.

The political implications of the humour are simply not articulated by author, narrator or characters, though they might be imposed, at least metaphorically speaking, by the modern reader. Furthermore, to define one's moral stance when considering texts such as *Les Quinze Joies* remains a matter open to a considerable degree of reader-choice. Politics apart, there are various strategies available. One might read the text as anti-feminist satire, but the limitations of this approach have already been indicated: it fails to exploit the sexual (and textual) dynamics of the different situations and plot-lets which form a context in which women are not punished but celebrated. Accordingly might one follow other cues within the text, cues perhaps planted by an author who, whilst not giving whole-hearted approval to the wives' actions, would reserve the right to view their feminine wiles with ironic admiration? This stand is somewhat against the narrator's susceptibilities, and a male readership might find it difficult to share the admiration of the vixen tricks expressed by the various female clans represented within the *Quinze Joies*. A third strategy might then be to fight back, so reactivating the sexual dynamics of the despised out-group, namely manhood. Nevertheless, a counter-attack by the male clan on the assembled bitches, shrews and castrating harpies represented in the *Quinze Joies* is inhibited by the fact that the male figures come out of their adventures so badly. Faced by their abject humiliation one might feel not sympathy, but merely disgust, nay even satisfaction that they will end their days in misery, as not having the virile wherewithal to stand up and change the sexual dynamics within their situation to their own advantage. At the end of the *7e Joye* the husband is pointed out in the street, called Jean Beausire (the cuckold's sobriquet) and mocked by one and all, and, cued in by such reactions, the satire directed against him has been seen more than once as the essence of this text: does he in fact deserve any more than he gets, for "ce n'est que la regle du jeu ... il n'est que une bête" (65)?

Extending this point of view, we can see on one side, in the triumphant and wily female, a representative of a clan which has achieved its self-expression via a comic reduction of an outsider, while on the other, in the defeated and woeful male figure, we have a scapegoat who happens to be a man, but who could in other texts or contexts be a cartoon character, a stuffed or cardboard dummy, a puppet or a stock butt for ridicule, like the Jewish schlemiel, all of which figures are defenceless or indefensible, or both. To this extent it is not the husband's role to fight back, but rather to be an ever more abject victim, loser or schlimazel, and no more than one yanks Guy Fawkes off the bonfire does one try to defend these classic victims of comic culture. Think of Woody Allen's neurotic persona and the Fiddler on the Roof who is his ethnic antecedent; think of Tony Hancock's attempts, as pathetic as Walter Mitty's fantasies, to better himself beyond the context of 23 Railway Cuttings, East Cheam; think of the court sycophant of the Middle Ages and later who is faced with the same problem of exclusion from a role which he apes with comic vanity; think of Bristow in the London *Evening Standard*, a desk-clerk tied forever to a petty office job in a firm the loathing of which is at the same time his entire raison d'être: for just as the hapless husband is defined by the very marital status which enslaves him, so if Bristow didn't work for the Chester-Perry organisation then he would not be Bristow, in fact he wouldn't be anyone at all.

This anomaly, expressed as fully in the *Quinze Joies* as in Thurber's far more gentle satires of the American male, is focused on that archetypal schlemiel, the cuckold. Were he not married, he would not be, as the *Quinze Joies* repeatedly puts it, "En la nasse ou finera miserablement ses jours" and therefore not himself. As cuckold he is a type imprisoned in a role in which he is as helpless as the fairground Aunt Sally or the toothless muzzled bear baited in the carnival riot (*14e Joye*), and reduced by the author and the other characters to being that "unheroic incompetent nonentity" that Richard Spencer so aptly described in his article of 1978.[7] To this extent he is scapegoated by male readerships and female readerships alike, and the sexual dynamic behind this reaction might be on the one hand one's gratitude for not actually being in a relationship with such a person, or, on the other hand, one's dread at being oneself reduced to such a status and plight. Was not this the psychology explaining the carnival charivaris inflicted on bad couples, or the *assouades* of which the cuckold was repeatedly made victim?

By contrast any identity which such a schlemiel may be given beyond that status and plight, as pathetic victim of a wife's infidelity or an adulterous lover's libido, is a threat to his role as archetypal cuckold and therefore to the essential humour deriving from it. Hence a further reading strategy would be to defend the husband by granting him some redeeming features, again cued in by authorial or narratorial support, and some background psychology which varies the pattern and draws him away from the travesty of married life which the *Quinze Joies* portrays, and into the real life which we flatter ourselves we, as real people with our legitimate married partners and our illicit sexual partners, all inhabit. Following this lead, some have seen the advantage the *Quinze Joies* has over its sources and analogues to be the use of dialogue, dramatic situation and observation of reality transmitted by the author in a series of "situations vivantes"[8] comprising the text. Satiric humour must be based on some version of real life in order for it to have any effective meaning, and within its broad spectrum we may create, at one extreme, a stuffed dummy to be the target of our comic contempt, while at the other we may find a fully biographied human being whom one cannot without grotesque injustice reduce to such a role. Painted skittles are there to be knocked over, but human beings deserve and may command our lovingkindness, and this is a strong inhibitor to splenetic humour.

Much of the time the husband is closer to the first extreme, but he may move towards the other as redeeming human features emerge, partly no doubt to add elements of personal interest to a sometimes monotonous series of comic misadventures. Like Charles Bovary, schlemiel and cuckold extraordinary, he is long-suffering and considerate – "est sage et ne vieult point faire de noise ne troubler sa famille" (30) – and this in a household where his wife rages round the house like a termagant, giving him no peace when he arrives home cold from his daily struggles in the outside world. Like Georges Dandin (*5e Joye*) he has the social disadvantages of a husband married to a nobler wife, and for fear of displeasing her will fain demand his conjugal rights when she rejects him, whereupon, caring as ever, he takes her petty ailments seriously when, like as not, they stem from sexual fantasies about her younger suitor. In the *13e Joye* he is himself a nobleman, keen to gain honour and *vaillance*, and forsakes a loving family for a war during which his death is reported and his wife remarries, only to be dishonoured when he returns. Then in the *14e Joye* the marriage is happy, the partners "come deux coulombeaux" (99), but the wife dies – and inevitably so, for it is unnatural that those in prison should enjoy it – and he marries a harridan widow, so creating a marriage almost as ridiculous as the old man with the younger wife, over whose fate the narrator chortles in gleeful anticipation. He will cough and spit all night long, farting and sneezing in a bed-chamber already rank with his halitosis: "c'est mervoille qu'elle ne se tue" (101).

Quite so, but if the situations belong to lived reality rather than comic fantasy, so their sexual dynamics change. Reality connotes ambiguity, and with it conflicting emotions in which the higher ones might predominate; hence as one teases out the contradictions of a real event as depicted in literature, so humour may disappear. It becomes both irrelevant and unworthy to reduce human problems to a mockery, thus the death of the young wife in the penultimate *Joye* is viewed quite seriously, whatever horrors await the widower when he re-marries. However when the situational detail of the *Quinze Joies* becomes so unambiguously depressing and negative as it often is, so it quickly invites one to leave reality behind (surely nothing is ever *this* bad?) and summon up a kind of marital house of horrors where everything precisely *is* that bad, if not actually worse. The comic incongruity thus resides in the juxtaposition of a reality recognisable via the detail which the author scatters through his text, and its textual travesty, which, despite the vitality of such detail, lumbers inevitably towards the worst-case scenario.

Moreover various stylistic and narrative tricks even within the telling of the tales impede the individuation of the psychology. For one thing that psychology is incoherent, the narrator insisting that the husband enjoys his sufferings in the trap of marriage long after that has ceased to be a credible possibility. In addition one notes how conjectural and provisional the narrated accounts are, witness how often the phrase *à l'aventure* (perchance) is used ("*A l'aventure* il a pere et mere ... *a l'aventure* il est seigneur de terre nouvellement ... *a l'aventure* el est fille de la meson, niepce ou parente, et est tellement avenu qu'elle est grousse*" etc.: 82-3), the author thus refusing, it seems, to fix the details of his story definitively, and preferring to talk in generalities and hypotheses rather than specifics: the married partners are never even named. Hence when all goes inevitably wrong, still no detailed, lived conclusion is provided. Maybe he goes mad or hangs himself, maybe he chucks her out, maybe he keeps her, maybe he even beats her for her deception: one does not know, but the one (comical) certainty is that he is "en la nasse dont il ne eschappera point, mais y sera en languissant tourjours et finera miserablement ses jours", a refrain delivered less with true sympathy for a human predicament than with the kind of bantering commiseration referred to by Joan Crow.[9]

So the author's role is less than fully clear. He is not a social commentator gifted with profound insights, even though he does give us some interesting local colour. Nor is he easily cast in the same role as that adopted by the misogynic narrator. It is apparent from a selective reading of the secondary literature on this text that far too often the narrator's comments have been taken as expressing the author's views, a very dangerous assumption but perhaps forgivable in a work which is somewhat crudely and naïvely, if not actually badly written. We hear of an "auteur terriblement sérieux",[10] clearly a member of the secular clergy,[11] of the again "sérieux" with which this author treats infidelity,[12] and of the "cri de révolte" which issues from his text against the constraint on freedom represented by a state of marriage which he regrets is permanent and indissoluble.[13] However to integrate the sometimes quite preposterous views textually expressed into the attitudes of an author of whom we have no absolutely certain knowledge (his name and dates, for instance, remain unreliably identified) is to make a leap of faith one is never obliged to undertake. Behind the woman-hating, misogamous, cynical narrator created by the text, there may stand an author of an entirely different complexion who is content to play on the incongruities endemic in marriage and the seemingly inexhaustible comic potential of the lover-wife-cuckold triangle in order to derive his comic effects, these comic effects being only heightened by the "froide férocité" with which the narrator judges the woman central to them.[14]

Certainly neither author or narrator is an effective ally of the threatened male. The latter grants him the preposterous support of state-ments whereby, for instance, God only imposes suffering on those able to withstand it ("quant à moy, je croy que Dieu ne donne adversité aux gens que selon ce qu'il les sceit et cognoist francs et debonnaires pour pacianment endurer" (29): hence, as we all know, God never inflicts cold on those unequipped to endure it, every winter's hypothermia figures bearing this out), and he uses vagueness and ambiguity to impede one's getting to know or admire him in the way in which, for instance, Flaubert finds himself reluctantly admiring his own schlemiel figures Bouvard and Pécuchet, if not in fact Charles Bovary as well. Meanwhile the author abandons the hapless husband to the female companies where he is inevitably outsmarted, to the chronotope of the household which, as we have argued, is the unquestioned domain of the wife, and within that household to the more intimate chronotopes of the bedchamber and marriage-bed, while his power is overthrown in the kind of carnival-esque *monde à l'envers* referred to above, and his authority progressively negated by the conniving sets of women (wife and daughters, wife and mother-in-law, wife and female servants, wife and female neighbours) who meet behind his back and always successfully plan his defeats. This may happen in the maternal bed-chamber (*8e Joye*), in the home of the mother-in-law (*11e Joye*) or in the gossiping circle (*15e Joye*), but the effect is consistent: to create a space in which not only the husband is emasculated but also the narrator, for the power of these women is such that it shoves him too into the background, his anti-feminist pleas becoming intermittent intrusions in a dialogue and a chorus which frustrate their realisation.

So although a strategic defence of the husband is possible, its pot-ential should not be over-stated, and for us these variations on the theme of comic or distorted wedlock, some of which are not even amusing or intended to be, produce less a psychological drama than a set of more or less ingenious twists in a skein of tales where the husbands are subject to laws other than those governing real life, and in no case gain enough realistic weight to support a meaningfully sympathetic approach. The detail is too fragmentary, being thrown at the reader in a few lines but scarcely ever carried over from one chapter to another. It relates predominantly to archetypes, rather than deriving from observation of real people, the husband being impulsive and gullible, jealous, decreasing in virility as he grows older, and the wife always faithless to a greater or lesser degree, and with various doses of vanity, vindictiveness and egoism thrown in. This is not the real world of the marriage guidance session where one talks difficulties through and sorts them out in terms of compromise solutions, but rather the parallel world of the music-hall comic where all of family life amounts to a female conspiracy against the hapless male persona that he portrays himself as being. So Rychner's insistence that in reading the *Quinze Joies* we are involved in "l'observation précise de la vie" in which a "réalisme impitoyable"[15] effaces the symbolism of former works must be amended. The old comic absolutes have merely been nuanced by some recognisably lived features, but it is those absolutes – the wife's perfidious wiles, the husband's desperate woes – that still determine the text.

Yet, however distorted be the description of marriage in the text, society still depends on this institution for its survival, and marriage itself survives, albeit in comically disfigured form, throughout the very text which seems to attack it. So, within, nay in terms of these comic incongruities, is there nothing one can do to defend the morally castrated victim of the social and sexual conspiracies they amount to? Yes, if one examines the again ambiguous psychological roots of one's reaction to him.

The schlemiel/husband, caught in the trap of the horror-marriage which is his determining identity, effects on one the kind of comforting reassurance always latent in the laughter at adversity. Thus the celibate is reassured that he has missed nothing in not being married, and the text can very obviously be read into the anti-matrimonial lore of the Middle Ages, the narrator's key role being to reinforce this aspect of the work when stating, unambiguously enough,

> celles .XV. joies de mariage sont a mon avis les plus grans tourmens, douleurs, tristesses et maleurtez qui soient en terre, esquelles nulles autres paines ... ne sont pareilles. (4)

However a significant number, even nowadays a majority of his readers are married or marriageable: where the reassurance for them?

Again the narrator is content with half-truths. For him those intending marriage are lost: they won't pay attention to the warnings, hence an entire seminar of Rychner's students of the *Quinze Joies* ended up married.[16] Whereas to those who are married the text can at least provide condolence:

> Ainxin, regardans cestes paines qu'ilz prennent pour joies, considerans la repugnance qui est entre leur entendement et le mien et de pluseurs aultres, me suy delicté, en les regardant noer en la nasse ou ilz sont si bien embarrez, a escripre icelles . XV. joies de mariage a leur consolacion; (5)

but what sort of *consolacion* can this be, given that, by his own admission, the married take the travails of marriage as often as not for joys, having been inured to them as a pack animal is to the burden he no longer feels?

No, we as (married?) readers have to take the initiative here and provide our own defence of the comic figures and impose a further and positive set of sexual dynamics as far as the text can accommodate them. The lover is easy to redeem. He is the image of our own lost youth: potent, vigorous, heedless of restraints and taboos, ready to sacrifice everything to the fulfilment of his, the race's, basic urge. The woman is his tool, but at the same time his mistress, and in both senses. As fulcrum of the adultery story, her will is compliant to the lover and rejecting of the husband, turning out of instinct, with both comic inevitability and daring irresponsibility, towards the new and against the old, just as her body, in the end alone, renews the generations and produces life, even in defiance of official values, including that symbolically absurd value which placed celibacy above the married state.

But the husband, the schlemiel, reviled and wretched as the outcast and the scapegoat: where does he stand?

In our view as reassurance that one (potentially or really) has a partner in ignominy. Frustration, exploitation, defeat, contempt, dismissal, rejection − sexual or other − one has known them all, incidentally if not repeatedly, and the schlemiel is a kind of totem set up in recognition of that fact, a totem which is at the same time a symbolisation of fears unrealised for those who have not actually been through these various mills, but feel they one day might. The cuckold is thus a kind of inversion of the Don Juan complex, being one caught on a treadmill of sexual, social and emotional failure no less than Don Juan is caught on the treadmill of his own tedious and unsatisfying sexual conquests. But even within or perhaps beyond this role has he not a curious appeal in his worm-like ability to cling on to the very bottom rung of the ladder of male self-respect, just as the Fiddler survives against the odds in clinging on to his roof, in the process even emerging as symbol of an entire community?

---

[1] I Timothy 2.12.

[2] q.v. Marbod of Rennes, Andreas Capellanus and the anonymous *De Coniuge non ducenda*, as cited in Alcuin Blamires ed., *Woman Defamed and Woman Defended* (Oxford, 1992), pp. 101, 123 and 128.

[3] Juvenal, *Satire VI*, tr. G. G. Ramsay (Loeb Classical Library, 1940), p. 119.

[4] All references to the text are taken from *Les XV Joies de Mariage*, ed. Jean Rychner (Geneva, 1967).

[5] cf. Rychner, p. 150.

[6] Toril Moi, *Sexual/Textual Politics: Feminist Literary Theory* (London, 1985), p.39.

[7] R. H. Spencer, "The Treatment of Women in the *Roman de la Rose*, the Fabliaux and the *Quinze Joies de Mariage*," *Marche Romane*, 28 (1979), 207-214 (p. 214).

[8] Rychner, p. xiv.

[9] "The *Quinze Joies de Mariage* in France and England", *Modern Language Review*, 59 (1964), 571-7 (p. 575).

[10] G. Mermier, "La Ruse féminine et la fonction morale des *Quinze Joies de Mariage*", *Romance Notes*, 15 (1973-4), 455-503 (p. 501).

[11] J. Wathelet-Willem, "Note sur les *Quinze Joies de Mariage*", in *Etudes offertes à Jules Horrent* (Liège, 1980), pp. 517-529 (p. 517).

[12] N. Kasprzyk, "Les XV joies d'un mariage", in *Mélanges Frappier* (Geneva, 1970), pp. 499-508 (pp. 506-7).

[13] J. Santucci, "Pour une interprétation nouvelle des *Quinze Joies de Mariage*", in *Le Récit bref au moyen âge* (Paris, 1983), pp. 153-179 (p. 169).

[14] J. Dauphiné, "Le Jeu de la transgression dans *Les XV joies de mariage*", in *Amour, mariage et transgressions au moyen âge* (Goppingen, 1984), pp. 471-9 (p. 474).

[15] Rychner, p. xx, quoting in the second case A. Coville.

[16] *Ibid.*, p. viii, n.

2. On Laughter in the Waning of the Middle Ages
Michael Freeman

Those of us who teach and research into the late medieval period in France are used to having conversations with colleagues working in other more modern fields, who have not read much of the literature of the century (or centuries) we study, but who nonetheless have a clearly defined view of it. Whatever we so-called specialists might have to say about the matter cannot usually persuade them that it was not in fact the "waning of the Middle Ages", an age of war and pestilence giving rise (understandably?) to a generalised feeling of despondency.

As for the French *homme moyen cultivé*, his knowledge of the period might extend to the poetry of François Villon, albeit reduced to a graphic description of the bodies of hanged men swinging on the gallows and to laments about the snows of yesteryear. He might also know one or two apparently naïve *ballades* and *rondeaux* by Charles d'Orléans – a poet generally dismissed as effete, perhaps because he was an aristocrat, or because he was captured and exiled, and thus a victim of the Hundred Years' War which, as we all know, was one of the main reasons for the terrible state of affairs which obtained in France.

He might perhaps know (or at least know of) a handful of farces, but would consider them to be coarse and unsophisticated, especially if he had seen them performed, as they usually are, by amateur or semi-professional troupes. To be sure, there is the *Farce de Maistre Pierre Pathelin*, but that is merely the exception which proves the rule, and in any case its anonymous author is usually put on a par with the early Molière, who, of course, went on to much greater things. And that's about it. *Notre-Dame de Paris*, Victor Hugo's delightfully anachronistic version of the life and times of fifteenth-century Parisians, with its hunchback, gypsies, evil priest, wayward students, and supporting cast of freaks and misfits, will be known to many, probably in one of its different film versions. Nevertheless, however much one might admire Lon Chaney and Charles Laughton, or for that matter Gina Lollobrigida and Anthony Quinn, one is forced to admit that even if it is *magnifique*, "ce n'est pas le XVe siècle".

What is the source of this *image d'Epinal* of fifteenth-century France as a time of depression and ennui? The answer is that it derives largely from the work of Johan Huizinga and his influential *The Waning of the Middle Ages*, which relays a particular and persuasive message, although one which has not always been fully understood. Even the title has given rise to some debate, the word "waning" apparently being more heavily loaded than the original Dutch title, which translates more correctly as "autumn". The book was first published in Dutch in 1919 and in English in 1924, and it is naturally in English that it achieved international status. The French translation bears in its title the no less unambiguous term "déclin", but whether or not it was meant by the author to be read as "waning" or "decline" or something less negative, the fact is that the title has had in itself an enormous impact.[1] As Daniel Poirion remarked concerning Huizinga's book,

> [Il] a fait redécouvrir le XVe siècle dans cette perspective du déclin, moins par ses analyses du détail que par son titre (tel qu'il est traduit dans toutes les langues). Parler de 'déclin' pour caractériser l'art franco-flamand de la cour de Bourgogne, dont les formes prédominent dans cette fresque critique, est injustifiable objectivement. On risque de confondre les valeurs de cette culture avec le destin de cette principauté, et de juger toute son histoire par le sort de Charles le Téméraire, dont la mort est l'accident d'une défaite militaire. Encore faut-il remarquer que la catastrophe culturelle, la dispersion de ses livres imprudemment aventurés sur le champ de bataille, s'accompagne d'une bonne nouvelle: cette année-là on imprime en France les premiers ouvrages, ouvrant une ère de progression sans limite.

Poirion suggests, moreover, that this notion of a decline of a certain age and way of life is a convenient one for the historian in that it allows him to

> marquer la transition entre les différentes périodes que l'on veut distinguer dans l'histoire. Que le Moyen Age finisse dans le déclin, c'est très commode: cela prouve qu'il y a bien eu un Moyen Age, ce dont on pourrait douter autrement;

and he goes on to list aspects of life and literature of the period which give the lie to the arbitrary choice made by Huizinga. The lavish courts, for example, of the Dukes of Berry, of Philip the Good and of René d'Anjou give no hint of a penchant for melancholy:

> C'est l'époque des grands banquets à la cour de Bourgogne. Olivier de la Marche raconte en 60 pages le Banquet du Faisan, de 1454. La coupe synchronique ne confirme nullement l'image d'un devenir déclinant.[2]

In other words it is all a question of perspective. Poirion's case seems to me to be unanswerable, and could have been made even stronger if he had mentioned the extraordinary musical activity of a period which included the likes of Josquin des Prés, Dufay, Binchois and Ockeghem; and stronger still – as we shall see – if he had chosen to make more of the abundant humorous writing of the times, mentioning the work of the many satirical poets and writers of *farces bonnes et joyeuses, sotties, sermons joyeux* and *contes pour rire*.

Such objections notwithstanding, there can be no denying the enduring influence of Huizinga's book, and its central theme whereby the fourteenth and fifteenth centuries in France and Burgundy (which embraced most of what is now Belgium) were a melancholy period of decline and despair, the inevitable consequence of war and insecurity. Once put back in its cultural context, however, the book can be seen to be very much part of the mental landscape of the time when it was itself written, and typical of much of its cultural historiography. Huizinga was born in 1872, and his formative years were spent in the *fin de siècle*. The portrait of an age which he provided and which appeared, significantly perhaps, at the end of the Great War, served to reinforce the consensus which had existed for some time that the world he was describing was one which had lost its way. Nor have things really moved on from there, except among specialists, of course, but they are perceived as being untrustworthy guides. As recently as 1969 Henry Hornik felt able to quote with approval Charles Lenient's *La Satire en France au moyen âge* (Paris, 1893), in which readers had been told that in the later Middle Ages one finds nothing but misery and unhappiness and, with it, a lack of literary inspiration:

> On ne voit plus les ménéstrels (*sic*) rassembler la foule sur les places publiques pour lui raconter les exploits de Roland ou les ruses divertissantes de maître Renart. Aux vifs et mordants couplets du sirvente, aux récits naïfs et malins du fabliau succèdent l'interminable roman en prose, chef-d'œuvre de stérilité et d'ennui; le pamphlet violent, haineux; le mystère et la farce assaisonnés de platitudes et de grossièretés. La vieille gaieté française a disparu un moment, étouffée par l'excès des maux publics.[3]

To the public of Lenient's day, particularly those fearful of being bored or shocked, that seemed to say it all, and it can have come as no surprise if many of them chose not to pursue their interest further. A very similar story is told in Henry Guy's pernicious *Ecole des Rhétoriqueurs* (1910) which helped impede the proper appreciation of the poets of the late fifteenth century in France and Burgundy: only fairly recently have its prejudices and misreadings been questioned.[4] Hornik predictably cites the "chaos of the Hundred Years War, the secularisation of the church as well as the constant waves of epidemics" as factors in the "general cultural upheaval", coming to the conclusion that "the fifteenth century would appear to prepare the modern era through the disintegration of the Middle Ages".[5]

The purpose of this chapter is to counter this prevailing view and, by examining what has been seen by more recent critics as a golden age of comic writing in France, to attempt to set out a new framework for looking at society and culture in France during the youth of François Rabelais, born 1484, and one of the greatest comic writers in world literature. It never was very likely, after all, that he created his sense of fun *ex nihilo*, nor that all the jokes he retails were his own. Like many others of his generation, he had a clear notion of the originality of his times and of its potential for improvement in the political, religious and moral spheres, but he never appears to claim that he wished to turn his back on the humour of the immediate past. The fact is that his sense of humour – and his sense of what is humorous – is grounded in that of his predecessors, of men and women living in what we have been wrongly taught to think of as the waning of the Middle Ages.

The ending of the Hundred Years War helped stimulate the new-found optimism which is typical of French writing in the second half of the fifteenth century. As so often happens after a period of suffering and want, it gave rise to a thirst for consumption and enjoyment, and signs of this post-war lust for life are everywhere. Paris, which had seen so much strife in the earlier part of the century, began to regain its *joie de vivre*. Its population had declined from about 200,000 in the middle of the fourteenth century to little over half that figure by about 1420. By the end of the fifteenth century it stood again at around 150,000.[6] Accordingly the 1460s and the decades that followed can be seen as boom years. Typical figures in this Paris after the Liberation were the young men jokingly referred to as *fringueurs* who spent their time showing off, wearing the latest fashions and looking for new ways of enjoying themselves, meanwhile deliberately cocking a snook at the older generations; they were, as I have suggested elsewhere, "comme des zazous avant la lettre",[7] and only in a period of social mobility and change could such individuals flourish. They provided much harmless fun and generated a certain amount of satire. The literature of the period stresses the ostentatious get-rich-quick atmosphere of the times, sometimes with amusement and approval, sometimes with frowns and threats.

As we shall see, the perfect guide to this ephemeral world devoted to fashion and snobbery is Guillaume Coquillart, writing in the late 1470s and early 1480s. While purporting to condemn it, he in fact celebrates a newly prosperous and confusing world of changed values. The point I should like to make here is that, whereas a contemporary audience would have understood this implicitly, modern critics have often failed to see the point, and have therefore taken what I have termed his "satire affectueuse" for tub-thumping denunciations of society's evils.[8]

Coquillart's work is a product of a world of youthful high spirits. Inevitably there were others who were less indulgent, and, as Jean Dufournet has suggested in his article on what he identifies as the "génération de Louis XI", sudden changes in society and in ways of seeing the world create their own tensions:

> Nos textes constituent une véritable éducation du lecteur, une éducation à la tromperie, mais aussi au conflit entre l'être et le paraître, entre la réalité et l'illusion, à cet équilibre si difficile à atteindre entre le dit et le non-dit, l'apparent et le caché, le cynisme et la naïveté.[9]

Guillaume Coquillart's description of the Paris of his day is hard to reconcile with Huizinga's thesis according to which the Middle Ages came to an end among wars, epidemics, and catastrophes, and the dominant cultural artefact was the macabre, seen as a natural reaction to these events. While it is indeed true that in the fifteenth century the *danse macabre*, or Dance of Death, was frequently represented in church décors, manuscripts and books, it is surely an over-simplification to see it as the symbol of the age. Alongside examples of melancholy there are innumerable cases of a fun which, even if not good and clean, was certainly fun nevertheless.

It is interesting that Huizinga, although clearly aware of this pattern, took the decision not to foreground it as an aspect of late medieval culture. As Bruno Roy pointed out in his illuminating study of the verbal humour of the period,

> Si Huizinga, qui s'affirma par la suite comme un théoricien du jeu (*Homo ludens*, 1944), avait eu le loisir de mettre ses théories en application, il aurait sans doute corrigé ses vues antérieures et concédé aux sociétés médiévales un plus grand potentiel ludique.[10]

Those who have read widely in the literature of the time will find it hard to disagree. But it would be a grave mistake to assume that this ludicity was in any way naïve or childish, innocent or transparent. There existed, as Roy puts it, a very definite "culture de l'équivoque": the fifteenth century was particularly fond of spoonerisms, innuendo and puns, especially if they involved smut, and here we can begin to see just where

Rabelais found the sources for his comic inspiration. Roy describes the word-games which were fashionable at the end of the Middle Ages, particularly in educated circles where what Guillaume Coquillart calls the "mondaines plaisances" were appreciated. Couples enjoyed swapping risqué jokes, vying with each other in a verbal inventiveness dependent on double entendre: "on s'amusait à des échanges verbaux, mimant l'improvisation, exigeant dans certains cas une gestualité appropriée, et faisant intervenir des partenaires de sexe opposé."[11] As a compilation of jokes dating from the end of the fifteenth century proves, the *contrepèterie* was already alive and well.[12] Moreover, any reader of the *Parnasse satyrique du XVe siècle*, published by Marcel Schwob as long ago as 1905, could not fail to be aware of this.

Sexual humour, mostly based on wordplay of the sort we have been discussing, is in fact one of the prominent characteristics of writing in fifteenth-century France. The difficulty is that many modern readers of medieval literature were determined to resist this interpretation, since it challenges the new received wisdom they were busy establishing. In a wide-ranging and thoughtful piece which throws light (if only incidentally) on the texts and the period we are examining, Sheila Delany has shown to what extent this applied to much scholarly writing on the Middle Ages.[13] Critics, often defensive about their period and its literature, felt that great authors should never allow themselves to be trivial, and that sophisticated audiences could not be seen to have been frivolous or sexually permissive. Also, the repressive morality of their immediate past continued to affect the academics producing a tradition of readings which were concerned to ring-fence the Middle Ages and protect it from accusations of levity: a clear case of special pleading, but wrong-headed for all that. What happened was that the prudishness of the nineteenth- and early twentieth-century literate classes was imposed on writers and works of a very different society which, inevitably, had no way of defending themselves. The past was appropriated and, to a large extent, misappropriated in a case of "no sex please, they were late medieval".

A good example of this approach can be found in Emile Picot's editions of *sotties* and descriptions of *monologues dramatiques*. Many of the texts he edits are bursting with vulgarity and high spirits,[14] but Picot chooses to ignore this important aspect of these works or to pretend that it is either incomprehensible or not worthy of consideration. As our critical guide (and, no doubt, a man of the world), he can be expected to understand the meaning of the text and sub-text, but prudishly (or per-haps as a covert expression of power?) spares the reader's blushes, as if he sought to shield us from these texts and from ourselves. What is more, he found himself in a delicate ideological position. Given that *fabliaux*, farces and late-medieval poets were part of the nation's herit-age, it was the literary historian's duty to make them better known, but not *tels qu'en eux-mêmes*. It was necessary to edulcorate them and make them palatable; in a word, to bowdlerise them.

A similar position to Picot's is taken by Italo Siciliano in his monumental work on François Villon. It is telling that his discussion of *équivoque*, word-play and even parody is consigned to a chapter on "La Décadence". Moreover Siciliano comes to the astonishing conclusion that "toute littérature arrivée à sa décadence, à sa fin, a connu, a dû connaître la parodie: le rire désespéré et méchant de ceux qui savent tout et ne savent plus que dire." For him, the key to an understanding of the mentality of this "siècle fourbe et méchant, vieux et sceptique" lies in its fondness for "malice" and "équivoque", and in his section on fifteenth-century humour the words "impudeur", "ordurier", "scatologique" recur continually, giving the distinct impression that he is reluctant to describe the phenomenon at any length. It is with evident relief that he moves on to his next chapter entitled... "La Vierge".[15]

Villon is at the heart of the problem. Whereas others could be safely marginalised, ignored or treated with condescension, he had, since Boileau, been seen as the first great French poet. There was no way out of the dilemma. There could be no pretending that he was not there; deformation was the preferred solution. Villon was made into a moral-istic and yet confused figure, summed up by the line (acontextually cited, of course) "je riz en pleurs". Often much of his subversive and caustic wit was often not even mentioned. Meanwhile, for lesser poets, things were easier: they simply ceased to exist. The case of Jean Molinet is symptomatic. Although he was "one of the most admired of French poets from the mid-fifteenth to the mid-sixteenth century",[16] writing poems of great feeling, versatility and pathos, alongside bawdy and what appear to be consciously transgressive ones, he has been dismissed as "a kind of fifteenth-century word-processor, with no more poetry in him than has a software spell-check glossary".[17] One cannot help feeling that it is the presence of so much undiluted eroticism in his work that has prompted an otherwise sensitive critic to express such a wayward opinion.

The trouble with Villon is that he simply cannot be air-brushed out of the picture in so cavalier a fashion. His work is often memorable and moving, but it is also satirical and vulgar, manifesting an obvious relish for puns and innuendo of a sexual nature. The solutions most often put forward to explain this rarely convince. To see him as an unstable *érotomane* will not do, nor will the Romantic vision of him as a man divided (neurotically) between tears and laughter. When in doubt, blame it on the times, as many scholars have traditionally done. The difficulty would appear to arise from the need to exclude from the range of what have been considered to be the acceptable facets of his work, the vulgar humour which is so typical of the age and which he clearly possessed in good measure. Once we accept that, like the majority of his contemporaries (and Marot or Rabelais after them), he saw nothing embarrassing about calling things by their common names, his place in their poetic canon, if not necessarily in ours, becomes clearer.

Not that his (or their) humour was always bawdy. It could be boisterous, without being crude or concerned exclusively with bodily function or misfunction. The *ballade* to which Villon's first editor, Clément Marot, gave the title "Ballade et Oroison" is a case in point:

Pere Noé qui plantastes la vingne,
Vous aussi, Loth, qui bustes ou rocher,
Par tel party qu'Amours, qui gens engingne,
De voz filles si vous fist approucher
- Pas ne le dy pour le vous reproucher -
Archedeclin qui bien seustes cest art,
Tous troys vous pry que vous vueilliez prescher
L'ame du bon feu maistre Jehan Cotart.

Jadiz extraict il fut de vostre ligne,
Lui qui buvoit du meilleur et plus cher,
Et ne deust il avoir vaillant ung pigne.
Certes, sur tous c'estoit ung bon archer;
On ne lui sceust pot des mains arracher;
De bien boire ne fut oncques fetart.
Nobles seigneurs, ne souffrez empescher
L'ame du bon feu maistre Jehan Cotart.

Comme homme beu qui chancelle et trespigne
L'ay veu souvent, quant il s'alloit coucher,
Et une foiz il se fist une bigne,
Bien m'en souvient, pour la pie juchier.
Brief, on n'eust sceu en ce monde sercher
Meilleur pïon pour boire tost et tart.

Faictes entrer, quant vous orrez hucher,
L'ame du bon feu maistre Jehan Cotart.

Prince, il n'eust sceu jusqu'à terre cracher,
Tousjours crioit: "Haro, la gorge m'art!"
Et si ne sceust onc sa seuf estancher
L'ame du bon feu maistre Jehan Cotart.[18]

Scholarly discussion of this *ballade* has frequently been centred on the identity of the legatee in an attempt to discover whether Villon was praising or satirising him, our reading of a satirical poem being naturally determined by the tone and the author's presumed intentions. Archival research has shown that, as an attorney in the ecclesiastical court, Jehan Cotart was a prominent figure in contemporary Paris, albeit not without one or two skeletons in his cupboard. He had been imprisoned in 1451, for example, and was later accused of withholding jewels belonging to a client. He died in January 1461, not long, in fact, before Villon started the final revision of his *Testament*, and, as is so often the case, it is impossible to gauge the exact nature of their relationship. Unlike most critics before him, Jean Dufournet has taken the view that the poem may well have been an attack on Cotart, an attempt to "ruiner définitivement la réputation de ce haut fonctionnaire ecclésiastique, d'ôter toute valeur à ses actes et à ses jugements", given that he is portrayed as a hopeless drunk,[19] and it is very likely that Villon is deliberately deriding an important yet shady establishment figure who has let his weakness for the bottle get the better of him. Have the newspapers not enjoyed revealing similar cases in the recent past, and will they not do so again? There is nothing that the iconoclast or the gossip likes better. But, as Dufournet persuasively argues, this poem takes on a significance which extends beyond that of one man in a particular time and place, for it is dedicated to a character

[qui] prend des proportions épiques. Il recule les limites du temps, il recule les limites de l'espace, puisqu'il arrive aux portes du paradis des buveurs. Dans l'envoi, en quelques mots, nous avons une sorte de dépassement mythique, un résumé de cette existence exemplaire, un passé, un présent et un avenir placés sous le signe du Vin, voués au culte du Vin.[20]

In fact this good-humoured poem is less of a satire or attack on a particular individual than an encomium not so much of wine, as of the extended family of drinkers in all their disinhibited silliness. It presupposes a knowing and learned audience, not unlike the one Rabelais claims to be addressing in the prologue to his *Gargantua*: "car à vous, non à aultres, sont dediez mes escriptz." Moreover, as every reader of the Bible knew, Noah and Lot had, just like Jehan Cotart, let themselves down when under the influence. While reminding the reader of their indiscretions, the poet makes it clear, in what amounts to a parenthesis central both to our understanding of this poem and to the more general relationship between Villon and his public, that no reproach is intended – "Pas ne le dy pour le vous reproucher" – and thus is the crucial tone of complicity established. These archetypal boozers (which is what the poet decrees them to be) are nonetheless referred to as "nobles seigneurs" and are asked to look kindly on the soul of a kindred spirit who drank nothing but the best. It was impossible, Villon recounts with cheerful hyperbole, to wrest the cup from his grasp once he had his hands on it.

The tone of complicity is reinforced by details purportedly taken from life. The third stanza has Cotart tottering home through the Paris streets, doing himself an injury as he goes. Who has not witnessed such a scene at some time or other? Villon's expectation of his public was that they would find this amusing, and in no way a cause for disapproval: whether it has much to do with the antics of the real Cotart is a moot point. As Rychner and Henry remark in their commentary on the poem,

> Cotart n'est pas tellement le procureur et le simple destinataire d'un legs satirique; il est le 'sujet' d'une ballade, fruit d'un travail personnel dépassant de loin la tradition. S'il y a sympathie, c'est pour le personnage né dans la création.[21]

In this *ballade* Villon fictionalises a well-known figure from contemporary Paris in order to create a mythical ambience in which the reader can participate and re-create himself. It as if we all become good-natured drunkards as we laugh at the comic misfortune of a man who has been remade in our image. There can be no mistaking the sense of complicity. Villon uses the device of colloquial speech to underline the point: "archer", "la pie juchier", "pïon", are all taken from the jargon of the tavern, and the message of the *ballade* is that the late Jehan Cotart has departed one convivial world for another, provided the lords of the vine mentioned here allow his soul to enter their bibulous paradise.

Villon is an advocate of good living, aspiring in his own words to a "maison et couche molle", and lovingly describing in his works the delights of the table. In this he is typical of his age. If those who lived in the waning of the Middle Ages did suffer from depression, they appear to have made every effort to eat and drink their way out of it. As the authors of a recent book on the subject remind us, the "cuisine of late-medieval France is one of the glories of that period. It contributed to the history of human culture an enormous amount that deserves to be remembered by us moderns".[22] It is yet another sign of cultural and physical well-being, even if it was restricted to those who could afford to eat well, namely the aristocracy and the (by the 1450s rapidly expanding) urban bourgeoisie.

Guillaume Coquillart's Paris shows all the symptoms of a society in rude health. His works form part of the *Basoche* repertoire, and were probably recited during those periods of more or less organised disorder in which the law students indulged for Twelfth Night or the Carnival season, or for their particular saints' days: one such was the broaching of the new wine on Martinmas in November. Coquillart's "affectionate satires" can be dated fairly precisely to the years 1478 to 1480. As with Villon, what characterises them is a certain knowingness, an amused tolerance of the follies of the world. The author of Ecclesiastes had taught that the *numerus stultorum infinitus est*, but Coquillart appears not to find this a cause for hand-wringing, and he assumes that his audience will feel the same. They are young (he calls them "enfans"), self-confident and sophisticated. His, and their, target is the bourgeoisie of which they will themselves one day soon be a part.

The bourgeoisie stands at the centre of Coquillart's world, and his *Droitz nouveaulx* are an exercise in social observation. Twenty years of prosperity under Louis XI have left France – or at least Paris – swimming in a sea of new-found wealth. Everyone seems to be on the move and everything seems to be up for grabs. A master of po-faced humour and mock indignation, Coquillart thus makes a show of berating Parisians for their sexual peccadilloes, acquisitiveness, and lack of decorum. Among his favourite targets are women who show off their breasts to titillate and seduce wealthy admirers, and who drop names with reckless abandon. A generation earlier, Villon had bid a fond farewell to "fillectes moustrans tetins / Pour avoir plus largement hostes", some of whom may well have been the mothers of the Parisian women Coquillart teases. It is a similar scenario, created with a similar lack of disapproval, but the genuine tone is one of amused admiration. Since there is so much new money around in Coquillart's Paris, new laws are needed, he suggests, to deal with the new social situation it has created. Meanwhile he provides the wealthy young snob with a tourist's guide to the fashionable Paris of his day, and also includes wonderful pen-portraits of would-be men-about-town. Those among them whose hair has turned grey are advised to squeeze onion juice on it to give it a blond tint, others whose beards are not thick enough are told to paint artificial stubble on their chins. The Paris of 1480 exudes prosperity and self-confidence. It is a new world, and one in which the carefree yuppies flourish, for, as the author states in his opening lines, this "monde nouveau" is peopled by "gens triumphans". It is this unmistakable spirit of triumphalism which characterises the times with a delight in consumption, ostentatious and sometimes frenzied, and a taste for risqué jokes and often outrageous behaviour. It has to be said that their taste and behaviour were scarcely those of nineteenth-century professors.

There is not a hint of seriousness in the *Droitz nouveaulx*, nor any sense of "decline" or "waning" or "melancholy". Paris had entered into a new period of enjoyment and extravagance, and Coquillart was there to celebrate it. He probably wrote this work for recitation in front of a *Basoche* audience during the traditional festivities at Epiphany or Martinmas. He provides his listeners with a code of social etiquette and a sort of do-it-yourself guide to seduction. He advises on whether a lover should ply a woman with presents, and tells him how to recognise the signs as to whether he is making any headway. In this he is following several other comic authors.[23] Where he perhaps differs is in his mock-serious social comment. Standards of behaviour are collapsing every-where, he announces with ill-concealed glee. People are living beyond their means and above their stations, all of which is causing havoc. He scoffs at their pretensions but, unlike moralists such as Olivier Maillard or Michel Menot, who were dismayed at the speed of social change and apparent immorality, he makes no attempt to censure, except in fun.

The new-found social mobility is nevertheless contained within fairly limited parameters. The phenomenon is above all Parisian; there are, for example, no peasants on the make. The country squire who comes to town to taste the good life for himself is roundly mocked, as is the new nobility, held up to the collective ridicule of the Paris young, who observe with a sense of youthful cynicism how hypocrisy, fraud and deceit are rampant. One imagines their reactions would have varied be-tween a shrug of the shoulders and a wry grin: they would not have been shocked or even surprised, for within two generations the urban and social landscape had been transformed. The detailed attention it paid to clothes, hair-styles, fashionable words and phrases as social indicators make Coquillart's work both topical in the extreme and difficult to annotate, but also render it invaluable, though less as a document of social history than as a guide to a caricatured reality. Yet that caricature renders reality recognisable nevertheless. The Parisian, and especially the street-wise Parisian, was clearly enjoying himself, as he mocked the pretensions of social climbers and the *nouveaux riches*:

> En Paris en y a beaucop
> Qui n'ont n'argent, vergier ne terre,
> Que vous jugeriez chascun cop,
> Alliez ou grans chiefz de guerre[24]

– that is until such time as they give themselves away with some social or sartorial *faux pas* – and there is something timeless about the description of the smartly dressed "gentilhomme d'honneur" who needs to hide the fact that he has only one coat. But the people who make up the city of Paris are less important as individuals than as ingredients in a collective sense of happy foolishness and well-being. The secret of success is to be fashionable: those who fail to keep up with current trends are quickly left behind, but to the great satisfaction at least of those who count themselves among the winners. Paris, with all her foibles, is the real heroine of the *Droitz nouveaulx*.

All in all, what makes this particular world go round is money. Coquillart reliably informs his listeners and readers that whereas some women enjoy making love – "pour avoir leur plaisance" – and deserve to be happy, others are merely on the make, and

> contrefont les amoureuses
> De quelque ung pour avoir argent![25]

As for men who have no money, gold chains or expensive jewellery about their persons, they can forget any thought of sexual advancement. The theme of the work is that graft and hypocrisy rule against a backdrop of loose money and even looser morals. But, as was true of Villon, the key to the poet's tone – and to his relationship with his audience – is summed up in the line from the *Ballade et oroison* to Cotart: "Pas ne le dy pour vous le reproucher." There is no hint of reproach or condemnation, except ironically, and the author's mask is crucial here. Villon and Coquillart created a sense of "jocular complicity",[26] a contract with their audiences based on a mutual understanding of what really matters in life. One finds it in the attack on the pastoral mode favoured by "Franc Gontier" in the *Testament*, with its description of a fat canon, *in flagrante delicto* on a soft bed with a lady of ill-repute, on whom Villon spies through a "trou de mortaise", inviting us to take part

in the peep-show. For Villon and his readers there is nothing dis-
honourable about this, whatever Siciliano might have thought.[27] It is,
rather, a demonstration of cleverness: his hypocritical couple have been
surprised and exposed not for our disapproval but for our amusement,
for the laughter of the fifteenth century was essentially a forgiving one.[28]
With this in mind, we can also see that only a critic led astray by notions
of pessimism and decadence in the waning of the Middle Ages could fail
to realise that Coquillart was sighing ironically when he pined for the
good old days when women could be had for a mere bauble, as opposed
to "aujourd'huy" when a would-be lover has to lay out a small fortune.

We see Coquillart at his tongue-in-cheek best in a slightly earlier
work, the *Plaidoyer d'entre la Simple et la Rusee*, probably written for
the *Basoche* entertainments of 1478, in which he has a comic lawyer
thunder against the dangers of sexual permissiveness. In this topsy-turvy
version of conventional morality, he worries about what would happen,
for example, if women gave away their favours without insisting on presents. The most unworthy men, he warns, would take advantage of them
(even the prettiest and sweetest ones). What is more, the profession of
prostitution would be ruined to the detriment of the "povres filles"
themselves. It clearly would not do! What would the world be coming to
if beautiful and gorgeous ("des plus gorgiases") women were prepared
to abandon themselves without playing hard to get? A frightening prospect! The case is put in a witty fashion which demands the
understanding of a sophisticated audience, together with an appreciation
of irony and mock indignation. There are no signs of naïveté or
melancholy here:

> Monseigneur, se tous ses moyens
> Estoient vrais, creés que on verroit
> Venir des inconveniens
> Bien grans. Car quoy! il s'ensuiveroit
> Que ung meschant homme se porroit
> Prendre aux plus succrees et drues,
> Et par ce semble qu'il ne fauldroit
> Qu'abbattre femmes en my les rues.
> Sy telles manieres indeues
> Couroient, tout seroit aboli;
> Povres filles seroient perdues
> Et le mestier trop avilli!
> Par quoy il n'y auroit celluy
> Qui ne gouvernast damoiselles.
> Et qu'il ne voulsist au jourdhuy,
> Sans foncer, avoir des plus belles

Et des plus gorgiases, s'elles
S'i vouloient habandonner
Comme il dist. Qu'elles feussent telles,
Dieu le me veulle pardonner!
Il ne fouldroit donc plus donner
Rubbis, diamans ne turquoises,
Mais dire franc, sans sejourner:
"Allons, faisons, ne vous desplaise!"
Chascun en feroit a son aise
Sans avoir langaige ou effroy,
La coustume en seroit maulvaise.[29]

By the time Villon came to write his *Testament*, his beloved Paris was recovering its social health. Twenty years later, in Coquillart's day, it was back to its frivolous, irreverent self. Both men laugh with it as much as at it, and in this they reflect the temper of the times. Theirs was not the France of the Renaissance – there are few signs yet of the revival of classical scholarship, of Italian influence, or of the printing boom which was launched in the 1480s – but it was definitely a France of renewal, and it was an urban renewal based on Paris and maybe one or two other large towns, all with an urban mentality and urban needs which were materialistic rather than spiritual, as one would expect of a post-war generation. Villon and Coquillart, and many others, could forgive it its extravagances. Huizinga found it less easy to do so. Or perhaps he simply found it uncongenial. Or incomprehensible.

The same good humour pervades farce theatre, the stories of the *Cent nouvelles nouvelles*[30] and the works of countless so-called minor poets. There is no denying that it is vulgar and that the jokes are sometimes obscene, but the modern reader is less likely to be shocked than was his counterpart of half a century ago by farces such as the *Farce du pect*, in which a woman refuses to admit that it is she who has passed wind. Her exasperated husband has no choice but to take her to court. The wife finally owns up but argues that the accident only occurred because her husband obliged her to carry a heavy bundle of clothes. Whose fault is it then? After some comically tortuous reasoning worthy of Baisecul and Humevesne the judge sums up by suggesting that couples must learn to live with the ups and downs of married life and that they must:

Accordez les nez et les culz
Ensemble à tous sentemens.[31]

When he drew up his list of farces in his influential *Répertoire du théâtre comique en France au Moyen Age*, published in 1886, the distinguished theatre historian Petit de Julleville was too embarrassed to give the title of this play. Nor could he bring himself to provide a plot-summary for it, merely stating that it was a "parade insignifiante et tout à fait plate [...] un échange d'injures et de coups entre un mari et sa femme". But as Claude Thiry remarks,

> Cette farce ne faisait certes pas rire Petit de Julleville, mais on veut croire qu'elle aurait amené au moins un sourire sur les lèvres de Pierre Dac... et on l'imagine, sans trop d'effort, jouée devant un public 'affamé de rire', où aurait pu figurer Maistre Alcofribas Nasier.[32]

The self-censorship which some scholars imposed on themselves in the nineteenth century not only prevented others from appreciating literary works of the past, but also helped to give a false impression of the age and its mentality.

The *Farce du pect* was not of course the only farce to incur Petit de Julleville's displeasure. The *Farce nouvelle et fort joyeuse des Femmes qui font escurer leurs chaulderons et deffendent que on mette la piece auprès du trou*, which must have seemed terrifyingly explicit to him, becomes in his list *Les Femmes et le Chaudronnier*.[33] By describing it as a "parade grossière et dépourvue de toute espèce de sel", he also appears to want to ensure that nobody should be tempted to read it. One would love to know whether he even understood some of the sexual and physiological allusions in this play, starting with the "chaulderon" which needed scouring... Other farce women *font rembourrer leur bas*, or *vendent amourettes en gros et en detail*, or require the services of a *ramoneur de cheminees*,[34] and I feel sure that Petit de Julleville would not have wished to draw attention to these titles, or their unmentionable contents, in mixed company at least. Would it have done to draw too much attention, either, to plays in which women are sexually demanding and more than a match in a variety of ways for their often impotent or inadequate husbands? Are these not further signs of a collapsing civilisation?

What we have seen demonstrates clearly enough that there was no lack of laughter in what has perhaps been too easily written off as a time of decline. It has also provided us with a useful lesson in cultural historiography, as we have seen how one age transposed to another its own attitudes and taboos. There may be those of us today who do not find the humour of the fifteenth and early sixteenth centuries to our taste, but we can no longer deny the vitality of an age which, even if it had its own inhibitions and preoccupations, did not share those of the late nineteenth century. What is more, a greater awareness of texts which were not easily available to scholars a century ago allows us to understand better the spirit of the times. By criticising the profligacy and extravagance he sees all around him, a moralist like Eloy d'Amerval (now at last available in a modern critical edition)[35] implicitly bears witness to the social revolution he appears to deplore. Unaware, as they went about their lives in a bustling and prosperous city, that they were living at the end of the Middle Ages, many Parisians of the fifteenth and early sixteenth centuries cheerfully set about laughing it into its grave. And they would have agreed with one of the outspoken women in the farce of the *Femmes qui font escurer leurs chaulderons* when she concludes that the best way to live your life is to surround yourself with happy people and to laugh with them:

> Rire avecques ceulx qui riront,
> Il n'est point de meilleure vie;
> Et puis laissez parler envie.[36]

So much for the waning of the Middle Ages.[37]

---

[1] The first edition in English was J. Huizinga, *The Waning of the Middle Ages: A Study of the Forms of Life, Thought and Art in France and the Netherlands in the XIVth and XVth Centuries*, tr. F. Hopman, London, 1924. It has been reissued in various forms since in Britain and the United States, probably reaching most people through the Penguin paperback edition.

[2] See D. Poirion, "Déclin ou décadence: une confusion du sens et des valeurs", in *Apogée et déclin. Actes du Colloque de l'URA 411, Provins, 1991*, Textes réunis par C. Thomasset et M. Zink (Paris, 1993), pp. 293-304 (pp. 300-1). In his introduction to the same volume Zink speaks of how, "s'agissant de la fin du Moyen Age, un préjugé très répandu veut qu'il existe une crise et un déclin de la littérature correspondant à une crise et à un déclin dans les autres domaines" (p. 10). Cf. the remarks made by G. Gros to the effect that "la notion de déclin appliquée à la dernière periode littéraire du Moyen Age paraît bien procéder de la rétrospection du regard moderne qu'influence, dans la conception théorique de l'évolution de l'art, le changement voulu par l'enthousiasme renaissant, et peut-être aussi la définition équilibrée de l'esthétique classique, implicitement tenue pour le critère de l'apogée". He goes on to make the very valid point that "il ne faut plus voir l'œuvre de Villon comme l'extrême avatar du désarroi consécutif à la Guerre de Cent Ans, une sorte de Testament du Moyen Age" (*ibid.*, p. 269).

[3] H. Hornik, "Three Interpretations of the French Renaissance", in *French Humanism 1460-1600*, ed. W. L. Gundersheimer (London, 1969), pp. 19-47 (p. 38). Hornik's article was first published in 1960 in *Studies in the Renaissance*; mais quand même...

[4] See in particular L. W. Johnson, *Poets as Players: Theme and Variation in Late Medieval French Poetry* (Stanford, 1990).

[5] *Art. cit.*, pp. 33-34.

[6] For discussion of these figures see A. Fierro, *Histoire et dictionnaire de Paris* (Paris, 1996), p. 280.

[7] As A. Beevor and A. Cooper's book, *Paris after the Liberation* (New York, 1994), illustrates, there are some uncanny parallels between two otherwise totally different epochs and mentalities. See my article, "Aspects du théâtre comique français des XVe et XVIe siècles: la sottie, le monologue dramatique et le sermon joyeux", in *Le Théâtre au Moyen Age* (Montreal, 1981), pp. 279-298, and especially p. 294: "Ce qui ne veut pas dire, loin de là, que tout le monde mangeait à sa faim aux alentours de 1480. C'est ainsi que les vantards des monologues d'amoureux sont, par leur préoccupation obsessionnelle avec le paraître, et par conséquent avec tout ce qui concerne la mode, avec leur *sex appeal*, comme des zazous avant la lettre. En racontant par le menu leur moindre exploit, ces esbroufeurs entendent peut-être nous faire oublier qu'ils ont connu la faim et la misère."

[8] See my article on "La Satire affectueuse dans les *Droitz nouveaulx* de Guillaume Coquillart", in *Réforme Humanisme Renaissance*, 11 (1980), 92-99, in which I show that Coquillart's original public was essentially an educated one of students and lawyers enjoying themselves on their traditional feast days. Bakhtin spoke of this "joyeuse littérature récréative des écoliers" which he saw as being close to popular culture. Those who appreciated most this learned humour, though, were the members of the "confrérie joyeuse" of law students and clerks who formed the *Basoche*. What I describe as Coquillart's "clins d'œil de complicité" were directed at them. They understood his use of irony, and also understood that his "rire est positif, jamais grinçant". It is worth pointing out that the two nineteenth-century editors of Coquillart's works saw him as an embittered moralist. Huizinga mentions him only fleetingly, but would have read him in these editions, and read their misguided introductions and notes.

[9] J. Dufournet, "La Génération de Louis XI: quelques aspects", *Le Moyen Age*, XCVIII (1992), 227-250. Cf. P. Ménard's comments: "Il faudrait aussi prendre garde au caractère trouble de certains rires. Dans les contes obscènes rien n'est net. Il serait exagéré de croire que l'idéalisation de la sexualité et l'atmosphère joyeuse du récit excluent toute inquiétude et toute angoisse. Les histoires sexuelles véhiculent toujours de secrètes inquiétudes. La gauloiserie n'est souvent que la face visible d'un ensemble beaucoup plus complexe", q.v. "Le Rire et le sourire au moyen âge dans la littérature et dans les arts. Essai de problématique", in *Le Rire au Moyen Age*, textes recueillis par T. Bouché et H. Charpentier (Bordeaux, 1990), pp. 7-30 (p. 25).

[10] See B. Roy, *Une culture de l'équivoque* (Montreal, 1992), p. 9. He gives a guarded welcome to Bakhtinian views which of course reflect a very different interpretation of medieval culture, but makes the point that festivity was not confined to carnival, nor was humour the preserve of the popular classes. Instead, he sees the Middle Ages as a time when "une société humoristique" existed, inspired by what he calls "l'*esprit* médiéval, dans tous les sens du mot, [qui] résultait alors d'une fascination pour la multiplicité des sens, pour la richesse des possibles, pour l'attrait chatoyant de l'ambigu" (pp. 9-10). J.

Le Goff's "Rire au Moyen Age", *Cahiers du Centre de recherches historiques*, 3 (1989), 1-14, makes some useful points about the theory (especially) and practice of laughter in the medieval period but is concerned mostly with earlier centuries. Our discussion is meant to focus mainly on the period following the Hundred Years' War, that is to say from about the middle of the 15th century.

[11] Roy, *op. cit.*, p. 96. His chapter on "Les Voies de l'humour érotique" (pp. 89-100) is an excellent introduction to the humour of the period, and to its penchant at all levels of society for obscenity.

[12] *Ibid.*, pp. 101-112.

[13] See S. Delany, "Anatomy of the resisting reader: some implications of resistance to sexual wordplay in medieval literature", *Exemplaria. A Journal of Theory in Medieval and Renaissance Studies*, 4 (1992), 7-34. I say "incidentally" because her arguments deal mainly with English literature and English-language critics. But much of what she says applies to French texts and their readers. She notes that the "main lines of resistance were well established in authoritative medieval scholarship of the earlier part of this century" (p. 11) and singles out for criticism C. S. Lewis, who did, of course, write the authoritative (as it were) guide to the *Roman de la Rose* in English. As she points out "despite the evidence some scholars have been reluctant to accept erotic wordplay as normative in medieval literature" which "announces attitudes originating elsewhere than in literary evidence" (p. 10). She shows how critical discourse frequently asserts that punning, for example, is "the lowest form of humour", and that, by its very presence in a text, sexual humour lowers the tone. What is more, critics of this traditionalist and conservative bent "depreciate linguistic play as offensive or trivial; assume the incompatibility of linguistic play with a humane temperament or with matters of high seriousness; and end with an appeal to morality or (the gentleman's version of morality) good taste" (p. 12).

[14] The *Recueil général des sotties*, 3 vol. (Paris, 1902-1912), remains an indispensable tool for anyone interested in comic and satirical writing in the fifteenth and sixteenth centuries. The texts are often too obscure to speak for themselves, however, while the editor's comments do little to make them more approachable.

[15] I. Siciliano, *François Villon et les thèmes poétiques du moyen âge* (Paris, 1934), pp. 169-199. His concluding remarks give a flavour of both style and sentiment: "Avec Villon, par Villon, poète vivant, enraciné dans le moyen âge, tirant toute son inspiration du moyen âge, le moyen âge est fini. Le reste n'est que survivance lamentable. Il faut que la Renaissance vienne. Mais celle-ci n'a rien déblayé, car rien n'existait plus" (p. 199).

[16] See Johnson, *op. cit.*, p. 236.

[17] J. Fox, *The Poetry of Fifteenth-Century France*, 2 vol. (London, 1994), I, p. 76.

[18] I have used the text given by J. Rychner and A. Henry in their edition of *Le Testament Villon*, 2 vol. (Geneva, 1974), I, vv. 1238-1265.

[19] See J. Dufournet, *Recherches sur le Testament de François Villon*, 2e édition, 2 vol. (Paris, 1971-1973), II, p. 410.

[20] *Ibid.*, p. 415.

[21] *Ed. cit.*, II, p. 184.

[22] See D. E. Scully and T. Scully, *Early French Cookery* (Ann Arbor, 1995), p. 7. They make the point that "despite our modern prejudices and presumptions, in many respects Western Europe in the fourteenth and fifteenth centuries was in fact a remarkably civilized place. In the face of the common double tribulations of warfare and disease, social organization in France in particular allowed two small classes of individuals,

landed aristocrats and relatively wealthy bourgeois, to develop the arts of comfort and pleasure to quite a high degree" (pp. 6-7).

[23] Works such as the *Arrêts d'Amour* by Martial d'Auvergne, the *Confession et Testament de l'amant trespassé de deuil*, the *Amant rendu cordelier à l'observance d'amour*, to name but a few. Now rarely read, they reached a wide audience (in manuscript) and provided much pleasure.

[24] See Guillaume Coquillart, *Œuvres*, ed. M. J. Freeman (Geneva, 1975), p. 173, vv. 887-890.

[25] *Ibid.*, p. 197, vv.1317-1318. Elsewhere he states that, according to the common saying, illicit sex is no sin, since everyone enjoys doing it: "Ainçoys, selon le commun son,/Habiter ce n'est pas peché,/ Chascun en prise la façon" (p. 147, vv. 372-374).

[26] Tony Hunt uses the term with regard to Villon in his *Villon's Last Will. Language and Authority in the Testament* (Oxford, 1996), p. 82: it applies equally well to Coquillart. Hunt's lively book is principally concerned with the textual strategies exploited by Villon to create "a close rapport with the audience and form part of a contract between the two" (p. 96), using irony, pseudo-confession and what he calls a "verbal wink" (p. 83). Following in the footsteps of Muhlethaler, Koopmans and others, he stresses the "ludic excitement of virtuosity and display" in the *Testament*, and the "play of meanings in a joyful heteroglossia" (p. 141). This could take place only within the context of a work written for performance, a sort of dramatic monologue depending for effect on the complicity of a reasonably learned and well disposed audience. It goes without saying that this would involve more laughter than tears.

[27] Siciliano, *op. cit.*, p. 417, sees it as "une posture triste et incommode", and a form of self-debasement. There is nothing sinister about Villon's show of voyeurism, in fact. It is rather an exhibition of playful one-upmanship. The joke is on the fictional fat canon, and we are invited to share it.

[28] J.- C. Aubailly made a similar point about the farce theatre of the time with regard to the characters it would appear to be satirising: "ce n'est pas un rire vengeur ou correcteur que la farce suscite à leur égard, mais plutôt une reconnaissance souriante faite de pitié bonhomme. Le rire n'est pas ici une arme, mais un pardon", q.v. *Le Théâtre médiéval profane et comique* (Paris, 1975), p. 182.

[29] *Ed. cit.*, pp. 37-38, vv. 540-566.

[30] Although they are Burgundian (i.e. from northern France and the Low Countries), they share a similar outlook and humour to the Parisian works of the period.

[31] The farce was recently published in a modern scholarly edition. See *Recueil de farces (1450-1550)*, tome X, ed. A. Tissier (Geneva, 1996), p. 63, vv. 297-298.

[32] See C. Thiry, "L'Altérité du rire médiéval: la farce et son public", in *Der Ursprung von Literatur*, ed. G. Smolka-Koerdt et al. (Munich, 1988), pp. 199-220 (p. 216).

[33] Published, with full commentary and explicit annotations by Tissier in tome IX of the *Recueil de farces* (1995, pp. 197-240).

[34] The titles left little to the imagination. The particular qualities of the *ramoneur de cheminées* are described in detail in the farce of that name, published by Tissier in t. IV (1989).

[35] Eloy d'Amerval, *Le Livre de la Deablerie*, ed. R. Deschaux and B. Charrier (Geneva, 1991).

[36] *Op. cit.*, p. 220, vv. 75-77. It is impossible to date this farce (like so many others) with any precision. Tissier suggests that it could be from the end of the fifteenth century. On the other hand, it was printed for the first time only in the middle of the sixteenth, hence

the other hand, it was printed for the first time only in the middle of the sixteenth, hence it may well have been written after *Gargantua*. The author seems to share Rabelais's belief in the power of laughter and his distaste for those afflicted with "envie".

[37] Philippe Ménard points out (*art cit.*, p. 10) that this was indeed a very productive period for comic literature, especially in the theatre, "mais il nous manque toujours une grande étude d'ensemble du rire dans cette littérature abondante". I hope that this modest contribution of mine will prove to be a nudge in the right direction.

3. Bergson and Rabelais: the twain who never met
John Parkin

The origins of this chapter lie at once close to home and far away, which is to say at the doors of two figures whom I admire equally and who may indeed have more than that in common: they are respectively Professor Walter Redfern and Mr Henry Miller. At the July 1995 International Society for Humour Studies conference at Aston University, in a heat-wave matched only by the intellectual temperatures generated within its seminars, I had the privilege of sitting, one might have said sweltering, through Professor Redfern's paper on Vallès ("Blague Hard") which I was delighted to hear punctuated with a semi-parenthetical remark describing Henri Bergson as surely the most over-rated humour theorist of the twentieth century, indeed it may have been of all time. At any rate "Hear! Hear!" to that, then as now. What struck me immediately, more-over, was that my other idol would have concurred with the pair of us. For Henry Miller, roguish and iconoclastic where Bergson is prudish and moralistic, repeatedly mentioned the theories of *Le Rire* with reserv-ations bordering on distaste. From *The Books in My Life* comes a remark condemning works on humour such as Bergson's (and Koestler's and Eastman's) as deadly[1] and in a later text entitled *Flash Back* he calls *Le Rire* a very abstract intellectual work, not at all provocative of laughter.[2]

Now the fact that Bergson appears as rankly humourless through-out the hundred or so pages of *Le Rire* need not detain us long. Humour is humour; humour theory is theory. It is a humorist's job to provoke mirth; it is a theorist's job to lend enlightenment. Moreover at least Bergson does not fall into Freud's trap of telling us that the next joke to come will be brilliant, whereupon it, or at least its translated version, falls as flat as one of those sidewalk stumblers who, he tells us, have us in stitches. No, books of humour theory have not necessarily failed in their function if they do not make you laugh. It is just an added bonus if they do.

At the same time, moreover, there is a jejune quality to Bergson-ian theory which does give one, along with Miller, pause. Consider the following paragraph:

> Un homme, qui courait dans la rue, trébuche et tombe: les passants rient. On ne rirait pas de lui, je pense, si l'on pouvait supposer que la fantaisie lui est venue tout à coup de s'asseoir par terre. On rit de ce qu'il s'est assis involontairement. Ce n'est donc pas son changement brusque d'attitude qui fait rire, c'est ce qu'il y a

d'involontaire dans le changement, c'est la maladresse. Une pierre était peut-être sur le chemin. Il aurait fallu changer d'allure ou tourner l'obstacle. Mais par manque de souplesse, par distraction ou obstination du corps, *par un effet de raideur ou de vitesse acquise*, les muscles ont continué d'accomplir le même mouvement quand les circonstances demandaient autre chose. C'est pourquoi l'homme est tombé, et c'est de quoi les passants rient.[3]

Small wonder that these trite and artificial notions appealed so little to a writer whose streets where filled not with crowds of onlookers tittering at their isolated comic victims but rather with the carnivalesque riots of lunacy which are the Paris of *Tropic of Cancer* or the New York of *Tropic of Capricorn*:

Every time I hit that runway towards dinner hour a fever of expectancy seized me. It's only a few blocks from Times Square to Fiftieth Street, and when one says Broadway that's all that's really meant and it's really nothing, just a chicken run and a lousy one at that, but at seven in the evening when everybody's rushing for a table there's a sort of electric crackle in the air and your hair stands on end like an antennae and if you're receptive you not only get every bash and flicker but you get the statistical itch, the *quid pro quo* of the interactive, interstitial, ectoplasmic quantum of bodies jostling in space like stars which compose the Milky Way, only this is the Gay White Way, the top of the world with no roof and not even a crack or hole under your feet to fall through and say it's a lie. The absolute impersonality of it brings you to a pitch of warm human delirium which makes you run forward like a blind nag and wag your delirious ears. Everyone is so utterly, confoundedly not himself that you become automatically the personification of the whole human race, shaking hands with a thousand human hands, cackling with a thousand different human tongues, cursing, applauding, whistling, crooning, soliloquizing, orating, gesticulating, urinating, fecundating, wheedling, cajoling, whimpering, bartering, pimping, caterwauling, and so on and so forth. You are all the men who ever lived up to Moses, and beyond that you are a woman buying a hat, or a bird cage, or just a mouse trap. You can lie in wait in a show-window, like a fourteen carat gold ring, or you can climb the side of a building like a human fly, but nothing will stop the procession, not even umbrellas flying at lightning speed, nor double-decked walruses marching calmly to the oyster banks.[4]

This is the incongruous habitat of the Pythonesque Silly Walker, of Hulot the patron saint of chaos, of Jarry, Handke and the Marx Brothers, all of whom compound their comic follies in a rich amalgam whereby their skills of supple improvisation and cultivated incongruity generate a humour which seeks out and rewards the unexpected rather than stubbornly deriding and condemning it. So let the human fly climb the wall and fall flat in the street, let the walruses urinate on him in the gutter, let even women buy mouse traps in shops, let anyone be, provided he be not himself and normal. For incongruity per se, the confounded refusal of things to be predictably themselves, is, Miller knew, one of the key sources of comedy, and that in itself as much as in the witty disapproval it can inspire.

Consider another of Bergson's preliminary examples.

> Voici maintenant une personne qui vaque à ses petites occupations avec une régularité mathématique. Seulement, les objets qui l'entourent ont été truqués par un mauvais plaisant. Elle trempe sa plume dans l'encrier et en retire de la boue, croit s'asseoir sur une chaise solide et s'étend sur le parquet, enfin agit à contre-sens ou fonctionne à vide, toujours par un effet de vitesse acquise. L'habitude avait imprimé un élan. Il aurait fallu arrêter le mouvement ou l'infléchir.[5]

Again he envisages a genuine comic situation: April Fool's Day or the prank against the uninitiate. But the comic effects he describes, effects of unpredictable outcome (mud for ink, or the pratfall), need not be linked to a failure of any sort. To be sure human behaviour is conditioned, but who could predict mud in an inkwell and who would foresee walruses on Broadway? These comic incongruities need not be targeted at someone who should have done this or that, changed stride or adapted the force of habit so as to behave in a way of which Bergson approves. Instead they can result from the kind of comic ingenuity which indeed has one fulfil a sudden notion to sit on the ground, and then lay a table-cloth there, setting out a meal of stewed dung and paving stones; and this is the same spontaneous zany which has an inkwell produce first mud, then a bouquet of flowers, then the Reichstag, then the continent of South America and finally Margaret Thatcher's bagpipes.

Arguing from a pre-established position *Le Rire* cuts out these alternative possibilities from the start, which clearly alienates those like Miller whose comic procedures are so open and experimental. Bergson, in contrast, pre-selects but those procedures which are targeted and judgmental, hence falling, much of the time, well beside the point. So, given that he limits his range so drastically, begging questions throughout his argument, why has it been felt almost *de rigueur* to bend the knee before the Bergsonian altar when sketching out one's own thoughts on laughter, at the same time generating sentences like the following: "The reader is left with a Bergsonian smile",[6] "Bergson – the most original of all the philosophers of the comic",[7] "Bergson, in one of the twentieth century's classic essays on humour, argues that 'the comic is that side of a person which reveals his likeness to a thing';"[8] and why did Miller instinctively follow the same path? For despite the antipathy separating them, Bergson sprang immediately to his mind on the subject of comic theory, just as he has done to authors in the formative stages of works like Keith Cameron's recent compilation *Humour and History*:

If we agree with Bergson (Le Rire) that laughter is society's weapon to criticise departures from the norm, from the expected, to punish and to correct idiosyncrasies, then it should be possible to detect a relationship between the use of humour and the course of history:[9]

whereupon, if I may say so, a most stimulating volume follows. Why finally does François Rabelais, Miller's favourite writer and undoubtedly France's greatest comic author, only get a single mention in *Le Rire*, while Molière, undoubtedly France's greatest comic dramatist, gets so many?

To clear some of the undergrowth it is necessary to repeat the main principles of Bergsonian theory and before doing so I apologise at once for teaching so many grandmothers and fathers to suck eggs. At the same time, a moment or two's refreshment is no bad thing.

Laughter for Bergson is first of all a human phenomenon, in that not only are human beings the only creatures to laugh, they are also the only creatures to provoke laughter, in so far as animals, say, are only risible to the extent that they call human beings to mind: a good example of this is the chimpanzees' tea-party, not to say the House of Commons at Question Time. Secondly, laughter is incompatible with sensitivity: "Le rire n'a pas de plus grand ennemi que l'émotion;"[10] so our stumbler in the street is risible only until he reacts painfully, at which point the onlookers' sympathy drowns out their mirth. Thirdly humour is communicative and social: it always seeks a response from other laughers. Hence, in a somewhat dogmatic conclusion to his first section, Bergson combines the three principles by arguing that the comic comes about when a group directs its laughter at one of their number whilst at the same time stifling their emotions and acting on the intellectual level alone.

Now these are the preconditions of humour, but not its stimulus. Rather does that stimulus reside, for Bergson, in a mechanical rigidity defying the supple adaptiveness of real life, which rigidity the watching group observes and then punishes with the emotionless laughter described above. Thus forgetfulness is risible in that the forgetter has lapsed into routine behaviour and not taken account of the new circumstances he has forgotten. Quixote is risible in that he continues mechanically to act out his fantasy of knighthood despite the repeated beatings and humiliations it causes him. Molière's Avare is risible in that he can be defined in terms of his vice alone, the vice of avarice to which all his acts can be related but of whose comical effect he remains unaware. Stimulated by the incongruity of their mechanical unlifelike behaviour-patterns, the laughter punishing these victims aims at the same time to impose normality on them at the expense of those same patterns and the fixed ideas and attitudes (forgetfulness, delusions of grandeur, meanness) from which they stem.

Fundamentally Bergson has the comic originate in a substitution of the inanimate object for the animate human being: so a real person becomes a jack-in-the-box or a painted skittle, Sancho Panza is reduced to a personified belly, De Gaulle, say, to a mere exaggerated nose, or Richard Nixon to a grossly heavy and permanently dark-shaded jowl. The examples could be extended at will, but it is in this context that Rabelais is mentioned. For one of the basic comic mechanisms which Bergson defines is the string puppet, a comic figure who has no independent power, who is ridiculous in not possessing the human faculty of free-will, and who, in more sophisticated terms, is the character believing himself to be in control of his actions when in fact he is being entirely manipulated by stronger forces. This is the comic pattern of the cat and mouse or pig in the middle, and it is exemplified in Rabelais by the frantic toings and froings of Panurge, who is unable to free himself of an obsessive worry concerning his eventual fate were he to marry.

Again a word of background may be in order. Panurge, without doubt Rabelais' greatest comic creation, is the companion figure to the heroic Pantagruel of whom he is at the same time the comic antithesis, Sganarelle to his Don Juan, Sancho Panza to his Quixote, Jeeves to his Wooster. Now in the first volume of Pantagruel's adventures, where he is invented, Panurge is predominantly a knave, remarkable for being sexually active, comically ingenious, a character at times heroic, more often amoral, and frequently immoral, in all a standard trickster figure of the type Alison Williams has worked on so promisingly during her thesis studies. However in the *Tiers livre*, which is paradoxically enough the second volume of those adventures, Panurge changes from a knave into a fool, and one who, though still affected by lust, becomes obsessed with his less comically admirable fears of cuckoldry. Before he does marry, he seeks to learn whether or not he should marry, and furthermore what guarantees he can have that, were he to marry, his wife would not take lovers, not beat him, not rob him.

This is where the comic manipulation comes in. For, structurally speaking, the entire *Tiers livre* can be seen as a set of attempts by Panurge to gain answers to these questions from a variety of oracles none of whom satisfies him, up to and including Pantagruel himself. So we have a comic portrayal of obsession, of a character locked into a mechanically repeated behaviour pattern whereby he continually seeks advice concerning a problem, but never finds in that advice a satis-factory solution to his problem, and this is unsurprising as the only solution is, as he is told from the outset by Pantagruel, to make his mind up, take the plunge and hope for the best.

Now thus far the Bergsonian criteria apply: Panurge is a travesty of a human being, reduced even below the status he enjoyed in the pre-vious volume. Given this reduction in status we need not sympathise with him – one can even regard his folly in the *Tiers livre* as just punishment for his knavery in *Pantagruel* – and in the jeering laughter which we aim at him we are grouped in several ways. We belong in the company of the other characters who to various extents make mock of him, we belong in the company of Pantagruelistes, that group of narratees to whom the author addresses himself, and over the head of his own characters, in devising the textual humour and comic character-isation there to be enjoyed, and we also are grouped as real Rabelaisants, sharing our responses via the ongoing dialogue of Rabelais studies which has continued, thank God, unabated since the sixteenth century.

All that is serious in life, Bergson tells us, comes from our freedom. The feelings and passions we cultivate, the acts which we decide upon and carry out, these are what constitute the drama of real living: witness for instance our own seriously taken but free decisions to marry or not to marry. To convert this drama into a comedy, all one needs to do is to remove that freedom, and convert human beings into puppets, the playthings of inevitability: the inevitability which makes of Panurge the perpetual victim of his own preoccupations and, although Bergson does not say it, the eventual victim, were he to marry, of that fate which so preoccupies him in the text. Forever suspended between his own desire to marry and his own fear of marriage, Panurge behaves as an object, a mechanical travesty of a real person. For that real person he is not, would in real life, which this is not, be coerced by his own free-will and self-awareness, reinforced by the punishing laughter which society directs at him, into making his mind up, adapting to his cir-cumstances and stopping making a fool of himself.

So far so good, for there is no point in denying that if one chooses to adopt Bergson's premises then a comic effect of this type may emerge from a reading of Rabelais. Panurge's absurd behaviour will be condemned by a hostile reader, the grotesques of Rabelais' giants will be laughed at as ugly deformations of the human norm, and Rabelais' vulgarity can likewise be used as a weapon to express good-humoured abuse towards the pedants, censors, kill-joys, prudes and obscurantists to whom the humanist author and bawdy narrator oppose themselves. Cajoled by the moral and literary power of these twin voices – author and narrator – and joining in a chorus of disapproving narratees, the reader issues a series of derisive responses towards these clowns who are travestying life as we know it, as Rabelais enjoyed it, and as we would want to live it.

But that all depends on one choosing to adopt Bergson's premises. Supposing one does not; and after all human life is for Bergson an expression of human freedom. Suppose one uses this freedom not to condemn the target figures but to side with them. Does this break the mould of Bergsonian theory, or is it merely a literary impossibility, an attitude so perverse as to deform the Rabelaisian, nay indeed the entire comic, experience? The figure to be mentioned here is Mikhail Bakhtin, by now established as the most influential student of Rabelais of our own century. The contributions he has made to Medieval and Renaissance studies, and also to the general theory of fiction specifically via his notions of heterogolossia, dialogism and the carnivalesque, these need scarcely be emphasised and cannot here be summarised, except in his key concept of carnival laughter.

For Bakhtin Rabelais' work is the culmination of a process whereby the laughter of the people, different in kind from the laughter of the intelligentsia, broke through into great literature during the Renaissance, having been maintained at a subcultural level throughout the Middle Ages. However the life of the Medieval folk, encapsulated in the unofficial world of the carnival, was an extremely rich one, and its effects are traceable via those relics of the carnivalesque which he analyses: folk rituals, farce theatre, doggerel verses, mock sermons, popular tales, joke-sequences, grotesque designs on churches and in manuscripts and so on.

Now the key debate in this area of Bakhtin studies has tended to focus on the extent to which these phenomena are genuinely popular, and to what extent maintained not by the people at all but rather by an unorthodox element within the cultural, nay socially powerful elites which Bakhtin says were alien to and subverted by the carnival tradition. However this debate need again not concern us centrally, important though it be. For the key point which I would like here to emphasise about Bakhtin's humour theory does not in fact depend on his sociology, but rather on his psychology. He argues that carnival laughter, gaining its strongest literary expression in Rabelais' work, was both mocking and celebratory. It was two-faced. It both crowned and dethroned. It both destroyed and created. It both reviled and revered. Hence its true temporality, like its true nature, is ambiguous. It belongs to and is sparked by an ambivalent time, festive time, which looks both forward and backward, destroying the old while creating the new. Accordingly the expressions of that trend of humour, for our purposes the Rabelaisian grotesque, are also thoroughly ambivalent, being objects of rejoicing as well as objects of contempt.

This possibility complicates the response to the comic very greatly, which is itself a laudable aim, for were Bergson right, then to laugh comically would always be to exert social coercion on a deviant: quite a monoform, not to say a dangerous pattern. I am reminded of O'Brien's statement to Winston Smith about the humour of the future as devised by the Party in *1984*: "There will be no laughter, except the laugh of triumph over a defeated enemy."[11] For Bergson, too, humour is unambiguously aggressive, there being no motive to laughter other than the desire to triumph over an enemy, although for him that enemy threatens less an ideology via his deviance, than life itself through his loss of vitality; he is not a heretic but a mechanical automaton.

Now I have sketched the features of Panurge as comic dynamo, this being his role in *Pantagruel*. Those features are knavery, sexual potency and ingenuity, and they can be fitted into Bakhtinian carnivalesque in that carnival was a time when pranks and tricks were tolerated, sexual licence became permissible, and people adopted an alternative identity composed of ingenious costumes, grotesque masks, inverted behaviour-patterns, foul language and generally relaxed social norms. So the knave is a carnival figure to the extent that he personifies certain aspects of carnival licence – his amorality and immorality are a part of this – but our comic celebration of the knave can only fit laterally into Bergsonian theory. Insofar as he uses his licence to attack targets deserving of attack, then he can be seen as fulfilling this punitive function. Panurge guys the university authorities, Panurge torments the haughty Parisian ladies, Panurge unseats the town police; and all of the vices they can be seen to enshrine – pedantry, vanity, pompous authority – these Rabelais can be seen to be victimising in much the same way as Molière does equivalent vices in his theatre, which as I have said is the much richer source of Bergson's examples.

However the role of deflating vice – let us say the satiric function – is not the essence of the knave. The essence of the knave is knavery: a refusal to accept the voice of conscience which argues that human respect is important, that property rights must be safeguarded, that society cannot survive without a moral consensus in the majority and a habitual obedience to that consensus. All of this social morality the knave defies, and the point can, as I say, be extended psychologically if not sociologically in the Bakhtinian direction to the extent that one's positive response to the knavish tricks of Panurge, Puck, Captain McHeath, Til Eulenspiegel, Reynard the Fox, Dorian in television's *Birds of a Feather* or Alan B'stard in its *New Statesman*, can be seen as at the same time a celebration of the very norms which are being subverted – as Bakhtin has it, the laughter is two-faced, a dethroning which is at the same time a crowning.

Now this of course does not make logical sense, but logic is not the whole of human awareness or of human life, a point which Bergson himself made, curiously enough, and with great consistency throughout his metaphysics. Hence alongside the mathematically scientific aspects of thought, which are determined by rational methods of analysis and quantity, Bergson also sought in works such as *Essai sur les données immédiates de la conscience, Matière et mémoire* and *L'Evolution créatrice* to give due importance to intuition, which alone could grasp the essential and qualitative aspects of life as it is lived through time, rather than as it is conceptualised in space. This is a laudable purpose. However to return momentarily to Panurge, it is a moot point whether the essence of his character has been grasped by the in fact highly reductive apparatus of *Le Rire*, and it is significant, moreover, that it is not as paradoxical knave, and a knave paradoxically loved throughout his life by Pantagruel (the point is made emphatically by Rabelais as of his first appearance),[12] that Bergson represents him in the first place, but rather in his less admirable identity of semi-paranoiac, anxiety-ridden fool.

This is the second version of Panurge, the Panurge of the *Tiers livre* who is to degenerate, Michael Screech would have us believe, into the contemptible beast of the *Quart livre*[13] where, during the storm which threatens the life of Pantagruel and all his companions, Panurge lies on the deck, a physical wreck, praying to save his skin rather than helping the common purpose.

> Be be be bous, bous, bous (respondit Panurge) frere Jan mon amy, mon bon pere, je naye, je naye mon amy, je naye. C'est faict de moy, mon pere spirituel, mon amy, c'en est faict. Vostre bragmart ne m'en sçauroit saulver. Zalas, Zalas nous sommes au dessus de Ela, hors toute la gamme. Bebe be bous bous. Zalas à ceste heure sommes nous au dessoubs de Gama ut. Je naye. Ha mon pere, mon oncle, mon tout. L'eau est entrée en mes souliers par le collet. Bous, bous, bous, paisch,

hu, hu, hu, ha, ha, ha, ha, ha. Je naye. Zalas, Zalas, hu, hu, hu, hu, hu, hu. Bebe
bous, bous bobous, bobous, ho, ho, ho, ho, ho. Zalas, Zalas. A ceste heure foys
bien à poinct l'arbre forchu, les pieds à mont, la teste en bas. Pleust à Dieu que
présentement je feusse dedans la Orque des bons et beatz peres Concilipetes, les
quelz ce matin nous rencontrasmes, tant devotz, tant gras, tant joyeulx, tant
douilletz, et de bonne grace. Holos, holos, holos, Zalas, Zalas, ceste vague de
tous les Diables (*mea culpa Deus*), je diz ceste vague de Dieu enfondrera nostre
nauf. Zalas frere Jan mon pere, mon amy, confession. Me voyez cy à genoulx.
Confiteor, vostre saincte benediction.[14]

Again then we have a comic victim, subhuman in his loss of
reason and self-respect, punished by the reader's laughter, as by his companions' oaths, for not fitting into the group ethic of all for one and one
for all, rally round the mast boys, and Rah! team, Rah! In the *Tiers livre*
oracle sequence he is paralysed by his own indecision, in the *Quart livre*
storm episode he is paralysed by his own panic, and the victory of the
corporeal and the physical over the mental and spiritual, the victory of
matière over *mémoire*, is evident as he rolls in his own tears, vomit and
shit, a pathetic inversion of the comic master of ceremonies we once
knew.

So we have three patterns, beginning with the archetypal rogue
figure who is celebrated for his comic daring. This archetype Bergson
has no way of handling, for by Bergsonian theory he ought to be made
the victim of a punitive laughter forcing him back into the social norms
he has defied. Yet he is not. On the contrary the laughter is, at least in
part, one which urges him to ever greater feats of knavery, until finally
tolerance or patience snaps and the joke is over. Secondly we have the
rogue used for satiric purposes. Here the Bergsonian pattern gains
relevance, as the laughter, aimed via the knave at his victim, becomes
punitive, value-based, social, and relatively indifferent to consequences:
our emotions are not stirred by Panurge's discomfiting of the high and
mighty, even, I submit, when his pranks bring about their death, as happens in a number of episodes, among them *Pantagruel* c. 16 when he
spreads the plague and the pox through Paris by spilling and mixing
noxious substances on the pavement. At least ten die as a result, but who
cares?

But what of the third pattern, that whereby the comic hero we
have enjoyed becomes a figure of self-travesty, like Miller's horde
"utterly, confoundedly not himself", and that without any specific reason
other than that this is the way to be in fun, in the parallel world of playful time-off? The said time can be the early evening in New York when
everyone is rushing from their work-place to their place of pleasure. It

can be the Medieval carnival when rowdy processions, motley exhibitions, bawdy street-theatre and riotous feasting replace normal living. It can be the kids' party when uncles and aunts get down on all fours and let the little ones ride round the floor on their backs. It can be the weekend in Skegness when the bank-manager dons his "kiss-me-quick" hat and sends saucy postcards to embarrass his colleagues in the High Street branch of Tunbridge Wells. But whatever their specifics, the whole essence of these occasions, and the time in which they occur, is that one make a fool of oneself, becoming nothing more than an obsessive hedonist, a foul-mouthed drunk, a hobby-horse for tots, a cheeky chappy rather than the self-respecting workaday bore one usually is. So when we see our hero descend to this level and become a mocking inversion of his former self, can our intuition not still find a basis on which to rebuild our loyalty to him, nay indeed our affection for him, in a concession or even an accession to this very time-off, even though the moral and spiritual mechanisms of the text are forcing us to condemn him?

What Bergson argues is that comic repetitions like the neurotic toings and froings of the frantic Panurge defy the law of irreversibility of phenomena whereby life, unlike the comic, does not repeat itself, ever.

> Considérée dans le temps, [la vie] est le progrès continu d'un être qui vieillit sans cesse: c'est dire qu'elle ne revient jamais en arrière, et ne se répète jamais.[15]

Not true! If one takes the linear temporality of an individual's life and makes it the only temporality applicable to that life, then this very tragic perspective might apply, and the clown's repeated living through of the same event-sequence become an absurd and unworthy reduction of a personal life-time. This is the comic pattern thrust violently at the audience in traditional Punch and Judy, where the traditional scenario is forever reiterated, it is the circular pattern of the mouse caught in pitch (an image actually applied to Panurge in the *Tiers livre*),[16] and it was recreated, quite ingeniously, in the movie *Groundhog Day*, where an antipathetic protagonist, Punch-like in his cynical indifference to others' sensibilities, is forced to live through the events of the same day to the point of a despair beyond which he finds redemption in the love of the woman he had forever desired but never deserved.

The film's humour draws on many sources, but temporally speaking it depends on a comically repeated event sequence. No matter how hard he tries to vary his day the hero always reawakens to the same radio-alarm at six o'clock on the same morning, and this repetition, comic to begin with, turns frightening and even potentially tragic. Quite aware of the cyclicity of his new life-pattern, the hero is at the same time trapped by it, *mus in pice*, for however greatly he perfects his own skills and knowledge, or however much he learns about the characters and the environment surrounding him, he is unable to change anything outside the confines of the single ever-repeated day which is his temporal prison. Time makes a fool of him by frustrating him to the point of desperation, but he finally achieves the yearned-for escape from the temporal cycle, an escape we ought to feel he finally merits, when he is reintegrated into that ongoing temporality from which he has been excluded, but which Bergson sees as definitive of life.

Definitive it may be, and particularly in an era like ours which privileges individual existence so mightily, but it is not exclusive. Were it so, then we would not be aware of it as a temporality, because there would be no other way of viewing existential time, and therefore no point of comparison for it. But no-one lives exclusively in terms of that temporality. To it one can oppose the cyclic temporalities of the seasons and the yearly calendar, which is the whole basis of Bakhtin's argument about carnival whereby every year normal life is suspended in order that it be reinvigorated. Repetition here becomes not something inhuman and mechanical, but rather something which patterns the fluidity of individual time and at the same time socialises and enriches it; hence the rituals of the children's party which celebrate another turning of the annual wheel as much as they do the fact that the kid is growing up.

One can also oppose to it the rhythmic temporality of religion, whereby, in regular church services, or, in a secular society, regular spiritual experiences such as periods of meditation, ecstasy, the fortnightly home game, even the weekly disco-rave, individual time is suspended within a repeatable experience which transcends it. Such experience may place the individual in the greater whole of an enduring institution, such as a church, or indeed a family in the regular meetings over the meal-table, or it may, in conjunction with some of these, place him in an entirely different temporality, that of the imagination, a faculty which does not age, even though the individual exercising his imagination does.

Now imaginative time invades the comic experience in the extent to which a comic text such as the *Tiers livre* or the *Quart livre* is suspended outside individual time in a sphere where we return to it, as we do to all our favourite passages of literature or our favourite comic sketches, at will, always taking the threads up at the same point, but otherwise devising the contours of the comic experience very much on our own terms: Panurge is always rushing obsessively from oracle to oracle, Punch is always left at home holding the baby, John Cleese in the famous *Monty Python* sketch is always in the pet-shop complaining about his dead Norwegian Blue while Michael Palin stands before him, always behind the counter and lying his head off about the same dead parrot. But who they are, where they are, why they are and when they are – these matters depend on our imagination, not on any social macro-structure or value-system.

In the *Capricorn* scene, by contrast, we know exactly where we are and when we are: this is New York at 7 p.m.; but the comic effect depends on the fact that this is not a 7 p.m., but any 7 p.m. For this time and place, this chronotope, to use the Bakhtinian term, is one which re-curs predictably, every day, relaxing and invigorating one's awareness via that "electric crackle in the air". All one needs in order to enjoy it is to imagine one is there with the jostling bodies, whistling and pimping alongside the persona himself and sharing his mood. In *Groundhog Day* it is different again. Here the imaginative leap required is that one accept the fantastic notion of the repeated day. But the temporality surrounding that day, and in fact permeating it in the different people there encountered, is substantially normal. We know exactly who the pro-tagonist is – he is a television journalist on a routine assignment – and he comes to know everything there is to know about all the inhabitants of Punxsutawney, for he has ample time to do so, and a supremely ordinary, unexciting and uncarnivalised bunch they are too.

The temporal nature of Panurge is, however, more complex and ambiguous than any of these examples, hence in part his status as great comic hero. Such polychrony is an essential matter which Rabelais critics confront in their own way and on their own terms. Panurge is a rogue: a comic anti-hero. To this extent his time is that of the inverted circumstances of revelry whereby one is tempted to accept naughtiness and devilment which in cases of extreme relaxation may go up to and beyond murder. A figure within such revelry, Panurge is also a master of revels, capable of ushering in carnival festivity by his very appearance in an episode. This may not always happen, and a key problem within the *Tiers livre* is who – hero or anti-hero, Pantagruel or Panurge – controls the space and the time in which the events are situated and performed, but these roles are discernibly a part of his literary identity. He cues in and personifies a temporality which challenges and takes one beyond routine concerns.

Still more, when one tries to set him in a social or personal context one will see to what degree he defies such realities, being in fact a man from nowhere and a man with no past. He defies the personal time of biography, and the historical time of dynasty. He has no family, no background, no roots, and precious little identity beyond his roguish or foolish anti-personality, and the love of Pantagruel which is itself determined by no reason. His very decision to marry, moreover, is an arbitrary one, in no way justified by his role in the plot or the dynamics of his group: on the contrary the longer they all remain unmarried, the longer may continue the adventures which are their literary *raison d'être*. To this extent all his companions, up to and including Pantagruel, defy that personal time into which the Groundhog character is finally reintegrated when he manages to conquer his cynical nature and win Rita's love.

Now Panurge makes a fool of himself at the beginning of the *Tiers livre*, just before the marriage question is raised, and specifically by appearing before Pantagruel in a new and peculiar costume.

> Au lendemain Panurge se feit perser l'aureille dextre à la Judaique, et y atacha un petit anneau d'or à ouvraige de tauchie, on caston duquel estoit une pusse enchassée ... Print quatre aulnes de bureau: s'en acoustra comme d'une robbe longue à simple cousture: desista porter le hault de ses chausses: et attacha des lunettes à son bonnet. En tel estat se presenta devant Pantagruel: lequel trouva le desguisement estrange ...[17]

as well he might. However when he asks Panurge what's up, the latter replies: "I have a flea in my ear: I want to get married." So we are not only observing a costume change, but also a temporal shift: this is a new Panurge in a new phase of his career. But what type of shift is it, and what kind of temporality does it involve? Is it a change of personal time, whereby Panurge is now an older but a sillier man who ought to know better than to dress up in absurd costumes and to contemplate marrying a girl in whom he would only inspire distress or contempt? If so, and of course one is quite free to take this option, then once again the Bergsonian approach applies, for in so doing we have tied him down within real time and irreversible circumstances, and activated the for me quite limited personal temporality Rabelais grants him. He is a quirky old fool and on the way to being a dirty old man, and in the process about to reveal a moral inertia as comical as the physical inertia causing the walker to stumble over a stone in the street: both figures in their own way come a cropper.

However the change of costume can also denote a different temporal shift, one from normal time into festive time, just as does the shift of Miller's narrator onto the fervid chicken run of Broadway. The costume then becomes a cue encouraging one not to apply the values of routine living, but rather to lay those values aside, just as one lays aside the moral outrage which Punch's infanticide might in real time and real circumstances provoke, or the logical exasperation which the dead parrot exchange might evoke were the pet-shop a real time or a real place. A funny costume, like the funny voices of Punch and the Python characters, inverts the normal harmony of character with appearance, as all ceremonial tends to substitute the rigid exterior (costume) for the fluid interior (personality). Hence the same funny costume is always latently ridiculous, as are the special voices ordinary people adopt during official ceremonials. However the response to a carnival clown, a man "utterly, confoundedly not himself", may, in the festive context of time renewed and redeemed, be not the condemning derision which would have clowns revert to the norm, take off their red noses, their baggy trousers and their size thirty boots, but instead precisely that "warm human delirium" of which Miller speaks, and on which their act depends. We want to relax from the arduous efforts of moral concentration, as from the sheer tedium of predictable living, and the time when the funny costumes come out can be just the time in which to do that.

Now Bergson proves himself aware of this opposition when, alongside his comic principle of *répétition*, which for him defines Panurge's foolery in the mechanical repetitions to which we have alluded, he sets that of *l'interférence des séries*, by which he really means incongruity:

> *Une situation est toujours comique quand elle appartient en même temps à deux séries d'événements indépendants, et qu'elle peut s'intepréter à la fois dans deux sens tout différents*[18]

and this he exemplifies via the quidproquo by which characters in a play take a situation as meaning one thing, when in reality it means something different – Shakespeare's comedies abound with mistakes of this kind. However the theoretical potential of the principle of *interférence* is far richer than Bergson realises. For it is in part via the *interférence* of these two temporalities, and the identities which are manifest in them, that comic surprises, jokes (especially practical jokes) and incongruous events gain their effect. Endless examples could be given, but the appearance and change of life-style of Panurge at the beginning of the *Tiers livre*, leading on to the obsessive behaviour which Bergson regards as defining his comic nature – he is a victim of his own mechanisation – can also be seen as the intrusion of festive time, with its outrageous costumes, absurd language and mad behaviour-patterns, into a non-festive environment: the castle of Pantagruel where, given the role imposed on the giant at this stage by the author, responsibility and moderation rule, at the expense of excess and folly.

So the repetition which Bergson sees as a key feature of comic mechanicalness – "This parrot is no more, it has ceased to be, it has expired and gone to see its maker: this is a late parrot!" – can be seen as a reductive distortion of real time – as war-time film-strips portrayed Nazi storm-troopers goose-stepping to the tune of the Lambeth Walk – and we can mock the speakers accordingly, as we were intended to mock the SS. But that repetition can also be seen as a necessary feature of festive time. The whole point about festive time and festive clowning is that they come back regularly, as the costumes are dusted off, the stock scenes re-enacted and the old stories reiterated. Where would the annual seaside holiday be without the funny hats, the saucy postcards, the wise-cracking layabouts and the bar-room rowdies? What would Christmas be without Pantomime and its ritual cross-dressings, its clan-calls of "Oh no there isn't!" – "Oh yes there is!", and the ever re-enacted happy endings which are as predictable as they are welcome and apposite.

It follows that the time-warp of Panurge's marriage complex, like the time-warp of the dead parrot debate, the time-warp of Punch's comic brutality, the time-warp of Groundhog Day, and the time-warp leading Cinderella from scullery to palace (and back again for the next perform-ance), is a distortion of time as we might live it during our own irreversible decisions about our own lives. But that fact can make Panurge at least as enviable as he is contemptible, insofar as his identity is sustained not by an individual will or intelligence, for in his case these are, as Bergson opines, fatally deficient, but by an imaginative time-scale which allows him to put off his decision forever, never demanding of him that he make his mind up and take the plunge. For, as all students of Rabelais know, and in the spirit of Panurge's own fecklessness, the author extends the hiatus of Panurge's indecision by himself never writing up either the final oracular pronouncement about his future, or his final resolution to wed or not to wed, or the ensuing marriage, or the eventual outcome of that marriage. Hence even at the climax of the unpublished further adventures of Pantagruel, which come after the

Quart livre and its sequence of visits to strange lands and weird adventures at sea, we do not experience the triumphant marriage or anti-marriage of the comic hero, but rather an ambiguous injunction by a high-priestess of Rabelaisian whimsy that we drink up and be companionably merry, perhaps, all in all, the best answer one could have to life's ongoing and in the end all-conquering vicissitudes.

So, set against the continuity of individual time, whereby life is about the creation of a consistent personality based on a series of moral decisions, one must also set the cyclic temporality of the day, the year, the community and the institution, all of which repeat themselves in order to pattern the individual lives which both experience them and apply them for purposes of self-definition: one is oneself only in so far as one is at once identifiable and yet contrastable with the enduring situations in which one's life is embedded. The humour associated with these cycles is, moreover, one which is itself repeatable (the same corny jokes reappear on birthdays and anniversaries), celebratory (the April Fool is not the victim of a coercive and conditioning laughter, but rather the often willing focus of a comic stunt sufficient unto itself), and finally unifying: it is via the traditional cracks, tales, costumes, japes and tableaux that the family, clan, tribe or township reunify themselves in terms of their own identity ("shaking hands with a thousand hands"), if not in terms of their own value-systems.

Moreover against both of these temporal patterns, the ongoing *durée* dear to Bergson and the regenerating cycle dear to Bakhtin, one must, or at least one may, also set the temporality of the immediate moment, the psychological chronon, which is a suspension, in Rabelais and Python a comic suspension, of both individual continuity and cyclic renewal. Whereas the linear temporality of the individual leads him through unrepeatable circumstances from a birth he is unaware of to a death which is his final oblivion, the cyclic temporality of the clan, the group or the society, fits the individual into a repeatable continuum which is greater than himself and which allows him to resolve his identity in a pattern of which he forms but an incidental part. However by this third temporality, the temporality of immediacy, life is lived not in terms of an individual quest for self-fulfilment, or in terms of the continuation of a cult or culture, but rather in and for itself. Seen thus, the superannuated adolescence of Panurge, beginning with the change of costume, and leading, beyond his author's death, to the shrine of the Holy Bottle and the priestess Bacbuc's injunction "Trinch!", is not a period in a life, nor a cycle of events, but specifically an over-extended chronon, a comic hiatus of massive proportions, a gag which never ends.

Let us reconsider Rabelais' storm sequence with these distinctions in mind. As a comically rich episode it exists in several temporalities: it is a polychrony. First we have the real time of danger, which threatens the collective enterprise of the journey and faces each individual with his own death. This situation demands of Panurge that he behave as a good crew-member, a role which of course he utterly fails to fulfil, and to this extent the abrasive denunciations of Frère Jan are satire in its most savage form and articulate all the reader's annoyance and frustration at his inadequacies:

> Il radote, dist frere Jan, le paouvre Diable. A mille et millions, et centaines de millions de Diables soit le Coqu cornard au Diable. Ayde nous icy hau Tigre. Viendra il? Icy à orche. Teste Dieu plene de reliques, quelle patenostre de Cinge est ce que tu marmottez là entre les dens? Ce Diable de fol marin est cause de la tempeste, et il seul ne ayde à la chorme.[19]

However against this real time must be set the festive time to which we have alluded already. By this temporality the characters are not faced with any real danger, but belong instead in a carnival pageant whereby their identities as real people facing real threats are submerged under a set of roles which convert them into their opposites. Bergson has some sense of this pattern, and even mentions the *monde renversé* topos in *Le Rire*, but his examples of inversion refer, mechanically, to comic punishments, and so they must, because to do otherwise would threaten his philosophical principles. So, for him, comic inversion is not the fluid and invigorating challenge to norms implied by the temporal habitat of carnival, but rather a mechanical procedure as inhuman as are his other comic principles of *répétition* and incongruity (*interférence des séries*). It represents an absurd or meaningless reversal of circumstance whereby, for example, Dandin is made to appear the adulterer when his wife Angélique turns the tables on him, or Pathelin is made the victim of that same cunning trick he taught his rascally client to use. When it occurs, it sets the characters' dramatic fate in inverse relation to their own deserts or intentions, and this relation is comic as being, unlike life, rigid in its inevitability.

What the treatment omits, however, is the positive side of inversion whereby what is normally condemned (adultery in Angélique, duplicity in Pathelin's shepherd) suddenly becomes triumphant and praiseworthy in a moral grotesque which involves as much recreation as destruction. So the craven Panurge is indeed the opposite of a good crew-member, and is verbally savaged for falling so far short of what is expected. But is the triumphant Frère Jan, voice of that verbal savagery, not himself the opposite of what he ought to be: that is the consoling, restrained and worthy man of God, ready to minister to his flock while the others sail the boat? Instead we see him drunk and cursing, orating, gesticulating and caterwauling, and going through precisely the routine of a clown on a carnival float who defies the conventions of his costume and annihilates respectability in the same way as does Miller's foul-mouthed persona and narrator in and throughout the *Tropics*. And don't we just love him for it?

> Par la vertus (dist frere Jan) du sang, de la chair, du ventre, de la teste, si encores je te oy pioller Coqu au diable, je te gualleray en loup marin; vertus Dieu que ne le jectons nous au fond de la mer? ... Je croy que tous les Diables sont deschainez aujourdhuy, ou que Proserpine est en travail d'enfant. Tous les Diables dansent aux sonnettes.[20]

Even Pantagruel, mostly silent during this episode, has a touch of the carnivalesque about him: clinging with all his strength to the ship's mast, he is here a giant once more, out of all proportion with his mortal companions, and giants are a stock feature of the carnival parade. However it is the mock priest who most clearly incites the festivity, as master of the comic ceremonial whereby the storm is nothing more than an excuse to profane God and his Word, inverting serious duties and respectable behaviour-patterns. So Panurge may beg for confession till the clocks run backwards, he will not jog Frère Jan's conscience, nay woe betide anyone who tries to shout him down or reimpose the norms he is defying. This is All Devils' Day and a time of moral anarchy.

So if this is a mock-storm as much as it is a real storm, and the story surrounding it far more a mock-odyssey than it is a real journey, can one not see Panurge in the same inverted perspective as one does Frère Jan, his boon companion who is yet, at this moment, his enemy? If, in this perspective, everything has become its opposite, then one can well ask why Panurge need abandon his spinelessness and help the common cause, any more than Svejk need abandon his and become a good soldier. For one does not demand that Alan B'Stard become a good MP, or Edina in television's *Absolutely Fabulous* a good mother or daughter, nor must one demand of Quixote that become the sensible old man he is on his death-bed. My point is that we can apply real values and personal time to these characters and event sequences, as Cervantes does in the final chapters of his novel, but one is no way obliged to. Moral anarchies allow the individual vast scope to impose their own value-systems, and it would be a poor text that allowed no alternative readings.

Accordingly it matters but little to me as critic how any reader judges Panurge as a character, and I suspect it matters equally little to Rabelais, in reading whom we apply such moral, characterisational and temporal structures as we choose, always provided they have some point of reference in the text. What is important is to see what choices that text lays open to the reader, not how that reader is or may be coerced into adopting one choice rather than another. For he should not, and perhaps cannot, be so coerced, given that the reader's imaginative freedom, wherewith he judges his characters precisely as he chooses, is something even a creative author, let alone a scholar involved in secondary writing, infringes at his peril.

Do we not then find that Bergson has guided us into a very narrow channel of humour wherein the quality of comic discourse, Panurge's blabbering, is prejudged as connoting failure, stupidity, mechanical repetition? All of these things it may indeed connote, but if one can situate this scene in the alternative temporality of the festival, the free inventiveness of his comic discourse can redeem the moral weakness which, set in a different temporality, one might also see it indicate. Considered thus, the ravings and blubberings of Panurge on the deck are a reflection of the way the body has taken over from the mind: viewed psychologically he is a person reduced to the motor responses of blind panic. But viewed as a carnival performer, and the storm is at least in part a carnival event, he can be celebrated for his verbal antics here no less than on many other occasions.

Two examples. On first meeting Pantagruel in *Pantagruel* c. 9 Panurge addresses him in a vast number of different languages, none of which Pantagruel understands and all of which are intended to conceal from him the very pressing needs (hunger, thirst and fatigue) from which Panurge is visibly suffering. Now read one way this episode can be seen as satire on polyglossy – a kind of *reductio ad absurdum* of the Renaissance cult of language which here serves no purpose and indeed thwarts the communication language is intended to allow. However the passage can be read alternatively, and I think much more effectively, as a piece of street theatre in which motive and self-expression are simply dislocated from one another, not in order to deride or humiliate anyone, but so as to travesty the stock epic encounter of hero and companion, of which this chapter remains an example.

One more. At the beginning of the *Tiers livre*, even before the marriage question has been raised, Rabelais describes Panurge's career as landed nobleman, we discovering that in this area of estate management he is quite simply a disaster. Following his victory in the previous volume, and in another stock episode, Pantagruel handed over to him lands which were to be his fief. Panurge, by improvident economics, and particularly by holding open house to all comers and on a perpetual basis, ruined the lands within days and got himself into a situation of perpetual debt. Called to account for this to his lord Pantagruel, he launches into a paradoxical eulogy of debt, telling him and the world at large that there is no greater human or divine invention than debt, that debt is what keeps the cosmos in place via the reciprocal influence of the heavenly bodies, just as debt is what keeps society alive owing to the interrelation of credit and debit in its economic system. The argument is daft (though not so daft as to be without any reasoned basis) and morally irresponsible (but then Panurge has always been this): so one's response to it can be negative. More positively, however, the argument is highly ingenious, linguistically rich and worthy of the best of those parodic eulogies which the humanists produced in their idle moments, or what they professed to be their idle moments: Erasmus' *In Praise of Folly* is the clearest example and certainly in Rabelais' mind:

> Debtes. O chose rare et antiquaire! Debtes, diz je, excedentes le nombre des syllabes resultantes au couplement de toutes les consonantes avecques les vocales, jadis projecté et compté par le noble Xenocrates. A la numerosité des crediteurs si vous estimez la perfection des debteurs, vous ne errerez en Arithmetique praticque. Cuidez-vous que je suis aise, quand tous les matins autour de moy je voy ces crediteurs tant humbles, serviables, et copieux en reverences? Et quand je note que moy faisant à l'un visaige plus ouvert, et chere meilleure que es autres, le paillard pense avoir sa depesche le premier, pense estre le premier en date, et de mon ris cuyde que soit argent content. Il m'est advis, que je joue encores le Dieu de la passion de Saulmur, accompaigné de ses Anges et Cherubins.[21]

In all three passages (the storm, the meeting, the praise of debt) the temporality of carnival is latent: in *Quart livre* cc. 20-1 Frère Jan, and not for the first time, is officiating at a kind of inverted holy day, in *Pantagruel* c. 9 Panurge is setting up the kind of linguistic practical joke appropriate to spontaneous theatre, in *Tiers livre* c. 2 the praise of debt is sparked off by a kind of perpetual party in which Panurge wasted all the resources conferred on him by his lord:

> Et se gouverna si bien et prudentement monsieur le nouveau chastellain, qu'en moins de quatorze jours il dilapida le revenu certain et incertain de sa

Chastellenie pour troys ans. Non proprement dilapida, comme vous pourriez dire en fondations de monasteres, erections de temples, bastimens de collieges et hospitaulx, ou jectant son lard aux chiens. Mais despendit en mille petitz bancquetz et festins joyeulx, ouvers à tous venens, mesmement tous bons compaignons, jeunes fillettes, et mignonnes gualoises. Abastant boys, bruslant les grosses souches pour la vente des cendres, prenent argent d'avance, achaptant cher, vendent à bon marché, et mangeant son bled en herbe.[22]

Again, given that carnival is a time of improvidence, then this behaviour is fully germane to the festive temporality that those fourteen days must have generated, and the praise of debt is merely the (il)logical extension of that time.

So the Bergsonian approach to these episodes, which would argue that their effect is one of mechanical jabbering which has lost contact with the realities of life, cuts across that cyclic temporality which legitimates them as comic inversions of the norm. It is as if someone were to find a Mardi Gras costume outrageous, or to criticise the expense involved in holding a Christmas party. At carnival time the outrageously extravagant becomes the norm, and the figure personifying it the hero and not the target of the occasion.

But what of the third temporality, the temporality of the immediate moment, whereby Panurge in the storm is not situated either in a time of danger, or in a festive pageant, but is merely creating a comic climax which we enjoy beyond any context, as a rich amalgam of linguistic effects and tricks? For although the storm bears elements of the carnival, it is not a carnival. It is an event sparked off by a bad omen (the sighting of a convoy of ships heading for the Council of Trent) and not by the coming of a particular season or day: so unlike carnival it will not return, to which extent its temporality is not cyclic. It involves violent struggle, but with the forces of nature, and not with the rival bands who form the enemy in Rabelais' carnival wars. Finally it occurs on board ship in a closed company, rather than in the market squares and public places where performers and audience mingle and applaud one another. We are the audience applauding (?) Panurge's ravings, for to the crewmen they are merely noises off in a dangerous crisis, and Pantagruel almost certainly cannot hear him at all, until the tempest is virtually at an end.

Again the Bergsonian approach to this and his other follies is available: his language is that of a silly fool in his litany of terror during the storm, in his meeting with Pantagruel and in his encomium of debt. But on all three occasions, and in many other episodes one could list, it is also, and each in its own different way, the language of a highly gifted and resourceful performer, raconteur, blarney-merchant, after-dinner speaker, equipped with a huge stock of references, topoi, quotations and languages, blessed with the ability to argue black white, and to cue in, as I have implied, that temporality of the immediate moment which certainly stands aside from the dogged morals and the even quite frightening social coerciveness which for Bergson motivates humour. Nor perhaps is it coextensive with the festive and cyclic temporality of licence whose theory Bakhtin virtually created and which at the same time does explain some, indeed much of Panurge. The response in terms of this third temporality – the temporality of the chronon – is then not to tut-tut on the basis of a condemning moral judgement: the blarney-merchant should not be tied down to the wisdom of the world, for to do so destroys him. Nor is it by definition a response which looks for parodic travesties and comic inversions which relieve inhibitions and invoke chaos over order. Rather is it a response which would wish to extend the joke in perpetuity, savouring its richness, enjoying its techniques, exploring its varied potentials, and separating it as a moment from all the structures in which it can be found. After all, the best jokes have no context. They are simply conjured up as ever repeatable quips, gags, anecdotes, sketches or scenes; hence the oft-repeated cue, "Tell us the one about ...". Similarly the best comic performances are the ones we don't want to end, as if Panurge's panic *tour de force* were to last not just for a couple of chapters, but for always.

Indeed so it does. As arguably the most sustained piece of comic writing Rabelais ever achieved, it stands as an extended chronon outside the career of the anti-hero and outside the festive fairground that is his current journey, a fairground in which each land visited is a separate comic side-show and each ship encountered a group of spectators as motley as the Pantagruelians themselves. So his behaviour and performance, with all its quips, gags etc., is as high or low a point of comic art as one chooses to make it, but, being an isolated chronon rather than a part of a developing pattern, it is never re-examined by the characters or the narrator. On the contrary, when Pantagruel finally asks what all the fuss is about, Frère Jan actually covers up for Panurge, saying drunkenness (and therefore not cowardice) is the reason for his terror, and while Pantagruel says that under the circumstances he would forgive fear in anyone, provided that they had done their job during the crisis, no-one then shops Panurge to him by saying to what extent he let them all down. And this moreover in a section (*Quart livre* cc. 22-4) when Panurge, with the storm over, is at his most irritating, not only lending a hand now that to do so is no longer necessary, but himself accusing Frère Jan of back-sliding and of panic. Is this the nadir of his comical blindness, or the acme of his comical cheek? Once again, as so often, the choice is yours.

So to read and enjoy Rabelais is not merely to evoke a kind of perpetual carnival – though it does help to have a bottle of wine at one's elbow – and it is certainly not just to go, remorselessly, through the motions of relearning, as Screech would have it, the folly of deviating from humanist norms,[23] important though those norms are within Rabelais' moral apparatus and conscience. To read Rabelais is also to enrich the individual moment, lending it a vitality and an emotional privilege of its own, and to look and look again for moments where our amusement and our laughter are generated not merely in malicious put-downs, nor even in a carnivalesque celebration of folly, unorthodoxy or waste, celebrated as the antithesis of the serious values one lives by in normal time; moments rather when our laughter is a great shout of joy at the potential each instant of our lives possesses for self-enrichment and self-transcendence.

The great humorist may have great moral awareness – as a good meal possesses positive nutritional value: that is its biological function. He may also generate a carnival – as a good meal takes place at best in a relaxed, positive and egalitarian company: that is its ideal social context. But a good meal must not only be wholesome and situated in a well-intentioned company. It must also please, with the tastes of well-cooked dishes: that is its sensual delight. So must great comic writing also please by creating whole series of individually memorable and imaginatively valuable moments which we willingly incorporate into our repertoire.

Hence against the temporality of *durée* – which of course exists as the perpetually unresolved *devenir* which is individual life – one can set the cyclic temporality of carnival, which is an unofficial but collective temporality at once subverting and yet fulfilling serious life. But one can also set against it the pattern of life as neither a *durée* nor a cycle, but rather a series of chronons: discrete but enriching experiences, be they comic experiences, religious experiences, sexual experiences, artistic experiences, or even tragic experiences, synthesised out of the potential our personalities, our social roles, our cultures, milieus and our environments provide, and repeatable to the extent that one says to one's friends, "D'you remember the scene when Panurge shat himself with fear?" As enjoying this temporality we come to know, love, seek out certain jokes, figures, people, themes as recurring catalysts within our own particular selection of great moments. At best this is what Panurge, if not Rabelais, is all about.

I repeat, Pantagruel loves Panurge throughout his life, unquestioningly, warts and all, and surely this paradoxical and comic travesty of a relationship has at its basis a far richer and more appealing vein of humanity than the kind of unending humiliation and imposed conditioning that Bergson sees at the basis of *le comique*. *Autrement dit*, if Bergson could not make of Panurge anything more than a dancing puppet or a pathetic clown, then it was Bergson who was the loser.

---

[1] H. Miller, *The Books in My Life* (Norfolk, Conn., n.d.), p. 24.

[2] *Ibid., Flash Back* (Paris, 1976), pp. 78-9.

[3] H. Bergson, *Le Rire* (Paris 1947), p. 7: author's italics.

[4] *Tropic of Capricorn* (Paris, 1939), pp. 102-3.

[5] *Le Rire*, pp. 7-8.

[6] M. Gauna, *The Rabelaisian Mythologies* (London, 1996), p. 37.

[7] T. Sprigge, "Schopenhauer and Bergson on Laughter", *Comparative Criticism*, 10 (1988), 39-65.

[8] G. Schrempp, "Our Funny Universe", *Humor*, 8.3 (1995), 219-228 (p. 223).

[9] K. Cameron, *Humour and History* (Oxford, 1993), p. 5.

[10] *Le Rire*, p. 3.

[11] G. Orwell, *Nineteen Eighty-Four* (Oxford, 1984 [*sic*]), p. 390.

[12] q.v. *Pantagruel*, c. 9: "Comment Pantagruel trouva Panurge, lequel il ayma toute sa vie."

[13] He is prone to "pathological ... brute-emotion" (M. A. Screech, *Rabelais*, p. 384), while glorying "in the grossest, foulest, ugliest apsects of our common humanity" (*ibid.*, p. 460).

[14] Rabelais, *Oeuvres complètes*, ed. M. Huchon (Paris, 1994), p. 584.

[15] *Le Rire*, p. 67.

[16] By Pantagruel in *Tiers livre*, c. 37.

[17] Rabelais, pp. 371-2.

[18] *Le Rire*, pp. 73-4: author's italics.

[19] Rabelais, pp. 586-7.

[20] *Ibid.*, p. 586.

[21] *Ibid.*, pp. 361-2.

[22] *Ibid.*, p. 357.

[23] *Op. cit.*, p. 3.

4. La Bruyère: a study in satire
John Parkin

In so far as humour is an essential constituent of La Bruyère's *Caractères* it is clear that that humour is predominantly satiric. This term I am using in the specific sense outlined in my own *Humour Theorists of the Twentieth Century*, and elsewhere, where I see it as not only humour which provokes thought – for just about anything can provoke thought, even this paper – but which does so on the basis of an explicit or implicit value-system which is the standard on which the victims of the satire are judged and condemned.

Bergson, rightly or wrongly, recurs as a leitmotif in French humour studies, both in general and in this volume: the debate on his status will continue. However, to reset my notion of satire in Bergsonian terms, satirical laughter is a punishment on the target figures whom he envisages, using La Bruyère as an occasional example,[1] and who are victimised for having imposed rigid and mechanical behaviour patterns on the fluidity of actual life. To my mind this description is too narrow, but it rightly adjudges satiric laughter (as inspired by *le comique*) to be aggressive, and more specifically as an aggression on the part of those upholding an agreed norm of behaviour on one (or more than one, since La Bruyère must nowadays be all but always read as generalising rather than particularising in his caricatures) who has fallen short of it. The laughter occurs, Bergson would have it, entirely without sympathy for the victim figure: I doubt if this is true or even possible, human emotions being as complex as they are, but certainly the laughter connotes more support for whatever social norm the *caractère* is unable or unwilling to live up to, than for the ridiculed figure himself. Were it the other way round, and the comic figure more appealing than the straight-man who objectively describes him, who actually confronts him, or to whom one imaginatively compares him, then the humour, although entirely possible, would be of a very different kind, and not a kind one can easily discern in La Bruyère's work.

A quick example. One of the first named pen-portraits in La Bruyère is Arsène (and it is significant that much if not most of the humour is expressed in these many sketches, rather than in the didactic and abstract paragraphs in which they are scattered):

> *Arsène*, du plus haut de son esprit, contemple les hommes, et dans l'éloignement
> d'où il les voit, il est comme effrayé de leur petitesse; loué, exalté, et porté

jusques aux cieux par de certaines gens qui se sont promis de s'admirer réciproquement, il croit, avec quelque mérite qu'il a, posséder tout celui qu'on peut avoir, et qu'il n'aura jamais; occupé et rempli de ses sublimes idées, il se donne à peine le loisir de prononcer quelques oracles; élevé par son caractère au-dessus des jugements humains, il abandonne aux âmes communes le mérite d'une vie suivie et uniforme, et il n'est responsable de ses inconstances qu'à ce cercle d'amis qui les idolâtrent: eux seuls savent juger, savent penser, savent écrire, doivent écrire; il n'y a point d'autre ouvrage d'esprit si bien reçu dans le monde, et si universellement goûté des honnêtes gens, je ne dis pas qu'il veuille approuver, mais qu'il daigne lire: incapable d'être corrigé par cette peinture, qu'il ne lira point.[2]

The value-systems on which the satire is based are, for me, modesty, lack of pretension and objectivity: Arsène is vain, pretentious and predisposed by vanity in his own favour. I say "for me", moreover, intentionally, for in applying a value-system or systems satirically one is acting subjectively – it cannot be otherwise – and it is up to others, here as elsewhere, to select their own set of responses on the basis of their own proclivities. All I will say in defence of my choice is that, in making it, I believe I have the narrator's clear approval, for in refusing to consider any work as having merit when compared with his own, Arsène is rejecting the very work containing this description (an interesting piece of literary irony), and ignoring the protests of La Bruyère's own mouth-piece. Two additional points: in this sketch Arsène is situated in a group (hence my point about plural rather than individual targets), and he also reflects La Bruyère's own theory of satire, whereby it is didactic and improving. The point about making fun of people is, for him at least, a kind of social reform: as Mazaheri has it, "Il prétend que sa raillerie à lui est au fond didactique. Son rire se veut positif et utile",[3] though the point is lost in this instance to the extent that the person reproved is too conceited to be bothered about the opinions of others.

Hence the first essential in creating a satirical framework, and this applies in any context, is the establishment of the value-system on whose basis the satire will operate. Without this common ground there is no secure guarantee that the satire will make sense to the readership, or that a point will be made or an improvement invited; hence the failure of sophisticated satires before an audience of simple people or of children who cannot understand the points at issue, which is to say why precisely the victimised figures are being made fun of. To establish a frame of reference is, however, not the same thing as to impose a system of beliefs. If the readership or audience fail to appreciate the satirical framework the author has created, this will radically diminish, if not destroy, their appreciation of the work applying it: anyone ignorant of the key to *Gulliver's Travels* will therefore miss out on many of the jokes intended, and the same applies, I am painfully aware, to uninitiated readings of *Le Canard Enchaîné*. However the reader need not actually share the writer's (or narrator's, or caricaturist's) beliefs in order to appreciate the satire once he has identified its value basis, and we see this, do we not, in the satirical material which Keith Cameron has included in this volume. Few of us care deeply about the issues it reflects concerning attitudes to the France's Imperial family of the 1860s. However the humour still works, up to a point, once we know what background, value-systems and satiric frameworks the satirist was alluding to and establishing as the basis for the humorous response from his public.

As I have argued, La Bruyère, adopting classical positions, sees satire as intended, at best, to shame or cajole its target into changing his ways, and hence, as Bergson would no doubt have it, re-entering the flexible and responsible modes of behaviour which comprise serious living: the highest aim of authorship is thus "le changement de moeurs et la réformation de ceux qui ... lisent ou qui ... écoutent" (61). Yet in fact the satiric effect can have very little indeed to do with this aim. In indulging satiric humour an audience can be adopting value-systems and satirical positions to which it is in reality quite indifferent: do we care if the Prince Imperial was a masturbator or not; in fact do we care if anyone is a masturbator or not? Nevertheless, for the purposes of the satiric effect, we have to toy with the value-judgements involved in a satiric shaft, so engaging in what one might call a willing suspension of moral disinterest, and in so doing we may at the same time be impersonating, or joining, an audience whose satiric common ground is quite alien to us, and responding to a satire which goes against the grain of our beliefs: by my reading it is helpful, if not indeed necessary, to adopt the value-system whereby court taste is superior to town taste in order to appreciate at all fully those sections of *Les Caractères* entitled *De la ville* and *De la cour*. However this response runs firmly against the preferences of one who has never in his life been in the company of an aristocrat, and who, to the unwitting relief of the entire English peerage, probably never will.

So one becomes a snob in order to appreciate the snobbery of a seventeenth-century court satirist, just as a certain change of spots takes place when misogynic jokes are cracked successfully to an audience of feminists, or anti-Jewish humour is displayed before an audience of Jews, nay even of Zionists. This can happen. Though the humorous effect so engendered may be rendered the more problematic for being thus situated in what is normally alien territory, and hence the more difficult for the humorist to make succeed, it is certainly possible to appreciate satire based on value-systems which one neither shares nor condones; and this effect, incidentally, changes satire into something very different from the reforming mode of humour La Bruyère sees it as being.

One might here make a distinction between reader and addressee. As actual person (the reader of a satire) one can provisionally take on the values assumed in the addressee (the narratee of the same satire, conjured up by its writer) so as to activate the satire and comply at least partially with its satirical effect. So, in order that he fit in with the mood of the theatre audience, the black is prepared to adopt the persona of a racist and laugh at racist jokes, or, more innocently, the Irishman to accept the false value-system assigning stupidity to all Paddies. These are sympathetic reactions. The unsympathetic reaction is to insist on one's genuine beliefs, denying the common ground of the value-system satirically implied: "I can't take jokes about the Holocaust: they imply that Jews are subhuman and can be so treated. Such humour is intolerable." Furthermore there is a more consciously unsympathetic response whereby the reader, rather than being unable to accept the value-system being applied, feigns not to appreciate what that value-system is. His reaction is thus, "I just can't see the point of any of this," when in fact he can, but chooses for whatever reason not to enter even into preliminary compromise with the satirist.

Such a total refusal to appreciate satire might be just as dishonest, moreover, as a total acceptance of it. To what extent are we not all, in our social behaviour or even our reflective evaluations, merely posturing in support of values rather than totally accepting them? The point is best resolved by a psychologist, but I would suggest that not merely some, but all satire may be based, to greater or lesser degrees, on provisional rather than essential norms: is there indeed such a thing an essential norm? And this reservation could in turn imply that satire is not that defining and somehow ultimate mode of humour that Bergson clearly felt it to be, but instead a comparatively superficial and parasitic mode, as being too bound up with serious patterns of behaviour, when we are all, as possessing a sense of humour in the first place, concerned with, and even committed to, unserious patterns of behaviour: that is what a comedy club, if not a literary clique at Versailles, is all about.

Referring back to La Bruyère, it must then be conceded how limited is the common ground on which his satire operates much of the time and, accordingly, how demanding he is of his reader, now if not indeed in his own times. Indeed, so obviously do the value-systems relate to the metropolitan, educated, tasteful and aristocratic echelons of the court of his day, that a theory of satire begins to emerge from his text, a kind of meta-satire, which implies that humour can only work if it is based on similar assumptions.

> Les provinciaux et les sots sont toujours prêts à se fâcher, et à croire qu'on se moque d'eux ou qu'on les méprise: il ne faut jamais hasarder la plaisanterie, même la plus douce et la plus permise, qu'avec des gens polis, ou qui ont de l'esprit. (165)

The implication is that not merely satire, but humour – he insists that he is thinking in very general terms – can only work within an audience of those to whom its value-systems are most clearly related, not because they alone understand it, but because they alone know how to respond to it. Moreover when the "sots" round on the in-group of the "gens d'esprit" – clearly La Bruyère's own élite clan – they are shunned:

> Rire des gens d'esprit, c'est le privilège des sots: ils sont dans le monde ce que les fous sont à la cour, je veux dire sans conséquence (166);

Shakespeare please note.

I have used the word clan very deliberately. For my theory of satire does not merely take account of value-systems (as, for example, the value of wit, which is the basis of the sneers which La Bruyère is here directing at those who, in not possessing it, are by their nature unhumorous), but also of clan divisions. Were satire based exclusively on moral issues it would be intolerably stuffy. However any caricaturist bases his initial comic effects not on a good or an evil, nay a right or a wrong, but on a beauty and a proportion which his satirically deformed targets fail to embody – see Cameron's Prince Imperial once more. Furthermore we have already observed La Bruyère, as satirist, invoke such amoral criteria as taste, breeding and intelligence, hence he ends his section *De l'homme* with an exclamation as to how many are the "âmes faibles, molles et indifférentes, sans de grands défauts, et qui puissent fournir à la satire!" (342)

Nevertheless, if not immoral, the tasteless lout and the ill-bred thicko are still satirised on the basis of value-judgements, and in the clique surrounding Arsène we have seen, have we not, how outsiders are mocked as not applying the standards of taste enshrined in Arsène's own work. Moreover, set alongside this type of value-based satire, there resides a clan-based satire which derides the satiric victim as a member of an out-group, and not primarily on the basis of the norms or systems applied in the incongruity apparent in that victim's behaviour, appearance or character: to this extent the Arsène coterie mocks you on the basis merely of its own exclusiveness, not because that exclusiveness is grounded in any definable value. Put more positively, and this time in terms of La Bruyère's own preferences rather than antipathies, if one is a member of the clan of the *gens d'esprit*, or aspires to join it, one will encourage humour at the expense of the *sots* much more readily than if one is, let us say, merely assessing the degree of clever wit or comical stupidity manifest in the remarks made at a social function, be it in the gaming-salon at Versailles or in the cocktail party at the local golf-club. It's always good to be in with an in-crowd, and to laugh at the right things and at the right times is one of the best ways of achieving such complicity.

In this context one might, perhaps must, also situate La Bruyère's narrator. In our day his reader will scarcely ever conform to the moral proportions of the narratee envisaged by an author who had achieved social and cultural recognition under the Ancien Régime. Much adaptation is here needed, just as some adaptation may always be needed, otherwise the reader/narratee distinction would have no meaning. However the narrator, as La Bruyère's mouthpiece in shafts such as

> Tout ce qui est mérite se sent, se discerne, se devine réciproquement: si l'on voulait être estimé, il faudrait vivre avec des personnes estimables, (166)

can certainly be seen to be promoting various value-systems on whose basis he creates satiric common ground with his narratee and ultimately, given their indulgence, with his readers too. At the same time he is also, more or less clearly, identifying with a discernible clan, membership of which is certainly an advantage if one is to enjoy in any way fully the satire which he is expressing. That clan has varying conditions of membership – good breeding, good taste, social poise, acquaintance with Versailles etc. – but it may be ultimately definable in terms of its own exclusivity, and not in terms of the value-systems which might, or might not, be enshrined in those conditions. Thus rival courts, or, in his case, rival factions within a court, might develop satires antagonistic to one another, and based simply on the fact that they were rivals, and not because one clan could honestly claim to be any better than another.

Curiously enough this precise eventuality is taken up by La Bruyère, but in the context of the *ville* rather than the *cour*, that is in the disdained if not despised out-group of Parisian rather than Versaillais society.

> La ville est partagée en diverses sociétés, qui sont comme autant de petites républiques, qui ont leurs lois, leurs usages, leur jargon, et leurs mots pour rire. Tant que cet assemblage est dans sa force, et que l'entêtement subsiste, l'on ne trouve rien de bien dit ou de bien fait que ce qui part des siens, et l'on est incapable de goûter ce qui vient d'ailleurs: cela va jusques au mépris pour les gens qui ne sont pas initiés dans leurs mystères. (203)

So these mutually hostile clans (the "diverses sociétés") are for him but subsets of a larger clan ("la ville") which he subjects to a satire based on the value-system of cultural sophistication on whose basis it loses out against the palace: part of his satire of Parisian society is thus based on its vapid cliqueishness. On the other hand such cliques can be recognised in any social context, and their humour reproduced endlessly at the expense of any outsider who happens to present himself: we see this happening as the main satiric function of the Arsène clique, which, one assumes, was a far from untypical court cénacle. At the same time it could easily be argued that what for La Bruyère divides Versailles from Paris is a clan loyalty rather than a genuine value-judgement, indeed many of his value-judgements on the court imply disgust. Meanwhile, to be sure, the *ville* might deploy its own counter-satire victimising members of the court including La Bruyère himself, let alone Arsène, and invoking open-mindedness and lack of prejudice as the value-systems on whose basis the snobbery of the courtiers would be held up to ridicule.

These patterns notwithstanding, much of the time La Bruyère seeks to build up the moral and philosophical content of his chapters, and not merely the prejudicial cliqueishness of their narrator: given his professedly didactic aim, he is anxious to appear a value-based rather than clan-based satirist, and this is not an aim unrealised. To investigate a case-study more fully, I here quote *Du souverain* paragraph one in order to demonstrate the way in which the satiric common ground is cleared, the reader being seduced into accepting the author's (or narrator's) value-systems as imposed on the narratee:

> Quand l'on parcourt, sans la prévention de son pays, toutes les formes de gouvernement, l'on ne sait à laquelle se tenir; il y a dans toutes le moins bon, et le moins mauvais. Ce qu'il y a de plus raisonnable et de plus sûr, c'est d'estimer celle où l'on est né la meilleure de toutes, et de s'y soumettre. (269)

That the passage is unhumorous is no surprise. It articulates a philosophical or at least social position rather than applying it; it presents no caricatured target figure; its literary qualities depend on simplicity and elegance of expression rather than the incongruity essential to humour; and these qualities are intended to seduce the reader into accepting what is at the very least a contestable moral position whereby one does best to accept the political status quo of the country of one's birth rather than seeking to establish effective comparisons between the different systems one encounters. The simplicity of expression has the advantage of reassuring the reader: it is easiest and best to adopt the safest and least contentious solution. To this extent the narrator postures as that voice of common sense often personified in the *raisonneur* speeches of Molière. They project a specific philosophical dimension into the text, using good style to make it easily appreciable, and then hand over to the techniques of satire the comic exploitation of that dimension via the ridiculous activities of people who fail to inhabit it.

So one way of inciting reader support for the satirically applied value-system is simplicity of presentation: the clearer the point, the easier it is to appreciate, and the more quickly one can be projected into the humour situation, if this is the order in which the satirist chooses to operate. Another way is by appeals to common sense. The *raisonneurs* may have a depressingly trite perspective on the world and on their comic interlocutors, but that banality is most often grounded in simple wisdom, see La Bruyère's second paragraph in *Du souverain* whereby "la tyrannie ... est la manière la plus horrible et la plus grossière de se maintenir ou de s'agrandir", a point so easy to recognise and assimilate that again one is not delayed by its elaboration, and one notes Floyd Gray's comment whereby La Bruyère "arrive souvent à des simplifications de jugement qui ne font qu'accuser sa propre aridité".[4]

A third technique involves rather more. Having dressed up home-spun wisdom in eloquent phrases, and reassured the reader that one is not operating in a difficult philosophical area, one can then become ingenious and subtle in pointing out further distinctions, confident that one has gained a measure of reader sympathy. This approach is applied in paragraph seven of the same section of *Les Caractères* where, I flatter myself, the author is doing more than merely saving his reader the bother of developing a complex comparative theory of government (see paragraph 1) or reassuring him (paragraph 2) that his immediate and trite responses to the politics of tyranny are not too superficial to be worth making.

His argument (unsupported either by examples or humorous presentation) is that some political evils are tolerable for the reason that they prevent greater evils, whilst others, having become institutionalised, cannot be eradicated without a greater evil being enacted (the point is owed, directly or not, to Montaigne). The relative and dialectical nature of morality makes some evils advantageous to the family whilst deleterious to individual members of the family, whilst others (for instance taxation) aid the State whilst harming the groups (for instance the families) within it. Such material is at least worth considering, and invites one to think further, rather than closing off discussion via glib aphorisms. Having thus appreciated that there is a philosophical substratum to the section, the reader is then taken in a further moralistic direction in paragraph nine via an attack on received opinion, the target being war.

This is an evil afflicting the individual, but which might be presented as advantageous to the community. By contrast La Bruyère overthrows his previous argument and stresses the fundamental inhumanity of war, which, although institutionalised by history and enjoyed as a source of exciting news by those not involved in it, does occasion the inevitable and arbitrary deaths of young men, nay the mutual destruction of whole populations, all dignified via the notion of an *art militaire* and the rewards of glory and fame. What happens in this section is that social values, far from being relativised as in paragraph seven, are rendered absolute by being projected against the ultimate value-system of respect for humanity, a value-system so general that it might be (and has often been seen as) essential rather than socially induced.[5]

So far, then, we have enjoyed an (in fact far from consistent) display of values on four levels: norms imposed by custom and tradition, norms vested in common sense, norms re-examined using intellectual subtlety, norms projected against a backdrop of human loving-kindness – the kind of backdrop all too often neglected in a society whose customs and traditions lionised inhuman war-mongering as source of the highest social honour. But what of humour? The vignettes which follow, personifying attributes with the kind of caricature at which La Bruyère the humorist tends to excel, play around the moral issues which the commonsensical but at the same time intellectually subtle and humanely pacifist narrator has raised.

First we have Démophile, a Jeremiah and a scaremonger, unbalanced in his reflections on events and unself-aware in his defeat-

ism, but overly self-interested when he foresees enemy occupation
threatening his personal fortune:

> il entend déjà sonner le beffroi des villes, et crier à l'alarme; il songe à son bien et à ses
> terres: où conduira-t-il son argent, ses meubles, sa famille? où se réfugiera-t-il? en Suisse
> ou à Venise? (273)

The caricature is then balanced by its opposite, the over-sanguine
Basilide who, a know-all on the subject of war, pre-emptively ascribes
victory to the French in every engagement. Anxious above all to participate in victory celebrations, he therefore talks down the power of
every enemy, talks up the strength of every ally, knows all the secret
dispositions which will lead to French success, and pounces on every
rumour to give grounds to his unthinking euphoria.

> Si les nôtres assiègent une place très forte, très régulière, pourvue de vivres et de
> munitions, qui a une bonne garnison, commandée par un homme d'un grand
> courage, il sait que la ville a des endroits faibles et mal fortifiés, qu'elle manque
> de poudre, que son gouverneur manque d'expérience, et qu'elle capitulera après
> huit jours de tranchée ouverte. Une autre fois il accourt tout hors d'haleine, et
> après avoir respiré un peu: « Voilà, s'écrie-t-il, une grande nouvelle; ils sont
> défaits, et à plate couture; le général, les chefs, du moins une bonne partie, tout
> est tué, tout a péri. Voilà, continue-t-il, un grand massacre, et il faut convenir que
> nous jouons d'un grand bonheur. » Il s'assit, il souffle, après avoir débité sa
> nouvelle, à laquelle il ne manque qu'une circonstance, qui est qu'il est certain
> qu'il n'y a point eu de bataille. (274)

Much of this reflects value-based satire, and, incidentally, fits
with Bergsonian theory. The warning stressed by the presentation of the
figures is that we avoid being foolish in forgetting ourselves to the
extent of allowing our patriotic fears or hopes to get the better of our
judgement: this one might call the primary value-system, which
generates the satiric incongruity. Underlying it, however, is a secondary
value-system, which, as often in La Bruyère, reflects moderation and
circumspection. Meanwhile, technically speaking, the moral caricature
of Démophile and Basilide depends on the fixing of an attitude or mood
in a character-sketch which corresponds to the artist's fixing of a
particular passing expression (frown, yawn, sneeze or whatever) in
exaggerated outline: the one is a travesty of the pessimist, the other a
travesty of the optimist. So, just as the target figure as drawn by the
caricaturist displays striking ugliness (a physical incongruity), so the
target figure as described by the satirist displays striking eccentricity (a
behavioural incongruity), and this is enough to secure some sort of
comical effect: whether it is reinforced by secondary value-systems or

by clan loyalties depends on contexts and attitudes not always as easy to predict as at this point.

The more interesting complication to this pattern comes with the diplomat, who, significantly perhaps, is unnamed, although to a certain extent completing the triangle. Unlike his unbendingly consistent counterparts, he is highly self-aware and very flexible: he is described as a *caméléon* and could be named Protée. To this extent he cuts right across the Bergsonian notions of comic rigidity, and indeed he does not provoke humour. He is unscrupulous, but highly skilled. In no way morally admirable, he is most adept in the techniques expected of him:

> Il a du flegme, il s'arme de courage et de patience, il ne se lasse point, il fatigue les autres, et les pousse jusques au découragement. Il se précautionne et s'endurcit contre les lenteurs et les remises, contre les reproches, les soupçons, les défiances, contre les difficultés et les obstacles, persuadé que le temps seul et les conjonctures amènent les choses et conduisent les esprits au point où on les souhaite. Il va jusques à feindre un intérêt secret à la rupture de la négociation, lorsqu'il désire le plus ardemment qu'elle soit continuée; et si au contraire il a des ordres précis de faire les derniers efforts pour la rompre, il croit devoir, pour y réussir, en presser la continuation et la fin ... Toutes ses vues, toutes ses maximes, tous les raffinements de sa politique tendent à une seule fin, qui est de n'être point trompé, et de tromper les autres. (278-9)

These skills place him high on the value-scale on which the others fall down, for he is an expert evaluator of evidence and circumstance, which they are not, and he harmonises precisely with a role in which they are manifestly inept. Anyone whose judgement is so clouded as that of Démophile and Basilide by the character defects which they portray could never be what he is: a highly useful diplomatic or political agent. However, though demonstrably strong where others are laughably weak, the character does not rank high on the value-scale of human-kindness, an important reservation because this is the value-system which can, and often does, redeem a victim of satire: "Don't be too hard on him, he may be a lousy academic, but he's always been very kind to his mother." So, rather than being sharpened by secondary considerations, hostile emotions can be softened by them, particularly when these considerations reflect a warmth and humanity clearly absent from the figure we have just considered.

What is happening in such cases as these is that the secondary value-system, instead of reinforcing the satire (as, in political cartoons, the differing value-systems enshrined in political loyalties reinforce the effect of the primary value-judgement made on the ugly figures depicted), is in fact weakening it, and softening the satiric judgement and also perhaps the laughter which that judgement generates. Accordingly the good satirist may close off avenues whereby these favourable secondary value-judgements might be invoked, because they have the potential to weaken his satire, and he does this especially by isolating his target figure within a specific context: so La Bruyère isolates him in satiric sketches which are rarely more than a paragraph long. Also he will simplify his character portrayal to the point where complex responses are inappropriate and unlikely: La Bruyère's *caractères* are not real people with backgrounds, personalities or even names; they are personified attitudes.

Under such circumstances the satire is quite strongly directed and the secondary (and tertiary, and quaternary) value-systems trimmed to a minimum. Nevertheless a doggedly sympathetic reader might still invoke the ultimate value-system of humanity and accordingly diminish the satiric effects. This might involve bad reading (who can say in any way meaningfully that Basilide, for all his faults, might have been a kind grandfather, or Démophile a loving husband?), but it is still a possible strategy, and in more complex satires (Molière's family dramas, for instance) one readily available. Meanwhile, putting things in a reverse perspective, it is interesting to speculate whether someone who scores not high, but low on the value-scale of human-kindness – in other words someone who is simply inhumane, as contrast inefficient, unself-aware, indecisive, unintelligent (that is low on one or more of the many primary value-scales which satirists seek to apply) – can be an object of satire. One can laugh at the eternal optimist, and at the eternal pessimist; but can one laugh at the eternal villain or the unremitting scoundrel?

Perhaps, in order to be thus attacked, such scoundrels need a caricatured grotesque quality as well: a weakness. Is it not necessary that there be a primary value-system set within the satiric framework, just as the personification of evil in the ogres of children's folklore is, in addition to being bad, also clumsy, stupid and ugly? In this way he can be a figure of fun whilst also being a focus of horror. However La Bruyère's Machiavellian agent (as contrast the ogre of the beanstalk or, more subtly, the hypocritical and manipulative Tartuffe) has no weakness: there is therefore no primary value-system invoked in the satire, and it is unfunny. Meanwhile Tartuffe is an equally skilled hypocrite, but he is undone by his own lechery, this undoing providing in many ways the comic climax of the play – see the table scene in Act 4 Scene 5. Is it this weakness, backed up by the secondary value-system of honesty (he is the archetypal *faux dévot*, much more famous than La Bruyère's own Onuphre),[6] plus the tertiary value-system of loving-kindness (he is thoroughly inhuman), plus all the further value-systems which are skilfully engaged by any actor portraying him, which brings him into the realm of comic satire?

There is, however, an important caveat to be made in this context. For in the areas of politics and war (*Du souverain*), or indeed those of court and town society (*De la cour*, *De la ville*), nay that of literature as well (*Des ouvrages de l'esprit*), one can imagine how the caricatured figure could, perhaps if things went wrong, achieve a certain glamour which would redeem him despite the adverse value-judgements cued in by the author. The braggart soldier might become a coward on the grand scale, the snob so outrageous that his attitudes attract rather than repel, the writing so dreadful that it becomes more memorable than the satiric text conveying it. By such means (though, for me, it rarely if ever happens in La Bruyère) is the entire mould of satiric humour broken (and Bergsonian theory refuted). There is of course a long tradition of comic anti-heroes, be they ruffians, villains or poltroons, who are the opposite of what they ought to be (brave, selfless and responsible) and who abound in moral weaknesses, but they are clowning parodies of a value-system (good soldiery, good politics, good living) rather than vehicles for the application and reaffirmation of that value-system. Such humour is the realm of Rabelais, not of La Bruyère, and it does not belong in a study of satire.

For La Bruyère, at any rate as narrator, the didactic intention of the humorist reigns supreme: in the very introduction to his text "le public" is advised that

> Il peut regarder avec loisir ce portrait que j'ai fait de lui d'après nature, et s'il se connaît quelques-uns des défauts que je touche, s'en corriger (61),

and, as value-based satirist, that narrator establishes quite clearly what values he respects and would seek to inculcate: see for example the concluding section of *Les Caractères* which is a panegyric of Christian teaching aimed satirically at the *esprits forts* who are now denying it. These values centre around the concept of *honnêteté* which the seventeenth century gave birth to and officially revered, hence the critique of extremes ("Ce que l'on prodigue, on l'ôte à son héritier; ce que l'on épargne sordidement, on se l'ôte à soi-même": 194), and the lauding of *médiocrité*.

Stemming from this position come some memorable comic vignettes which ridicule eccentricity – particular favourites are

Hermippe the gadget-freak, Hermagoras the classical scholar who knows the kings of Babylon in order, but thinks that Henri III was father to Henri IV, and Diphile, the aviculturist who has become a bird:

> il passe les jours, ces jours qui échappent et qui ne reviennent plus, à verser du grain et à nettoyer des ordures; il donne pension à un homme qui n'a point d'autre ministère que de siffler des serins au flageolet et de faire couver des *Canaries*; il est vrai que ce qu'il dépense d'un côté, il l'épargne de l'autre, car ses enfants sont sans maîtres et sans éducation; il se renferme le soir fatigué de son propre plaisir, sans pouvoir jouir du moindre repos, que ses oiseaux ne reposent, et que ce petit peuple, qu'il n'aime que parce qu'il chante, ne cesse de chanter; il retrouve ses oiseaux dans son sommeil, lui-même il est oiseau, il est huppé, il gazouille, il perche; il rêve la nuit qu'il mue, ou qu'il couve. (390-1)

The primary value-system is more than clear, the secondary ones (good parenting, for example) almost equally evident. However the cult of moderation has its limits: it is possible to be excessively unexcessive, witness Narcisse who

> se lève le matin pour se coucher le soir ... lit exactement la *Gazette de Hollande*, et le *Mercure Galant*; il a lu Bergerac, des Marets, etc., ... se promène avec des femmes à la Plaine ou au Cours, et ... est d'une ponctualité religieuse sur les visites. Il fera demain ce qu'il fait aujourd'hui et ce qu'il fit hier; et il meurt ainsi après avoir vécu (208),

and is thus ridiculously banal.

To maintain literary vitality La Bruyère has to shift his moral position, or at least its emphasis, however the consistency of the satirist's line is only an issue if one chooses to question it, instead of merely enjoying it as being oneself a member of the clan comprising his responsive readership: the La Bruyère fan club. For there is no doubt that this clan exists, and that part of La Bruyère's authorial skill (rather than narratorial posturing) is exercised in sustaining it. Membership is based in part on one's being subtle enough to discern the various value-systems operating within the situations as they are described, however, as we have seen, often the value-basis to the satire is so obvious that we need scarcely compliment ourselves on fulfilling that criterion. Other conditions are more disquieting. The clan is clearly polite and intelligent (*honnêteté* again), but is also male, aristocratic (hence his lamentations about the rise of the *nouveaux riches*) and courtly: thus

> Paris, pour l'ordinaire le singe de la cour, ne sait pas toujours la contrefaire; il ne l'imite en aucune manière dans ces dehors agréables et caressants que quelques courtisans, et surtout les femmes, y ont naturellement pour un homme de mérite, et qui n'a même que du mérite ... Une femme de ville entend-elle le brouissement

d'un carrosse qui s'arrête à sa porte, elle pétille de goût et de complaisance pour quiconque est dedans, sans le connaître; (210-1)

and here we might see a clan-based satire taking over. Though the *cour* may claim superiority of taste over the *ville*, the delight in such vignettes lies less in the advancing of that value (which for me is the true purpose of value-based satire), than in the consolidation of the clan as such.

Evidently both patterns are punitive, but the punishment is of different kinds. We have seen La Bruyère claim that the aim of value-based satire is to reform (hence his reference to the "fléau du ridicule" in Molière):[7] I feel this is an aim so rarely achieved as to be virtually spurious. However a humorist may advance a value if not by actually changing people's behaviour, then at least by reassuring those who already respect that value. Thus the victims of an oppressor will be reassured when the values enshrined in that oppressor are derided. On the other hand clan-based satire aims merely to consolidate and reinvigorate the clan generating it and responding to it: its target is not being structurally criticised or, by intention, reformed, so much as merely scapegoated. Hence the comic role of the Parisian townswoman is to be a Parisian townswoman, and the incongruity basic to that role resides there, and not in the behaviour-patterns which confirm her inferiority. To shift the satiric co-ordinates down to my level, the Spurs supporter derides the Arsenal supporter, both at the same time claiming that their team is better, but what generates the satire is the clan division between the supporters' clubs, not the value-system of good football.

To be sure, this is a complex distinction, and the more complex for being so subjective in its operation. People define, formally or out of instinct, the membership rules of their clans; people choose, consciously or unconsciously, to uphold certain values both in their behaviour and in the humour which forms a part of it. They will often, moreover, claim superior status for their clan, so smuggling value-systems into the loyalty they feel towards it. By contrast they may also affect support for a certain value-system in order to be accepted into a certain clan, this being one of the ways whereby one might explain that willing suspension of moral disinterest in the behaviour-pattern mentioned above. So value-judgements and clan loyalties can merge into one another in a highly fluid manner, and it is not always clear what precisely lies behind the privilege which La Bruyère grants, despite grave reservations in some areas, to the court, the nobility, the French, nay even Christendom.

Also curious is the way in which, despite being in part a clan-based satirist, he in fact proceeds to satirise such satire. As we have seen, this happens by implication in the Arsène *vignette*. It is more clearly theorised in a later passage from the same section (*Des ouvrages de l'esprit*):

> Les connaisseurs, ou ceux qui se croyant tels, se donnent voix délibérative et décisive sur les spectacles, se cantonnent aussi, et se divisent en des partis contraires, dont chacun, poussé par un tout autre intérêt que par celui du public ou de l'équité, admire un certain poème ou une certaine musique, et siffle tout autre. Ils nuisent également, par cette chaleur à défendre leurs préventions, et à la faction opposée et à leur propre cabale: ils découragent par mille contradictions les poètes et les musiciens, retardent les progrès des sciences et les arts, en leur ôtant le fruit qu'ils pourraient tirer de l'émulation et de la liberté qu'auraient plusieurs excellents maîtres de faire, chacun dans leur genre et selon leur génie, de très beaux ouvrages. (80)

In his chapter *De la société* he builds this antipathy into a satire of the small town ("Il y a une chose que l'on n'a point vue sous le ciel, et que selon toutes les apparences on ne verra jamais: c'est une petite ville qui n'est divisée en aucuns partis": 165), and in *Des biens de fortune* he notes how the laughter of the clan surrounding a wealthy man will be turned on the outsider who dares to mock him for his stupidity: "Un projet assez vain serait de vouloir tourner un homme fort sot et fort riche en ridicule; les rieurs sont de son côté" (177-8). Thus can the value-bases and the clan-loyalties in a comic situation oppose rather than reinforce one another.

The scapegoat figure, or pharmakos, as victim of clan-based satire, has received extensive theoretical treatment.[8] His role is, willy-nilly, to suffer, as La Bruyère the man truly suffered owing to his own defects and less than exalted birth. He has, however, a counter-part in the anti-pharmakos who, as studied by Northrop Frye, is set up as a figure via whom is mocked the whole of that society which is shunning or punishing him. Here we find a satire which is once more value-based (if one does not admire the anti-pharmakos for some important reasons, then the satire in which he is situated will not work), but which, in its extreme form, has an interesting dimension in terms of clan membership. For just as the scapegoat can be isolated from the clan via its punitive humour, so the anti-pharmakos can be situated in a clan of one member, denouncing the whole of the rest of society, nay humanity, even including, by implication, himself.

This is a satiric pattern not infrequent in La Bruyère, and, unsurprisingly perhaps, his section *De l'homme* furnishes examples as of its first paragraph:

Ne nous emportons point contre les hommes en voyant leur dureté, leur ingratitude, leur injustice, leur fierté, l'amour d'eux-mêmes, et l'oubli des autres: ils sont ainsi faits, c'est leur nature, c'est ne pouvoir supporter que la pierre tombe ou que le feu s'élève. (289)

Here the narrator as the anti-pharmakaos is condemning humanity as self-seeking, greedy, mendacious and indifferent to virtue. Even that social acme, the court, merely disgusts one with the court: "Un esprit sain puise à la cour le goût de la solitude et de la retraite" (247). Meanwhile, in an eloquent conclusion to the section *Des jugements*, mankind is attacked for attributing to itself the faculty of reason, while having also invented war with all its destructive technology:

Mais comme vous devenez d'année en année plus raisonnables, vous avez bien enchéri sur cette vieille manière de vous exterminer: vous avez de petits globes qui vous tuent tout d'un coup, s'ils peuvent seulement vous atteindre à la tête ou à la poitrine; vous en avez d'autres, plus pesants et plus massifs, qui vous coupent en deux parts ou qui vous éventrent ... etc. (383)

The satiric technique is a standard one whereby the anti-pharmakos adopts the perspective of an *ingénu*, pre-empting all the sophisticated cultural baggage of civilisation and seeing things with what masquerades as a natural lucidity. However the technique has its appeal. In some contexts the humour might be branded cynical, in the sense that the satirist refuses to nuance his hostile point of view, and prevents the introduction of alternative value-judgements à propos of humanity at large, in much the same way as we saw him over-simplify the individualised vignettes whereby specific character-traits were held up to ridicule. Thus Doris Kirsch opines:

A travers de multiples cas particuliers, où toutes les classes et tous les groupes sociaux sont représentés, c'est toute la société de son époque qu'il rejette comme étant dépourvue de sens et de valeur humaine.[9]

Cynicism there may be in La Bruyère, but once again it is unwise to confuse the postures adopted by the narrator with the attitudes more subtly encouraged by the author, and, to return to the clan-basis of this general satire on humanity, we can see how the author is once again establishing a rapport with us as readers (seducing us back into complicity with him) while his narrator arraigns humanity (the clan from which we, paradoxically enough, find ourselves alienated) as being a race of hypocritical and vainglorious butchers.

The point is that such a generalised satire cannot work, except as an ironical posture on the part of the narrator. Society, as the source of "valeur humaine", cannot be deprived of "valeur humaine", and the ultimate value of human-kindness to which we have already alluded is once more the system which softens the satiric blow. When he says that we should not condemn humanity for its inhumanity, the author, if not the narrator, means it. To do so would be inhuman. So, for me at least, the unspoken value redeeming *l'homme* is that same human-kindness which La Bruyère also applies in his satires on war. At the same time as being confronted with this value-system, moreover, are we not also being drawn, symbolically and by the narrator's same paradoxes, back into the ultimate clan – humanity – into which, ideally speaking, all sub-clans can be dissolved? Just as one's adherence to all values may be minimised when one is confronted by a case of innocent human suffering, so one's clan loyalties may find their limits when one is faced with ultimate questions of human brotherhood. Frequently, therefore, La Bruyère looks beyond the class-ridden, clique-ridden, and clan-ridden society he is denouncing, to speak for a common humanity, and the exhortation quoted above ("Ne nous emportons point contre les hommes") can be seen as quite a gentle piece of irony, rather than a savage piece of cynicism, if one reads into it the ultimate value of human-kindness, perhaps that postulated essential norm which might ultimately redeem all satirised villains, or if one reawakens the clan loyalty of humankind, which consolidates all human beings on an instinctual if not (as professedly for La Bruyère) a religious basis.

It remains an interesting exercise to examine how incompetently, or at least insensitively, La Bruyère handles other types of laughter. I have entitled this chapter "a study of satire", so it might seem inappropriate to condemn an author for not doing what he has not set out to do: as we have already observed, we are not here dealing with Rabelais. However the point is relevant to the extent that, Rabelais apart (and La Bruyère does of course mention him),[10] he chooses to satirise other types of humour, much as we saw him satirise that type of satirist which he does not wish, at least professedly, to be.

The theoretical basis of his position is at least clear, it being expressed, for instance, in the following aphoristic piece of meta-satire: "Il semble que l'on ne puisse rire que des choses ridicules" (315). However he continues:

> l'on voit néanmoins de certaines gens qui rient également des choses ridicules et de celles qui ne le sont pas. Si vous êtes sot et inconsidéré, et qu'il vous échappe devant eux quelque impertinence, ils rient de vous; si vous êtes sage, et que vous ne disiez que des choses raisonnables, et du ton qu'il les faut dire, ils rient de même. (*ibid.*)

This could be a response to several things, not least to the clan which has chosen to scapegoat the court satirist who has, on whatever basis, been satirising it. It could also be a satire of inanity – an attack on the importunate glee of those gigglers who can't take anything seriously: in vain would La Bruyère's narrator tell them what they ought to be laughing at, they would simply, like children, laugh at him. However in the sketch of Ruffin (*De l'homme*) he reopens his attack on vapid gaiety, situating it in a character who, though "gai, jovial, familier ... [qui] rit de tout son coeur, et ... rit tout seul et sans sujet" (331), lives on the fringes of idiocy to the extent that he cannot even take seriously the death of his only son. Death and laughter sit ill with one another in any case, as he tells us in *Des esprits forts*:

> Toute plaisanterie dans un homme mourant est hors de sa place [Mercutio please note] ... c'est une chose bien sérieuse que de mourir: ce n'est point alors le badinage qui sied bien, mais la constance. (451)

So the idiotic laugher, the death-bed comic and the inane giggler are all criticised and marginalised as unworthy of one's attention or company. Yet the types of humour they represent – whereby value-systems are not imposed, but rather challenged, inverted or suspended – is an immensely rich one, and it is only by La Bruyère's preference that satire is placed above it. The problem reappears in the forever paradoxical figure of Socrates, whom Rabelais portrayed as a rowdy toss-pot who concealed his wisdom under a grotesque exterior, and of whom La Bruyère recalls the judgement classing him as a "fou tout plein d'esprit" (365):

> Quels bizarres portraits nous fait ce philosophe! quelles moeurs étranges et particulières ne décrit-il point! où a-t-il rêvé, creusé, rassemblé des idées si extraordinaires? quelles couleurs, quel pinceau! ce sont des chimères. (*ibid.*)

Accordingly, Socrates is converted into your humdrum satirist: "Socrate s'éloignait du cynique, il épargnait les personnes, et blâmait les moeurs qui étaient mauvaises" (*ibid.*) and one wonders if the apparatus of La Bruyère is capable of handling the complexities of the fool figure: has he not already received bad notices elsewhere in the text?[11]

Socrates is a special case, there being as many of him as there are of his admirers, but the philosophical point whereby comic extravagance (even of a Ruffin) may serve a different purpose from the humour (or humours) of satire is not one unknown to *Les Caractères*.

> Voulez-vous quelque autre prodige? concevez un homme facile, doux, complaisant, traitable, et tout d'un coup violent, colère, fougueux, capricieux;

imaginez-vous un homme simple, ingénu, crédule, badin, volage, un enfant en
cheveux gris; mais permettez-lui de se recueillir, ou plutôt de se livrer à un génie
qui agit en lui, j'ose dire, sans qu'il y prenne part et comme à son insu: quelle
verve! quelle élévation! quelles images! quelle latinité! Parlez-vous d'une même
personne? me direz-vous. - Oui, du même, de *Théodas*, et de lui seul. Il crie, il
s'agite, il se roule à terre, il se relève, il tonne, il éclate; et du milieu de cette
tempête il sort une lumière qui brille et qui réjouit; disons-le sans figure: il parle
comme un fou, et pense comme un homme sage; il dit ridiculement des choses
vraies, et follement des choses sensées et raisonnables; on est surpris de voir
naître et éclore le bon sens au sein de la bouffonnerie, parmi les grimaces et les
contorsions; qu'ajouterai-je davantage? ... il est bon homme, il est plaisant
homme, et il est excellent homme. (362)

Such incongruity is essentially that of Rabelais' Socrates, nay of
Erasmus' Moria, and it operates simply by conjoining two incompatible
structures within the same character – be they costumes, verbal registers,
or, as here, behaviour-patterns – and allowing the humour to develop. As
such it is akin to others we might feel we had seen elsewhere
condemned, as in, for instance, the inconsequential humour of the jester
or, witness the passage following (from *Des ouvrages de l'esprit*), in the
crude vitality of popular theatre:

Ce n'est point assez que les moeurs du théâtre ne soient pas mauvaises, il faut
encore qu'elles soient décentes et instructives. Il peut y avoir un ridicule si bas et
si grossier, ou même si fade et si indifférent, qu'il n'est ni permis au poète d'y
faire attention, ni possible aux spectateurs de s'en divertir. Le paysan ou l'ivrogne
fournit quelques scènes à un farceur; il n'entre qu'à peine dans le vrai comique. (82)

But surely, in no way can a satiric and still less an improvingly didactic
principle be allowed to determine the comic patterns of parodic incongruity, otherwise Quixote and Sancho, Falstaff and Hal, Pantagruel and
Panurge would simply be enacting moral fables.

By my reading, the comic patterns of La Bruyère's text defy his
own satire and meta-satire at numerous other points. One could mention
the travestied married couple in *Des femmes* where, in unwitting echo of
the *Quinze joies*, the wife wears the trousers to the extent that her
husband needs only to give birth in order to take on her role entirely.
One could mention Théodecte, the loud-mouthed dinner-guest: "Il
mange, il boit, il conte, il plaisante, il interrompt tout à la fois" (153),
and, as a distant cousin of Rabelais' Frère Jean,[12] he might well have
been a better laugh than the narrator who walks out on him:

les rieurs sont pour lui [n.b.]: il n'y a sorte de fatuités qu'on ne lui passe. Je cède
enfin et je disparais, incapable de souffrir plus longtemps Théodecte, et ceux qui
le souffrent. (*ibid.*)

Finally one might recall the figure of Drance (in *Du coeur*), who is the more interesting in this context for being, in some ways like our trio of Panurge, Falstaff and Sancho, a social inferior who sets himself above his betters, and specifically his master:

> *Drance* veut passer pour gouverner son maître, qui n'en croit rien, non plus que le public: parler sans cesse à un grand que l'on sert, en des lieux et en des temps où il convient le moins, lui parler à l'oreille ou en des termes mystérieux, rire jusqu'à éclater en sa présence, lui couper la parole, se mettre entre lui et ceux qui lui parlent, dédaigner ceux qui viennent faire leur cour, ou attendre impatiemment qu'ils se retirent, se mettre proche de lui en une posture trop libre, figurer avec lui le dos appuyé à une cheminée, le tirer par son habit, lui marcher sur les talons, faire le familier, prendre des libertés, marquent mieux un fat qu'un favori. (144-5)

Again the value-judgements are imposed with unsubtle vigour: who is this upstart who seeks to break into the clan of his superiors, yet only succeeds in rendering his own pretensions ridiculous?[13] However, the incongruity of the servant who masters his master is far richer in its implications than La Bruyère's reductive treatment of it would imply, and I for one would encourage Drance to break the conventions in a time-honoured carnivalesque tradition which reaches from Jeeves back to the comedies of ancient Greece, and whose eternal function is roguishly to challenge the social order, rather than humbly to submit to it.

Perhaps aware that humour can never be bound over to keep the peace in any society, La Bruyère is happy to allow his narrator to produce a number of inconsistent positions, posing alternatively as cynic, moralist, voice of the people and thorough-going snob, and allowing the reader to flit between them, enjoying such variety in approach for the freedom it gives. Meanwhile, ever the satirist when called to account for his own position, he is yet prepared, when the mood takes him, to denounce satire itself, or at least the instinct for satire, saying:

> C'est une chose monstrueuse que le goût et la facilité qui est en nous de railler, d'improuver et de mépriser les autres; et tout ensemble la colère que nous ressentons contre ceux qui nous raillent, nous improuvent et nous méprisent (316),

which observation of course begs several questions including that as to whether we do respond to raillery with anger rather than self-mockery. After all, just as the victim of satire need not be lacking in humanity, so one responding to satire need not be lacking in comic perspective, even when the satirist then rounds on him for being so ready to laugh in the first place. For it is this same sense of perspective which has allowed one to join the author in ridiculing those for whom one may well feel no antipathy.

Some adjustment in terms of clan associations and value responses is necessary on the part of the audience or readership whoever is taking the satiric lead. Might it not be that the successful satire is less that which shows one how to improve one's own behaviour or thought-patterns, than that which enables an agile, guiltless and yet enlightening shift of humorous response?

---

[1] q.v. the treatment of Ménalque in the section *Du comique en général*.

[2] La Bruyère, *Œuvres complètes*, ed. J. Benda (Paris, 1951), pp. 71-2: all subsequent bracketed references are to this edition.

[3] H. Mazaheri, *La Satire démystificatrice de La Bruyère* (New York, 1995), p. 47.

[4] F. Gray, *La Bruyère: amateur de caractères* (Paris, 1986), p. 43.

[5] Rousseau is a case in point, he arguing that primitive man, an asocial being, still felt pity for the suffering of his fellow-men with whom he did not live, to whom he did not speak and from whom he had nothing to gain.

[6] q.v. "De la mode", § 24.

[7] "Des ouvrages de l'esprit", § 38.

[8] cf. Northrop Frye, *Anatomy of Criticism*, Essays 1 and 3, and R. Girard, *Le Bouc émissaire*.

[9] D. Kirsch, *La Bruyère ou le style cruel* (Montréal, 1977), p. 134.

[10] cf. "Des ouvrages de l'esprit", § 43, where he is condemned as incomprehensible and inexplicable, filthy and corrupt, despite being, at his best, "exquis" and "excellent".

[11] "De la société", § 56, cf. *supra*, p. 91.

[12] See his performance in *Gargantua*, c. 39.

[13] The code-breakers would have it that he is the Comte de Clermont-Tonnerre, and his "maître" the king's brother.

5. Humour and Propaganda under the Second Empire

Keith Cameron

A book on French humour would not be complete were it not to take into account a facet of that humour which is close to the heart of every Frenchman. I am of course referring to the art of satire and caricature. It is not surprising, given what makes a French person laugh, that Henri Bergson in his essay on laughter should highlight the mechanical element and the caricatural deformation of the norm as being prime factors in his analysis of the comic process. Although I have no statistics and no hard proof to support my observation, I feel that the French, given their innate belief that they know what good taste and "le beau" are, are more prone than many to find humour in an unexpected departure from the graceful. Laughter can lead to ridicule and be a powerful weapon if one wishes to discredit the object of that laughter.

I should like, for present purposes, to concentrate on one small aspect of this complex issue and consider satire and caricature as a political tool. In this connection, I am going to look at the use of caricature as a means of social and political criticism, which will therefore bring together the two items in the title of this chapter, namely humour and propaganda. Although I am more familiar with the use of satirical propaganda in the sixteenth century, I was, if not astounded, then interested, to find that under the Second Empire the satirical and caricatural assaults on Napoleon III corresponded significantly with the salient traits discernible in attacks made against his royal predecessor Henri III, the last of the Valois.

As Norbert Elias has pointed out,

> History is constantly being rewritten because the historian's way of seeing the connection between the details documented merely reflects his attitude to the extra-scientific issues of the day,[1]

and although I am aware that my reading of the past may be greatly influenced by my reading of the present, especially in view of recent conflicts between the media and public figures in the West, I want to draw attention to some of the aspects of propaganda under the Second Empire against the back-cloth of what I have gleaned from my study of an earlier period, and of what I have observed in our contemporary society.

> Le pamphlet et l'image! Deux armes redoutables pour le système du bon plaisir
> que l'imprimerie va mettre aux mains du public,

observed John Grand-Carteret,[2] but there are pamphlets and pamphlets, pictures and pictures. They all bear witness to the deep-rooted belief in the right of free speech and the will to spread one's views amongst one's readers and viewers. My brief here is, however, to examine the way in which pamphlets and images can also be used to deform reality, to convey an exaggerated picture, whether it be verbal or graphic, of a person or an event, often with the intent to amuse, but also with the intent to discredit and so make a political point.

Caricature consists in exaggerating physical traits and, thereby, creating from the normal something abnormal, which in turns generates an element of surprise, which in its turn often leads to a smile and humour.

> Combien de profils soi-disant immortels, ont été descendus de leur Olympe, pour
> peu que la Caricature se soit seulement amusée, par manière de passe-temps, à
> donner une de ces chiquenaudes crayonnées qui consistent à exagérer les
> contours d'un nez ou à aplatir un menton séducteur.[3]

At the time of the Second Empire, in Victorian England *Punch or the Charivari* was taking caricature into houses and gentlemen's clubs up and down the land; meanwhile, in France, Daumier was at the height of his powers, and many of his drawings and etchings have transcended the nineteenth century to become part of our artistic heritage. The problem with caricature is that one must be able to recognise the person or the thing being caricatured to appreciate all its satirical humour and bite. Both graphic and verbal humour change, and it is rewarding, if indeed often puzzling, to look at the *Punch* of 140 years ago and then try to work out what the elements of the humour are. The language has altered in resonance and now seems particularly archaic. It may, as do the pictures, contain many references to contemporary events which, although they would have been known to the contemporary reader, are often a mystery to us. Indeed some of the drawings can seem definitely unfunny because of the distancing which has inevitably occurred owing to the passage of time and to our ignorance of their specific cultural referents.

The Second Empire, as a historical term strictly applied, signifies the period between December 1852 and September 1870. It was an era of wars, economic growth, social change, imperial designs and military defeat which novelists and historians have chronicled well. It is too great a period for us to study in detail here, nor am I expert enough to be able to do so. If we consider it within the confines of this chapter, however, and therefore by reference to humour and propaganda, we first of all have to make the point that the press and the theatre were gagged.

To consolidate his regime Napoleon III sought by many means to stifle opposition. Hence as early as February 17, 1852, a decree had been promulgated which virtually imposed strict censorship on the press,[4] meanwhile theatre censorship was reinstated on December 30 of the same year. Many of the opponents to the regime had left France after the coup d'état of December 2, 1851, amongst them Victor Hugo, who made his way via Brussels to Jersey and then Guernsey. It was from there that he was to publish *Les Châtiments* in 1853, and this work, bearing the imprint of Geneva and New York, is symptomatic of much of the opposition to Napoleon III in that it was published outside France, Brussels and England being favourite locations. Although the censorship laws were relaxed somewhat in 1868, it is only after the outbreak of the Franco-Prussian War that one sees a real upsurge in mordant political satire in metropolitan France. To use the somewhat dramatic words of the Duc d'Aumale,

> La France, soumise au doux régime de la loi dite de sécurité générale, courbe la tête, en gémissant, sous le joug; la presse, bâillonnée, ne peut plus faire entendre sa voix, et la pensée, chassée du territoire de l'empire, s'est réfugiée hors de ses frontières, en protestant.[5]

During most of the Second Empire, caricaturists such as Daumier had to modify their subjects in the light of censorship, and they concentrated on the social aspects of the new era.[6] Humorous caricatures of daily events are to be found in journals such as *Le Charivari*, *Le Journal amusant*, *La Vie parisienne*, *L'Eclipse*, *Le Boulevard*, *La Lune*, *Le Hanneton*, etc. For example, in 1858, the fashion of wearing the crinoline inspired Daumier's amused and amusing pen to draw the rear view of a bourgeoise so attired and passing along a wintry street beneath not only a load of snow but also under the bemused eye of a female sweeper (Figure 1). Such engravings reveal not only a sense of humour, but also an awareness of social differences.[7] Similarly, in 1862 Daumier turned his attention to that relatively new mode of transport, the locomotive, and in a somewhat tame sketch showed the dangers of travelling in a compartment with a cigar-smoking male! (Figure 2) One can but wonder whether he could have drawn such a picture at the end of the twentieth century now that the dangers of passive smoking have been realised: what in 1862 was a humorous situation would in the 1990s be considered in extremely bad taste and decidedly lacking in humour.

Figure One

Figure Two

Other prints of the period by other caricaturists highlight such issues of the moment as the existence of "La Légion vésuvienne", a women's political movement founded in 1848, and which was to fall victim to traditional male chauvinist mockery (Figure 3).[8] Attention in such a work is drawn to the allegedly natural role of women in society, which is to raise children and not to enter political life. Recent discussion had focused opinion on divorce, and the old shibboleths about women were given new meaning in "Les Divorceuses" (Figure 4).[9]

I could also mention the *Salons caricaturaux*, which were "comptes rendus en images humoristiques des oeuvres, peintures ou sculptures, exposées au Salon officiel"[10] which was held in Paris from 1840 onwards: they occupied several pages in the contemporary press and were at their height during the Second Empire. However, for real criticism of the political regime, and for hostile comment on events in France, we often have to go to the foreign press, Belgian for example, where we find a print satirising the Crimean War,[11] an event which was not looked upon with favour or understanding by Napoleon's subjects, since it was so costly in both lives and funds (Figure 5).[12] The print, which allegorises the war in the form of a dragon swallowing armies, arms and treasuries, would not have required great expertise for one to interpret its allegorical meaning, and the appropriateness of the title, "Peace satisfies the appetite and War sharpens it", would not have gone unnoticed at virtually any level of opinion.

In England, too, Napoleon had his critics. His book on the *Histoire de Jules César* of 1865 was viewed as showing his imperial designs for a dynasty. Such ambition is admirably satirised in a sketch in *Punch* in which César is shown trying to blow up a balloon in the shape of Napoleon I to the size of a statuesque Caesar (Figure 6). *Punch* was equally scathing of the Emperor's flirtation with Prussia and Bismarck in 1866; this engraving (Figure 7) follows within a fortnight the revelation that Napoleon had approached Bismarck with a suggestion that Prussia should concede to France the frontier of 1814 plus Luxembourg, and again, on July 29, that she should abandon all German territory on the left bank of the Rhine. On August 6, that is within a week, Bismarck had refused what he called a tip (*pourboire*) or an inn-keeper's account (*note d'aubergiste*), and passed on the suggestion to the correspondent of the Paris *Le Siècle*.[13]

In France herself one notes, at least on the surface, the clear absence of an orchestrated campaign against the Emperor and his policies. In reality, however, as Pierre Silex informs us in 1871,

Figure Three

Une Patrouille de la Légion Vésuvienne

- **Caporal, faites donc taire votre moutard ou donnez-lui à téter. Il va faire fuir les voleurs avec ses cris.**

Figure Four

LES DIVORCEUSES

**Tout est porté à l'émancipation des femmes ...
... par des femmes déjà émancipées**

Figure Five

Le Dragon Actuel

La paix nourrit, la guerre affame

Figure Six

NULLUS AUT CAESAR

Louis (an ambitious boy): "Aha, mon ami!
I shall make 'im so big as you!"

Punch, 11 March 1965

Figure Seven

PEACE - AND NO PIECES

Bismarck: "Pardon, mon ami! But we really can't allow you to pick up anything here!"
Nap (the chiffonnier): "Pray don't mention it, M'sieu! It's not of the slightest consequence."

Punch, 25 August 1866

> Sous le règne de Napoléon III, alors que le théâtre était soumis à la censure la plus rigide et que la presse était muselée, il fallait bien que l'esprit français, ce vieux coq gaulois qui ne veut pas mourir, trouvât une autre issue.[14]

He takes obvious pleasure in recounting the tales that circulated around the salons, and in repeating the biting little puns that were in vogue. One could quote for example the riddle as to why the Emperor's wife had to be a blonde: "Il l'a prise blonde parce que la consigne est de fermer les grilles des Tuileries à la brune";[15] or the *bon mot* whereby Napoleon III was known after the Crimean war as "fearlead":

> Cambronne a dit le mot
> Craintplomb a fait la chose.[16]

These are but trifles, but they point to a healthy humorous and critical undercurrent within French society. What I find most revealing is the innuendo to be found in certain of the prints, especially after 1870, and in the nature of the campaign mounted by Napoleon's opposition outside France. For it is here that we get down to the very stuff of political satire and the nitty-gritty of character assassination. Accusations of sleaze are a common feature of life in the Britain of the 1990s. The Royal Family, eminent politicians, diplomats, company directors and pop stars all share in this bad press, and it has been suggested that a certain member of the British community, to seek revenge for the failure to provide him with a British passport, has deliberately leaked stories of infidelities and corruption to the newspapers so as not only to embarrass the miscreants but also to discredit them.

This is an old technique. One of the best exponents I know of the art of political assassination through innuendo and accusations which cannot be refuted, either because the person is dead or because their word stands opposed only by the accused, is Suetonius in his *Lives of the Caesars* (*De vita Caesarum*). It is one of those quirks of human behaviour that although someone is accused of a heinous sexual act of which he is subsequently acquitted or proves his innocence, we tend to remember the alleged crime and not the eventual verdict. We also tend to regard respectable private sexual behaviour as a precondition for the holding of public office, as though there were a correlation between sexual orthodoxy, whatever that may mean, and probity. It is not surprising, therefore, that if someone wants to bring down someone in authority, that person will begin to spread rumours about the adversary's conduct. Napoleon III is no exception.

In actual fact we know very little about Louis Bonaparte's real self, and what we do know comes often only through the filter of propaganda.

> As he was not in the habit of speaking his mind openly and unambiguously, even to his close relations, his contemporaries have left only very superficial portraits of him, at first accompanied by the extravagant praise of courtiers, and soon after submerged by an onslaught of judgements warped by blind and often unfair hatred. One can retain from all this a series of images of the emperor [...] and a catalogue of his faults and qualities: it has been said that he was a sexual maniac, that he was curiously devoid of moral sense, that he had no respect for the law and was no doubt full of contempt for men: but much has also been made of his peculiar charm, his good-heartedness, his generous loyalty to his old friends and his absence of cruelty.[17]

In short, his personality, as we can judge it, is enigmatic.

If we are to believe his detractors, he was a man much addicted to vice. His critics not only denounced the Emperor, but all his forebears and his ancestry too. For example a work which first appeared in 1854 entitled *Prostitutions, Débauches et crimes de la famille Buonaparte* besmirches his whole family, his aunt, Pauline Bonaparte, being, by the by, a courtesan:

> Pauline Bonaparte commença le métier de courtisane à l'âge de quatorze ans et continua longtemps à se prostituer sous les yeux maternels.[18]

According to Hippolyte Magen, the author of this work of defamation, Napoleon III was already a criminal before he became emperor:

> avant d'être César, le neveu [i.e. of Napoléon I] fut lui-même un conspirateur et un assassin.[19]

He was addicted to drink. This is implied by references to Ratapoil, a caricatured figure representing the populace which had voted Louis Bonaparte to the Presidency and thence to the Imperial position:

> Mais ce qu'on admire particulièrement en [Monsieur de Ratapoil], c'est la facilité avec laquelle il boit, sans en être ému, des quantités incroyables de rhum. Sa Majesté qui passe, avec raison, pour avoir en ce genre, comme en tant d'autres, un mérite qui souffre peu de rivaux, disait gaiement, à la suite d'un combat malheureux, qu'elle renonçait désormais à la prétention de vaincre un aussi rude champion: ce n'est pas un homme, ajoutait-elle plaisamment, c'est un alambic.[20]

He was, it was also claimed, the Antichrist; at least this was the view expressed by the Reverend M. Baxter in a broadsheet published in Philadelphia in 1866 and entitled *Louis Napoleon, the Destined Monarch of the World and Personal Antichrist* (Figure 8),[21] and doubts had even been expressed about his being the true son of Napoleon I's brother,

Figure Eight

1806 TO 1815.—THE ROMAN EMPIRE UNDER NAPOLEON I., who represented the Napoleon dynasty—the seventh governing head of the seven-headed and ten-horned Wild Beast.—(Dan. vii.; Rev. xiii., xvii.

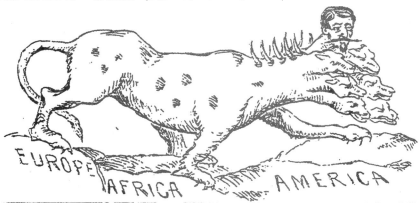

1815 TO 1852.—THE ROMAN EMPIRE HEADLESS.

1852 TO 1871-73.—THE ROMAN EMPIRE UNDER NAPOLEON III. who represents the Napoleon dynasty—the seventh revived, or eighth head of the Wild Beast, healed of the deadly wound it received at Waterloo in 1815. He is comprehensively termed the Wild Beast itself, and is also called the *Assyrian* (Is. x., xiv., xxx.); the *Little Horn* (Dan. vii., viii.); the *Wilful King* (Dan. ix. 21—45); the *Antichrist* (I. In. i. 24); the *Man of Sin*, destined to perish at the personal descent of Christ (II. Thes. ii. 3—8.)

Louis, thereby challenging the legitimacy of his claims and position. His mother Hortense had been allegedly in an advanced state of pregnancy when she got married. "But was Louis Bonaparte the father?" asked E. Ramier in *Les Mémoires de Badinguet*:

> Hortense, disait-on, était dans une position intéressante pour tous... excepté pour les yeux d'un époux de la veille.[22]

The above references are to authors who may have entirely disappeared from currency, but they show that a certain form of moral criticism of Louis Napoleon was being set in place. It was in Jersey that this same Hippolyte Magen, using the pseudonym of L. Stelli, had published a pattern for this type of attack. In a scurrilous work entitled *Les Nuits et le mariage de César* (1853) and sometimes attributed to Victor Hugo, whose legendary opposition to Napoleon III renders such an attribution not unlikely and gives added weight to its virulence, he made political capital out of the Emperor's physique by drawing attention to his face and basing his analysis on physiognomy:

> Au premier aspect de cette face impériale, l'oeil se détourne: un teint bilieux et jaunâtre indique "une sensibilité intérieure, une force morale, propres, ordinairement, aux plus grands crimes"... un nez, au large profil [...] l'intervalle bucco-nasal se développe trop aux dépens de cet organe mal dessiné; ce qui donne au bas du visage, "un caractère d'âpreté animale".[23]

The shape of his head receives an unfavourable phrenological explanation:

> sur le côté de la tête, au-dessus des oreilles, l'organe de la destructivité se développe à l'aise; il n'a cette large protubérance que "sur la tête des meurtriers qui agissent de sang-froid;" on la remarque sur la tête de plusieurs suppliciés et du marquis de Sade, - sur les bustes ou portraits de Caligula, de Néron et de Charles IX.[24]

Furthermore, Magen claims that Louis Bonaparte dressed up and lusted like a young girl – "le fils d'Hortense farde ses joues, à la manière de Henri III"[25] – and that unsuccessfully, the reader will be no doubt pleased to learn, as "le pied d'un laquais le jette à la porte, en s'appliquant à la partie inférieure où le dos change de nom".[26] Napoleon was also the owner of three brothels in New York, and an abuser of young girls, etc.[27] His wife, Eugénie, had a mother who was promiscuous:

> 1I faudrait remonter à l'histoire romaine ou du Bas-empire pour trouver les analogues du caractère de la mère Montijo; en un seul mot, sachez qu'elle est bien digne d'apparaître quand revient l'ère des Césars.[28]

Louis, like Henri VIII, protects his lascivious wife:

> A l'imitation de Henri VIII, qui décréta la peine de mort contre quiconque oserait
> médire, mal penser d'Anne de Boleyn, Louis-Bonaparte ordonnait l'arrestation,
> et, sans doute la transportation de quiconque oserait mal parler d'Eugénie de
> Montijo.[29]

These traits and accusations, which Stelli/Magen so vehemently
formulates, are a facet of the propaganda which was mounted against
Napoleon III. The word hatred (*haine*) occurs in it regularly, witness
another pamphlet, this time in verse, by Joseph Cahaigne, also eman-
ating from Jersey in 1853 and which savagely denounces the new
Emperor:

> Ce livre est-il dicté seulement par la haine? Non, c'est le cri d'une âme
> douloureusement atteinte, indiquée à la vue de cette honte incarnée, de ce fumier
> ambulant, de cette monstruosité à pieds et mains qui souille, qui dégrade la
> France, et dont la désignation a cours en Europe sous l'étiquette de Louis
> Napoléon Bonaparte![30]

His indictment of the Emperor is largely based on his immorality:

> Toi, l'infâme ouvrier de tant d'ignominie;
> Toi, pour qui la vertu, gémissante, bannie,
> Sans temple, sans asile, erre par les chemins;
> Toi, fils de l'adultère et des crimes humains;
> Ah! puisses-tu bientôt [...]
> [...] mourir de rage en quelque infâme lieu.[31]

These jibes, coloured by the exaggeration of the satirist's pen, are
to be found repeated in satirical prints, as what was poetic licence and
rhetoric becomes visual reality: a number of these prints have been
included by Steve Murphy in his work *Rimbaud et la ménagerie
impériale*.[32] The infidelities of the Empress are satirised by Alfred Le
Petit in a print showing Napoleon in the form of a "taureau" who is
"cocu" as well as "cornu" (Figure 9).[33] The Leboeuf is probably
Maréchal Leboeuf, one of Napoleon's ministers, for both he and Eugénie
were said to have been in favour of the war with Prussia.[34]

In another print, this time by Faustin, Eugénie is portrayed naked
on a billiard table, surrounded by leering males (Figure 10):

> Le lecteur n'aura pas de mal à saisir la métaphorique sexuelle, conventionnelle,
> du jeu de "poule" ou de billard, ni la pertinence des ornithonymes qui servent à
> désigner l'Impératrice. Et si l'Eugénie caricaturale porte très souvent un tambour,
> c'est à la fois pour rappeler ses origines espagnoles et pour proposer une
> insinuation sexuelle: tambouriner signifiait à l'époque "jouir d'une femme", en
> frappant son ventre à coups de cette baguette qu'on appelle le membre.[35]

Figure Nine

LE BOEUF PAR ... ZUT

**Eugénie: Je vous en prie, ayez un peu de tenue,
mon cher Leboeuf!**
**Leboeuf: Mille pardons, belle dame, ce n'est pas
moi qui suis le boeuf ... c'est lui!**

Figure Ten

Even the Prince Imperial was subjected to similar calumnies about his sexual prowess and his intellectual ability. Murphy provides an intriguing and revealing commentary on these images, which occur in the cycle known as *La Ménagerie impériale*. He stresses that in Hadol's *Le Serin* (Figure 11) the Prince's eyes reveal that he is prone to excessive masturbation,[36] and in the anonymous *L'Education d'un prince*, the young man is somewhat perplexed by his introduction to sexual activities by a naked woman who is trying to seduce him against a background composed of the imperial coat of arms (Figure 12).[37]

The subject matter of these images as well as the latent reference to phrenology in the depiction of the Prince Imperial were to be found in the pamphlets and publications to which we have referred above. Hippolyte Magen had also clearly tried to establish a relationship between Napoleon III and historical figures such as Charles IX, Henri III, Henry VIII, Caligula, Nero, etc.[38] This parallel was also one which Louis Bonaparte, as we have already mentioned, sought to develop himself in his *History of Julius Caesar*, but this literary foray on his part was greeted with scathing comments:

> Ce parallèle [i.e. between Bonaparte and Caesar] nous semble peu favorable à la cause de l'Empire français, et nous croyons que Napoléon III eût bien fait dans son intérêt de ne pas l'établir; car les vices et les crimes des Césars et de leurs partisans loin de voiler ceux du second empire français ne font que les mettre en lumière. Si un autre que Louis Bonaparte se fût permis cette comparaison, il l'eût certainement fait poursuivre et condamner à l'amende et à la prison, par excitation à la haine et au mépris du gouvernement et insulte envers l'Empereur.[39]

It is precisely these references to the past and to the sexual and immoral proclivities of the Emperor, of his wife and of his son, that make this publicity campaign against him more convincing and yet, paradoxically, so artificial. It follows a pattern that had been established long before the start of the Second Empire: Marie-Antoinette had known its force, as had Napoleon I, Charles X and Louis Philippe. It first seems to have been established as part of the political scene in France, and here I refer to the combined force of both pamphlet and image in the virulent campaign led against Henry de Valois or Henri III in the second half of the 1580s, he being the very monarch to whom Napoleon's polemicists so often refer.

Henri III came to the throne on the death of his brother Charles IX in 1574. At the time he was king of Poland and he left that country in stealth and haste to claim the crown of France. He was the last of the Valois kings, and at first was praised and admired. It soon became

LA MENAGERIE IMPERIALE
Le Serin

Figure Twelve

L'Education d'un Prince

apparent, however, that his style of kingship did not meet with the approval of all. In the midst of intermittent civil Wars of Religion he found himself opposed both to the Catholic faction of the Guises and the Protestant forces of Henri de Navarre, the future Henri IV. The latter sought to foster the Reformed Church, the former gave their support to the Holy League which aimed to re-establish the Catholic Church as the one true church in France.

Henry was intelligent and autocratic but also weak. Like Louis Napoleon, he had personal failings – he was superstitious and probably a transvestite; at the very least he enjoyed dressing up in female garb. He succeeded in arousing the opposition of the Protestants and the Catholics – no mean feat. In the 1580s his position became desperate, more particularly after the death in 1584 of his brother and heir apparent, the Duc d'Anjou. The new heir was deemed to be Henri de Navarre, an avowed Protestant, but this situation antagonised still further the supporters of the Holy League and the Guise faction, and their opposition to the king grew. In December 1588 Henry had the Duc de Guise and his brother the Cardinal de Guise assassinated at the Château de Blois; in 1589 Paris put up barricades to prevent the king from entering the city; and on August 2 of the same year Henri III was stabbed by a "mad monk", Jacques Clément, at Saint Cloud on the outskirts of the capital.

During the last few years of Henry's reign there had grown up an intense and vituperative propaganda campaign against him. This campaign took the form of pamphlets, books and engravings all aiming to discredit him in the eyes of his supporters, and all trying to justify the actions of the opponents to the monarch. It was important for ideologues of the period to show that the king was, owing to his immorality, unfit to be God's representative, unfit to reign, and consequently a legitimate subject for deposition. As I have treated this matter more extensively elsewhere,[40] I shall now refer but briefly to one or two aspects of the satirical iconography of Henri III.

As we have seen, Napoleon was attacked for his hypocritical and lascivious behaviour, and so was Henri. He was accused of arrogance, sacrilege, murder, rape, cruelty, etc. (Figure 13)[41] One study for an engraving shows him as an allegorical monster (Figure 14) on which the lion's wig suggests luxuriance, vanity, audacity, arrogance, bloodthirstiness, courage, etc. The Cordon around the neck symbolises order, but the female breasts highlight his effeminacy and how he draws his strength from his people's blood. In his right hand he bears a portrait of

Figure Thirteen

REPRESENTATION DE L'ORGVEIL de Henry de Valois, enuers la Noblesse de France, au commencement de son retour de Poulougne.

POVRTRAICT DV COVRONNEMENT de Henry de Valois, lors que par sa prodiguée & auquel le Couronne luy tomba deux fois de dessus la teste, qui afloit un mauuais presage à l'aduenir.

POVRTRAICT DV SACRILIEGE FAIT par Henry de Valois, en la sainte Chapelle à Paris.

REPRESENTATION DE LA CRVELLE ET BARBARE recompense, pour tant de bons offices qu'ont faict ce magnanime Duc & se predecesseurs à la Couronne de France, par vn Henry de Valois.

REPRESENTATION DE LA CRVELLE MORT COMMISE en l'innocence de Monsieur le Cardinal de Guise, personne sacree & dediee à Dieu : par Henry de Valois.

LES ARMOIRIES DE HENRY DE Valois, trainees par les boües, & brisees par vn executeur de Iustice, en plain marché, à Cracouie : pour auoir par luy esté de perfidie enuers les Poulonois.

FIGVRE DE LA VIERGE Religieusse, vendue à Paris par Henry de Valois.

FIGVRE DES CRVAVTEZ QVE Henry de Valois a fait executer enuers les gens de bien, qui se trouueyent bons sers mauuais deportemens.

Figure Fourteen

Portrait Monstrueux et Allégorique d'Henri III

Machiavelli, and in his left a rosary, this indicating his hypocrisy and how he used religion to cover up his evil deeds. The monstrous form ends in a fish's tail so as to stress how through his infamous acts he has reduced himself to the level of brute animals. Instead of feet, the monster has claws which show symbolically how through taxes and exploitation he gains sustenance from his people. The wings and the dragon's tail bear witness to his pact with the devil, and the knife in the bottom left-hand corner refers to massacres he has ordered and to the fact that he was destined to be massacred himself.[42]

Although some of the satirical prints appeared as broadsheets, a number came from biographies of Henri III.[43] These biographies, purporting to be accurate descriptions of the king's life and activities, were in reality consolidated attacks against his person and had recourse to the most vile accusations. As I have shown elsewhere,[44] many of them may well have been produced by English Catholic Refugees who had found safety across the Channel and who were on the side of the Guises against the king. Their satirical claws had, as it were, been sharpened in their attacks against Elizabeth I, especially after the death of Mary, Queen of Scots, in 1587.[45]

Whoever they may have been, it is certain that the sixteenth-century polemicists had read their classics and also their books on rhetoric, such as the *Ad Herennium* in whose Book Two are given all the tips on how to use character assassination to win one's case. A particular source is Suetonius, and indeed one could argue that very often the polemical biographies of Henri III and of Napoleon III were most similar to those of *De vita Caesarum*, so similar in fact that one could believe that the life of the French sovereign had been made to fit a classical immoral mould.[46] These attacks had as their prime mover a form of humour, but this is a humour which has as its aims the reformation, the transformation and perhaps even the subversion of society.[47] André Blum remarks that Napoleon III was shown no mercy at the hands of his detractors:

> Aucune injure n'est épargnée à Napoléon III. Indépendamment de la politique, aucun détail de son existence privée n'est respecté par les humoristes, qui s'en prennent à sa femme, à ses maîtresses, à ses débauches.[48]

The intensity of the outbursts and of the accusations increased during the Franco-Prussian War. The caricature becomes offensive and the humour is often difficult to appreciate when the print is coloured with emotional condemnation, as for example in Figure 15 – F. Talons's

Figure Fifteen

Qu'un sang impur abreuve nos sillons!!!

Qu'un sang impur abreuve nos sillons!!! – where a line from the Marseillaise is given a horrifying interpretation in the blood from the severed heads of the three traitors – the Kaiser, Bismarck and Napoleon III.[49]

As early as 1871, Bertall, the well-known contemporary caricaturist, had remarked in the *Revue comique* of October 15 upon the tragic aspect of certain humorous cartoons:

> Ce n'est pas en France, dans le pays où Rabelais, Montaigne, Voltaire, ont écrit, qu'il est possible de nier que si le sérieux a son côté comique, le comique puisse avoir à son tour son côté sérieux.[50]

The Roman Emperors, Henri III and Napoleon III were all guilty of certain misdemeanours and unethical political moves – few politicians are not. What I have tried to emphasise in this chapter is not so much that history repeats itself, or that the propaganda campaign against Napoleon was modelled on that against Henri III, but rather that the techniques of character assassination – exaggerated allegations of immoral behaviour, of anti-national activity, of diabolical intentions and relations, of, in short, sleaze – were employed both in print and in prints, and formed part of the rhetoric of defamation. Many of the allegations can be traced back to a factual event which could no doubt be construed differently within its context; but by taking it out of its context the satirist can endow it with damning proportions.

The polemicist and the humorist have in common the trait whereby they select and exploit the foibles and the weaknesses in human behaviour. Their exaggeration of the "departure from the norm" is normally amusing and comic. Where there is a divergence, however, it arises when the humour turns into ridicule and the ridicule, tinged with emotional involvement, turns itself into indictment. Similar techniques can have vastly different outcomes. Whereas humour allows us to chuckle at our own follies through another, orchestrated polemics can change respect to hatred, forbearance to revolt, and cause the mighty to fall. Perhaps we should be more wary of the political cartoon.

---

[1] N. Elias, *The Court Society* (Oxford, 1983), p. 34.

[2] J. Grand-Carteret, *L'Histoire - la vie - les moeurs et la curiosité par l'image, le pamphlet et le document (1450-1900)* (Paris, 1927-28), Vol. l, p. 41.

[3] *Ibid.*, p. 59.

[4] "Tout ce qui pouvait le mieux étouffer la pensée française avait été réuni dans ce décret pour rassurer une tyrannie peureuse et pour lui permettre de tailler en plein drap, de disposer, à son gré, des finances de l'Etat sans qu'elle ait à redouter les murmures de la

probité publique réduite au silence", Hippolyte Magen, *Histoire du Second Empire* (Paris, 1878), pp. 148-149.

[5] Henri d'Orléans, duc d'Aumale, *A Napoléon III. Qu'avez-vous fait de la France? Complément à la lettre du 15 mars 1861* (London, 1867), p. 15.

[6] See R. Passeron, *Daumier* (Oxford, 1981).

[7] See *Die Karikatur zwischen Republik und Zensur*, ed. R. Rutten et. al. (Marburg, 1991), p. 372.

[8] See S. Strumingher, "Die Vesuviennes: Bilder von Kriegerinnen im Jahre 1848 und ihre Bedeutung für die französische Geschichte", in *Die Karikatur*, pp. 260-276.

[9] See Lucette Czyba, "Feminismus und Karikatur. Die Scheidungsfrage im Charivari von 1848", in *Die Karikatur*, pp. 277-284.

[10] See *Les Salons caricaturaux*, ed. T. Chabanne (Paris, 1990), p. 4.

[11] Taken from *Le Charivari belge*, March 18, 1855. See *Die Karikatur*, p. 309.

[12] See J. M. Thompson, *Louis Napoleon and the Second Empire* (Columbia UP, 1983), p. 152.

[13] *Ibid.*, p. 267.

[14] P. Silex, *La Chronique Bonapartiste scandaleuse. Histoires véridiques, anecdotiques et galantes* (Brussels, 1871): "Au lecteur". See also the amusing and ironic satire on court life, purporting to be by Napoleon's dog Nero (and perhaps inspired by Bonaventure des Périers' *Cymbalum mundi*), *Le Testament de Néro tel qu'il a été dicté le 19 janvier 1867 à son très humble et dévoué sujet Georges Sauton* (Paris, 1868).

[15] *Ibid.*, p. 8.

[16] *Ibid.*, p. 10.

[17] A. Plessis, *The Rise and Fall of the Second Empire, 1862-1871*, tr. J. Mandelbaum (Cambridge UP., 1979), p. 5.

[18] Hippolyte Magen, *Prostitutions, Débauches et crimes de la famille Buonaparte* (London, 1871), p. 40.

[19] *Ibid.*, *Les Tyrans et le Tyrannicide jugés par l'histoire* (London, 1858), p. 21.

[20] Nicolas Bruncaux, *Vie de M. le Baron de Ratapoil, sénateur* (London and Geneva, 1871), p. 18 [also Bruxelles: V. Puissant, 1850].

[21] See *The Man of His Time. The Story of the Life of Napoleon III. By James M. Haswell. The Same Story as told by Popular Caricaturists of the last thirty years* (London, 1871), p. 321.

[22] E. Ramier, *Les Mémoires de Badinguet* (Brussels, London and Leipzig, 1869).

[23] H. Magen, *Les Nuits et le Mariage de César, par L. Stelli* (Jersey, 1853), p. 17. The British Library possesses another edition of this text bearing a different title which attributes the work to Victor Hugo: *L'Organographie physiogno-phrénologique de Badinguet, d'après Gall et Spurzheim, par Victor Hugo* (London, 1871).

[24] *Ibid.*, p. 20.

[25] *Ibid.*, p. 31.

[26] *Ibid.*, p. 32.

[27] *Ibid.*, p. 57.

[28] *Ibid.*, p. 66.

[29] *Ibid.*, pp. 68-9.

[30] J. Cahaigne, *La Couronne impériale, satire. A Louis-Napoléon-Werhuel, dit Bonaparte* (Jersey, 1853), Avant Propos.

[31] *Ibid.*, p. 34.

[32] S. Murphy, *Rimbaud et la ménagerie impériale* (Presses Universitaires de Lyon, 1991).

[33] *Ibid.*, p. 45.

[34] See Magen, *Histoire du Second Empire*, pp. 464 ff.

[35] See S. Murphy, *op. cit.*, p. 39.

[36] *Ibid.*, pp. 69-70.

[37] *Ibid.*, p. 70.

[38] The parallel between Napoleon and the Caesars was widespread, cf. E. Ramier, *Les Mémoires de Badinguet*, p. 9: "Les Césars de la décadence en agissaient-ils autrement? ... Il suffirait d'interroger les courtisanes d'Italie, les tripots de New-York et de Londres, pour faire surgir un Suétone." Other critics of his regime suggested that he was in league with the devil, cf. G. Waldstedt, *Des Teufels Minister, Zeitdichtung* (Oserburg, 1870). Napoleon's supporters, however, made more favourable comparisons: cf. M. C. Sosthène-Berthellot who compares the Emperor, and to his advantage, with Henri IV, in his *Essai sur le caractère et les tendances de l'Empereur Napoléon III d'après ses écrits et ses actes* (Paris, 1858), pp. 336-339.

[39] P. Vésinier, *L'Histoire du nouveau César, Londres* (London. 1865), p. 436.

[40] See K. Cameron, "Henri III - a maligned or malignant king?", in *Aspects of the Satirical Iconography of Henri de Valois* (U. of Exeter Press, 1978).

[41] Reproduced from D. Kunzle, *The Early Comic Strip* (U. of California Press, 1973), p. 45.

[42] See K. Cameron, *loc. cit.*, pp. 77 ff.

[43] Figure 13, for example, is a non-attested but credible broadsheet assembled by Kunzle from the woodcuts in J. Boucher, *La Vie et faits notables de Henry de Valois* (Paris, 1589).

[44] K. Cameron, "Suetonius, Henri de Valois and the Art of Political Biography", *International Journal of the Classical Tradition*, 2 (1995), pp. 284-298.

[45] See K. Cameron, "L'Illustration au service de la propagande contre Henri III"", in *Le livre et l'image en France au XVIe siècle* (Paris, 1989), pp. 89-104, and "La Polémique, la mort de Marie Stuart et l'assassinat de Henri III", in *Henri III et son temps*, ed. R. Sauzet (Paris, 1992), pp. 185-194.

[46] See Cameron, 1995.

[47] See S. Lambert, *The Franco-Prussian War and the Commune in Caricature 1870-71* (London, 1971).

[48] A. Blum, "La Caricature politique en France pendant la guerre de 1870-1871", *Revue des études napoléoniennes*, 8 (1919), 301-311 (p. 301).

[49] See *Die Karikatur zwischen Republik und Zensur*, p. 444.

[50] Quoted by Blum, *art. cit.*, p. 310.

6. Bergson Revisited: *Le Rire* a hundred years on
William D. Howarth

Bergson's *Le Rire* appeared in the *Revue de Paris* in 1899, and in mono-
graph form in 1900, hence the approaching centenary of its first
publication seems an opportune time to attempt a critical evaluation of
the reception and influence of this little text. I was prompted to choose
the subject, among other reasons, by references to Bergson made by
more than one speaker at the colloquium whose papers are here collected, and which were mostly so disparaging as to appear to suggest that
Bergson on laughter was hardly to be taken seriously.

I say "Bergson on laughter", because of course his essay has *Le
Rire* for its title, and is always referred to in translation as "Laughter".
However, it is at least debatable whether or not this is the author's true
subject. Bergson's subtitle is "Essai sur la signification du comique", and
one recent interpreter, Marie Collins Swabey, goes further, suggesting
that "comedy, rather than the comic, may be said to be the implicit
theme of Bergson's essay *Le Rire*".[1] I will return to this later, for it is a
fruitful approach, and her distinction between "comedy" and "the
comic" will need further exploration. However, we must surely
recognise from the outset that what Bergson offers is a personal and
original contribution to the study of comic drama, and in particular of
that tradition of comic drama which runs from Menander through
Plautus, Terence and the Italian Renaissance dramatists, to Molière and
his successors, and on via Beaumarchais to the *comédie-vaudeville* of
the nineteenth century. He is less interested in what we might call the
mechanics of laughter than, for instance, Koestler, or in the psychology
of laughter than Freud, or again in the connection between this and its
physiological manifestation than Saulnier; but he is a remarkably acute
and still, I would maintain, a most valuable analyst of that form of comic
drama which requires the response of laughter from its spectator or
reader.

Indeed, in the absence of any text deriving from the ancient world
which deals with comic drama with anything like the authority of the
Poetics, one might even be tempted to invest *Le Rire* with a unique
status, and to see it as taking the place, *faute de mieux*, of Aristotle's
missing treatise. The American scholar Lane Cooper did, it is true, offer
an ingenious adaptation of the *Poetics* in the 1920s in order to supply the
missing Aristotelian definition of comedy, and proceeded to amplify this

by linking it to the *Tractatus Coislinianus* as an early expression of an arguably Aristotelian approach to the analysis of comic drama; his definition reads in essence as follows:

> A comedy is the artistic imitation of an action which is ludicrous (or mirthful) ... as for the end or function resulting from [this] imitation ... it is to arouse, and by arousing to relieve, the emotions proper to comedy.[2]

A further development amplifies the last phrase as follows: "through pleasure and laughter effecting the purgation of the like emotions", and it was this hint at a comic catharsis, corresponding to tragedy's "purging of the passions", that provided the starting-point for my own article of 1973.[3] Cooper's justification for publishing the *Tractatus* was that,

> schematic though it be, [it] is by all odds the most important technical treatise on comedy that has come down to us from the ancients. And modern times give us nothing of comparable worth in its field.[4]

In fact both bibliography and index reveal a distinct paucity of references on Cooper's part to modern works on comedy and laughter. There are a handful of allusions in the text to Meredith and Freud, plus a mention of Eastman in the bibliography, but although his textual citations of Molière are equal in number to those of Shakespeare, and considerably outnumber those of Plautus and Terence, there is no mention of Bergson either as a theorist of the comic or as a secondary source with regard to Molière's theatre.

One shortcoming of Cooper's blueprint for an Aristotelian theory of comedy would seem to be that it remains so external to its subject. To say that a comedy presents "an action which is ludicrous (or mirthful) ... in such a manner ... as to arouse, and by arousing to relieve, the emotions proper to comedy" is to leave undefined the very terms which are specific to the comic genre: for example "ludicrous", "mirthful" and "emotions proper to comedy". On the other hand, the virtue of *Le Rire* is that Bergson goes straight to the point, defining in his opening pages the specific features that he sees as essential to the comic process. He starts, it will be remembered, with three "observations fondamentales":

> (i) Il n'y a pas de comique en dehors de ce qui est proprement *humain*.[5]
> (ii) Le rire n'a pas de plus grand ennemi que l'émotion: ... Le comique exige ... pour prendre tout son effet, quelque chose comme une anesthésie momentanée du coeur. (3-4)
> (iii) Notre rire est toujours le rire d'un groupe ... [le rire est] une fonction sociale. (5-6)

This is followed by his working definition: "Le comique naîtra, semble-t-il, quand des hommes réunis en groupe dirigeront tous leur attention sur un d'entre eux, faisant taire leur sensibilité et exerçant leur seule intelligence" (6). However the most original and striking feature of Bergson's theory is surely the contrast he draws between the suppleness of living forms and the automatism of a lifeless machine: "Les attitudes, gestes et mouvements du corps humain sont risibles dans l'exacte mesure où ce corps nous fait penser à une simple mécanique" (22-3): and this leads on to his central formula defining the comic process as "du mécanique plaqué sur du vivant" (29). The development he gives to this idea, encapsulated in his other memorable formula "plutôt raideur que laideur", has been most fruitful in its application to the process in Molière.[6]

So far so good; however, in the second part of his essay Bergson seems to shift his ground with regard to a fundamental aspect of his analysis of laughter. Where he had begun by presenting this as a spontaneous intellectual reaction to our perception of a kind of incongruity (in particular that between *le mécanique* and *le vivant*), he now seems to insist on its moral character, it becoming a "moyen de correction". Indeed his definition of laughter as "toujours le rire d'un groupe ... une fonction sociale" was already a pointer in this direction, a development which comes out more clearly still in the appendix added to his text in later editions. Replying to a critique by Yves Delage in the *Revue du mois* of 1919 (both contributions appeared in the same journal in the same year), Bergson takes up the point made by his critic: "Pour qu'une chose soit comique, il faut qu'entre l'effet et la cause il y ait désharmonie" (155); and counters with the observation that such "désharmonie" is a "condition nécessaire" of the comic effect in question, but not a "condition suffisante" (156):

> Il reste donc à chercher *quelle est la cause spéciale de désharmonie* qui donne l'effet comique; et on ne l'aura réellement trouvée que si l'on peut expliquer par elle pourquoi, en pareil cas, la société se sent tenue de manifester. Il faut bien qu'il y ait dans la cause du comique quelque chose de légèrement attentatoire (et de *spécifiquement* attentatoire) à la vie sociale, puisque la société y répond par un geste qui a tout l'air d'une réaction défensive, par un geste qui fait légèrement peur. C'est de tout cela que j'ai voulu rendre compte. (157)

This implies a fascinating throwback to the most fundamental of all divergences of opinion on the nature of laughter in the post-Renaissance period, namely the opposition between various forms of what one might call the moralist interpretation, whereby laughter is occasioned by a corrective urge, a desire on the part of the one who laughs to score off his victim, and the view that laughter is spontaneous, occasioned by the perception of a risible incongruity of some sort, and morally neutral. On the one hand we have Hobbes's "superiority" theory according to which we laugh at a fault or deformity perceived in others:

> Sudden glory is the passion which maketh these grimaces called laughter; and is caused either by some sudden act of their own, that pleaseth them; or by the apprehension of some deformed thing in another, by comparison whereof they suddenly applaud themselves;[7]

that of Descartes, for whom laughter is caused by disapproval of others:

> La dérision ou moquerie est une espèce de joie mêlée de haine, qui vient de ce qu'on aperçoit quelque petit mal en une personne qu'on en pense être digne: on a de la haine pour ce mal, on a de la joie de le voir en celui qui en est digne; et lorsque cela survient inopinément, la surprise de l'admiration est cause qu'on éclate de rire;[8]

the view of Du Bos, who writes of "le rire et le mépris que les incidents de la comédie excitent en nous";[9] and the magisterial fulmination of Bossuet quoting the words of St Basil: "Il n'est permis de rire en aucune sorte, quand ce ne serait qu'à cause de la multitude de ceux qui outragent Dieu et méprisent sa Loi."[10]

On the other side of the debate we find Pascal giving the clearest possible illustration of the intellectualist view of laughter: "Deux visages semblables, dont aucun ne fait rire en particulier, font rire ensemble par leur ressemblance;"[11] and, on this subject, it is interesting to see Voltaire for once siding with Pascal. Indeed Voltaire goes further in actually contrasting what I have called the moralist and the intellectualist interpretations:

> Les raisonneurs ont prétendu que le rire naît de l'orgueil, qu'on se croit supérieur à celui dont on rit. Il est vrai que l'homme, qui est un animal risible, est aussi un animal orgueilleux; mais la fierté ne fait pas rire. J'avais onze ans quand je lus tout seul, pour la première fois, l'*Amphitryon* de Molière; je ris au point de tomber à la renverse; était-ce par fierté?[12]

One of the clearest of early attempts to formulate an objective, or intellectualist, theory in abstract terms, must be that of the Scottish philosopher Beattie, writing in 1776:

> Laughter arises from the view of two or more inconsistent, unsuitable or incongruous parts or circumstances, considered as united in one complex object or assemblage, or as acquiring a sort of mutual relation from the particular manner in which the mind takes note of them.[13]

At about the same time, in 1781, Kant was giving expression to a variant of the incongruity theory. For him, laughter is "an affection arising from the sudden transformation of a strained expectation into nothing",[14] which is to say the frustration of our expectation by the sudden revelation of incongruity in two things apparently congruent. This formula was to be expanded by Schopenhauer, who may be seen as combining Beattie with Kant:

> The cause of laughter in every case is simply the sudden perception of the incongruity between a concept and the real objects which have been thought through it in some relation ... All laughter then is occasioned by a paradox, and therefore by unexpected subsumption, whether this is expressed in words or in actions.[15]

A particularly clear formulation of the incongruity theory is that of Léon Dumont, whose *Des Causes du rire* was published in 1862:

> [Est risible] tout objet à l'égard duquel l'esprit se trouve contraint d'affirmer et de nier en même temps la même chose; c'est en d'autres termes ce qui détermine notre entendement à former simultanément deux rapports contradictoires ... la connaissance d'un objet donne d'abord à notre entendement une certaine impulsion, et stimule son activité dans une certaine direction; mais immédiatement une impulsion contraire lui vient d'une autre qualité de ce même objet, et imprime à cette activité, avec une assez forte secousse, la direction contraire.[16]

Although it is derivatives of these objective interpretations of the nature of laughter as a morally neutral phenomenon which seem to have dominated the literature in the last hundred years, there are two notable expressions of a contrary view to which it is worth referring before we return to Bergson in an attempt to situate *Le Rire* in the context of the whole range of modern writings on the subject. The first is Meredith's essay *On the Idea of Comedy and the Uses of the Comic Spirit*, initially published in 1877. A typical example of Victorian belles-lettres, this relies heavily on literary metaphor and simile· rather than on prosaic analysis. Primarily concerned with the purpose or function of comic drama, it does incidentally appear to commit its author to the view that laughter is moral or corrective in its effect, and for students of Molière it is notable above all for the celebrated comment, "Never did man wield so shrieking a scourge upon vice":[17] there can have been few authorities who have expressed so debatable a view of Molière's theatre in such extravagantly forthright terms. And secondly Freud, although the chief emphasis of his views on comedy is on laughter as a relief of tension – an approach which follows on from those of Kant and Schopenhauer – nevertheless harks back to the superiority theory when he writes:

> a person appears comic to us if, in comparison with ourselves, he makes too great an expenditure on his bodily functions and too little on his mental ones; and it

cannot be denied that in both these cases our laughter expresses a pleasurable sense of the superiority which we feel in relation to him.[18]

If we now consider Bergson's essay once more and try to situate what he puts forward in *Le Rire* within this development of what appears to have become the dominant attitude to laughter as a spontaneous reflex morally neutral in character, it seems evident that his formula "du mécanique plaqué sur du vivant" fits squarely into that tradition, both in its abstract formulation and in the illustrations he offers.

I must say I have always liked the non-dramatic examples he gives – examples which are not far from the notion of "le comique à l'état pur" – such as his anecdote about a Channel steamer which foundered off the French coast. Customs officers, behaving with great courage, succeeded in saving a few passengers, and as they got them into the rescue vessel, "commencèrent par leur demander 's'ils n'avaient rien à déclarer' " (35-6); or this anecdote, "plus subtile", says Bergson, about a deputy in the Assemblée Nationale reporting a murder which had taken place on the railway, in the following terms: "L'assassin, après avoir achevé sa victime, a dû descendre du train à contre-voie, en violation des règlements administratifs" (36). The two examples taken together, Bergson suggests, illustrate "l'idée d'une réglementation humaine se substituant aux lois mêmes de la nature" (*ibid.*), and this leads him directly into a consideration of the "déformation professionnelle" illustrated by the doctors in Molière's theatre. He quotes Sganarelle replying to Géronte's observation that the heart is on the left and the liver on the right: "Oui, cela était autrefois ainsi, mais nous avons changé tout cela, et nous faisons maintenant la médecine d'une méthode toute nouvelle" (*ibid.*); and this passage from the consultation between two doctors in *Monsieur de Pourceaugnac*:

> Le raisonnement que vous en avez fait est si docte et si beau qu'il est impossible que le malade ne soit pas mélancolique hypocondriaque; et quand il ne le serait pas, il faudrait qu'il le devînt, pour la beauté des choses que vous avez dites et la justesse du raisonnement que vous avez fait. (*ibid.*)

Bergson comments thus: "Nous pourrions multiplier les exemples; nous n'aurions qu'à faire défiler devant nous, l'un après l'autre, tous les médecins de Molière" (36-7). What he does not point out, however, is that there is a significant difference between the two examples he gives. Unlike the two pedants from *Pourceaugnac*, Sganarelle is not a real doctor, but a "médecin malgré lui", and the juxtaposition of the two illustrations surely requires us to consider the whole question of laughing at and laughing with, which is so central to any appreciation of the comic process in a dramatic context.

I shall return to consider this question shortly, but let me give one further example from *Le Médecin malgré lui*, and one that illustrates very well the autonomous status of pure verbal comedy. This is the little exchange from the argument between Martine and Sganarelle at the beginning of the play:

> – J'ai quatre pauvres petits enfants sur les bras.
> – Mets-les à terre;[19]

an illustration, Bergson would no doubt have said, of his dictum: "Est comique tout incident qui appelle notre attention sur le physique d'une personne alors que le moral est en cause" (39). There can hardly be any doubt that such examples of purely verbal comedy support the notion of laughter caused by spontaneous intellectual perception rather than any theory based on the superiority of those who laugh.

This is the right place, I think, to introduce a consideration of the contributions of two writers I have already referred to: Claude Saulnier in *Le Sens du comique*, and Arthur Koestler whose *The Act of Creation* develops the ideas of his earlier text *Insight and Outlook*.

Saulnier's starting-point is the moral neutrality of the comic process. For him,

> L'essence du comique n'est pas l'intention mauvaise, mais l'irréalité joyeuse, même si le rieur prend part à une effective méchanceté. La personne qu'on brime est ridicule, parce qu'elle paraît, ainsi que tout objet ridicule quel qu'il soit, momentanément et alternativement revêtue d'un caractère d'irréalité et de fiction esthétique ... Il n'y a pas de risible à l'état latent: du côté de l'objet, tout peut être risible et rien ne l'est.[20]

The essence of Saulnier's interpretation is that "le risible" is the product of this "oscillation" in the mind of the one who laughs "entre le réel et l'irréel, le fictif et le sérieux, l'illusoire et, comme disent les enfants, le 'pour de vrai' "; and this leads him to his "définition provisoire du rire":

> Le rire est provoqué par la conscience d'un changement de clef, qui fait passer brusquement d'un plan quelconque (moral, immoral, tragique, familier, étrange), mais toujours considéré comme réel, à un plan opposé et tout autre, où le fictif est éprouvé comme tel. Ainsi, loin d'être un rassurement, le rire est plutôt une déception; mais cette déception ne va pas sans joie intellectuelle, car le rieur a conscience de son faux-pas. Le rire du comique est une déception agréable ... Il commence par un jeu de bascule; il se poursuit et se maintient par un jeu d'oscillation.[21]

In Koestler's case a similar theory is expressed through the concept of "matrices of thought", which he chooses as an umbrella term for "'frames of reference', 'associative contexts', 'types of logic', 'codes of behaviour', and 'universes of discourse' ".[22] Laughter, says Koestler, results from the fusion of two normally distinct matrices – and the stronger the moral or emotional charge accompanying such a spontaneous reaction, the more violent the physical explosion of laughter will be. In other words,

> The sudden bisociation of a mental event with two habitually incompatible matrices results in an abrupt transfer of the train of thought from one associative context to another. The emotive charge which the narrative carried cannot be so transferred owing to its greater inertia and persistence; discarded by reason, the tension finds its outlet in laughter. (59)

Let us look at one or two examples of "le comique" which there can be no difficulty in accepting as illustrations of Koestler's "bisociation", and beginning with one borrowed from Freud which he relates in these words:

> Chamfort tells a story of a Marquis at the court of Louis XIV who, on entering his wife's boudoir and finding her in the arms of a Bishop, walked calmly to the window and went through the motions of blessing the people in the street.
> "What are you doing?" cried the anguished wife.
> "Monseigneur is performing my functions," replied the Marquis, "so I am performing his." (33)

Another, well enough known, apparently originates with Schopenhauer: "A convict was playing cards with his gaolers. On discovering that they cheated they kicked him out of gaol." (36) The two frames of reference are easy enough to identify in both of these examples; in the following one, the matrices are created by two levels of verbal usage:

> In the happy days of *La Ronde* a dashing but penniless young Austrian officer tried to obtain the favours of a fashionable courtesan. To shake off this unwanted suitor, she explained to him that her heart was, alas, no longer free. He replied politely: "Mademoiselle, I never aimed as high as that." (36)

Another familiar example, attributed by Koestler to a fellow Hungarian refugee of his acquaintance, shows a more subtle clash of matrices. It is the one about a Jewish mother in New York who confessed to a friend that her son's teacher had recommended that he see a psychiatrist:

> "Well, what's wrong with seeing a psychiatrist?"
> "Nothing is wrong. The psychiatrist said he's got an Oedipus complex."

Pause. "Well, well, Oedipus or Schmoedipus, I wouldn't worry so long as he's a good boy and loves his mamma." (33)

It is Koestler who is responsible for one of the most pertinent critiques of the shortcomings, as he sees them, of Bergson's theory by comparison with his own. He finds fault in particular with the latter's *mécanique/vivant* explanation of the comic process, as being but one specific illustration of the more general principle of bisociation; but he seems to be rather hard on the Frenchman when he writes:

> Surprisingly, Bergson failed to see that each of the examples just mentioned [of the "dualism of subtle mind and inert matter"] can be converted from a comic into a tragic or purely intellectual experience, based on the same logical pattern - i.e. on the same pair of bisociated matrices - by a simple change of emotional climate. The fat man slipping and crashing on the icy pavement will be either a comic or a tragic figure according to whether the spectator's attitude is dominated by malice or pity. (46)

This objection is surely catered for by Bergson's notion of an "anesthésie momentanée du coeur"; however Koestler is perhaps on surer ground when he disagrees with Bergson's proposition that we only laugh in the presence of others:

> presumably because this fitted his theory of laughter as an act of social correction ... No doubt, collective giggling fits do occur in dormitories at girls' schools, and no doubt one laughs with more gusto in company than alone. But the infectiousness of emotive manifestations is a well-known phenomenon in group behaviour, which equally applies to hysteria, panic, even to infectious coughing of theatre audiences: it is not a specific characteristic of laughter, and contributes nothing to its explanation. (61)

Finally, Koestler somewhat patronisingly congratulates his predecessor on a near-miss:

> In his discussion [of comedies of situation], Bergson came closest to the essence of humour: "A situation is always comic", he wrote, "if it participates simultaneously in two series of events which are absolutely independent of each other, and if it can be interpreted in two quite different meanings." One feels like crying "Fire", but a couple of pages further on Bergson has dropped the clue and gone back to his hobby: the interference of two independent series in a given situation is merely a further example of the "mechanization of life". (78)

With Saulnier and Koestler we are a long way from the notion that I have already discussed, that is of laughter as correction, and to conclude this review of some of the more important contributions to this important debate since Bergson's day I should like to look briefly at two or three further titles.

Charles Lalo's *Esthétique du rire* is one of the most uncompromising expositions of the superiority theory – to the extent that he is at pains to annex in his support writers like Saulnier. His own "essai de synthèse" is placed, he tells us,

> sous le signe de l'idée de valeur, ou plus précisément, de dévaluation, c'est-à-dire de passage d'un niveau supérieur à un inférieur dans la hiérarchie toute relative des estimations individuelles ou sociales. C'est par cette opération de décalage que le rire nous semble être l'une des expressions les plus normales de la vie humaine: une permanente mise en question de ses valeurs sous la forme d'un jeu polyphonique, jeu esthétique qui est, suivant les cas, un substitut, une préparation ou une dispense des réformes sérieuses de nos moeurs. Polyvalence qui justifie à la fois l'enthousiasme confiant des amis du rire et l'ombrageux état d'alerte, sinon de guerre, proclamé par quelques moralistes moroses.[23]

Francis Jeanson's *Signification humaine du rire* contains a sustained critique of his distinguished predecessor. Compared with *Le Rire* itself, and with other post-Bergsonian works that have come my way, I must confess that I find Jeanson's writing characterised by an almost impenetrable abstraction, though one *trouvaille* is the fact that he quotes from Marcel Pagnol's *Notes sur le rire*, a work otherwise unknown to me. Pagnol is evidently a believer in the superiority theory: "Le Rire est un chant de triomphe; c'est l'expression d'une supériorité momentanée, mais brusquement découverte du Rieur sur le Moqué";[24] and this is illustrated by his analysis of the banana-skin topos:

> Il y a aussi l'exemple classique de la chute imprévue d'un passant. Cet homme, qui vient de glisser sur une peau de banane, et qui a fait des gestes étranges et désordonnés avant de tomber brutalement assis sur son derrière, je ne le connais pas, je ne lui en veux pas, je ne tire aucune satisfaction de sa mésaventure personnelle: mais comme je suis content que ce ne soit pas moi! Moi, la peau de banane, je l'avais vue de loin ... et je ris tout seul des compliments que je me fais.[25]

Jeanson himself finds Bergson lacking in consistency: is he dealing with "le rire" or with "les procédés de fabrication du comique", and are we to understand that for Bergson laughter is an individual phenomenon or a social act?

As we have already seen, Bergson does seem to occupy an ambivalent position in respect of this important debate. It is not easy to account for the apparent contradiction between his recognition of the autonomous nature of laughter as the spontaneous reaction to the juxtaposition of two opposites (*mécanique/vivant*; *physique/moral*) and the framework into which he seeks to place this process as serving a corrective, moralising function. The answer would surely seem to be that he is trying to do justice both to the phenomenon of laughter itself, as an automatic act on the part of the individual, and the literary or dramatic contexts with which he seeks to give a larger meaning to this immediate comic effect. If we look back at Meredith, he also uses his rather fanciful image of a "fly in amber" to express something like what I have in mind:

> I do not know that the fly in amber is of any particular use, but the Comic idea enclosed in a comedy makes it more generally perceptible and portable, and that is an advantage.[26]

It is true that what Meredith means by his "Comic idea" would appear, as far as one can determine from his over-literary prose style, to be somewhat more abstract than Bergson's relatively straightforward version of the comic process, but at least the text I have quoted has the merit of directing our attention towards the important difference between the container – comedy – and what it contains: in Meredith the "Comic idea", in Bergson and others the process by which laughter is aroused. A semantic difficulty arises here, moreover, for as a noun "the comic" comes uneasily to an English ear, while French is much happier with its well established concept of "le comique", and it will perhaps be more helpful for us to use this form as much as possible.

Thibaudet is one who enables us to take an important step forward in this direction. In his article "Molière et la critique" he defines, simply and with complete clarity, the subject which is so very central to Bergson's *Le Rire*. The installation of Molière and his company in Paris in 1658 was the beginning, he says, of:

> une période de deux siècles et demi pendant lesquels Paris va demeurer pour l'Europe le laboratoire et le centre d'exportation du comique théâtral, j'entends le comique qui fait rire d'un rire de foule un à deux milliers de spectateurs réunis dans une salle.[27]

However, the analysis of this "comique théâtral" depends on an essential distinction between its two constituent elements, and he makes this point equally effectively in another article, entitled "Le Rire de Molière":

> Molière n'est pas seulement un homme qui fait rire et un inventeur de comique: c'est un créateur de ces êtres organisés, complets, vivants, que sont ses comédies ... La comédie, c'est le comique plus le mouvement organisateur, et quand ce mouvement organisateur est puissamment et pleinement présent, le comique lui-même passe au second plan.[28]

Expressed as clearly as this, Thibaudet's point must seem to be a statement of the obvious. However it is the lack of an appreciation of this essential contrast between "le comique" and "la comédie" that has led a number of scholars working in this field – French as well as Anglo-Saxon – to follow false trails. When critics write of the corrective or the didactic nature of laughter in Molière or other playwrights, they are not always mindful of the fact that the morality that resides in comic drama is conveyed by features such as characterisation, plot or denouement as well as, and frequently rather than, by the purely comic process which generates our laughter. Whether this is what Swabey means when she writes that "Comedy, rather than the comic, may be said to be the implicit theme of Bergson's essay", I am not sure, but what she says in continuation seems to be a thoughtful development of this distinction:

> Yet in appreciating the comic our attitude is not entirely aesthetic, for instead of being disinterested it is unconsciously utilitarian, expressive of society's secret intent to correct eccentricity and enforce conformity to social life. Besides being largely free of emotion, comedy aims at the general or typical, a feature in which it differs from all the other arts. Indeed, for Bergson it is not too much to say that comedy, in its use of external observation, abstraction, and classification, resembles the inductive sciences, that it stands midway between art and nature as a kind of artifice imitating life - in its lower reaches suggesting children's games played with puppets, dolls, or mechanical toys, although in its higher forms it sometimes approximates to real life so closely that scenes from real life might be transferred to the stage without changing a word.[29]

Closely allied to the distinction between *le comique* and *la comédie* is the contrast, which provides the starting-point for Edith Kern's study, between the two types of *comique* that she calls the "absolute" and the "significative". I find these terms somewhat rebarbative in their English form: they are of course adapted from the French, and appear to owe their origin to Baudelaire's essay "Sur l'essence du rire", but most of us, I imagine, would prefer terms in more general currency, at any rate in academic discourse, namely the "mimetic" and the "ludic". At all events, such a contrast goes beyond Thibaudet's distinction between "le comique" and "la comédie", and enables us to characterise two trends in the history of comic drama. Within the French tradition the ludic predominates in mediaeval farce, the *commedia dell'arte*, eighteenth-century fairground *parades*, *vaudeville* and whatever in our own day looks back to the disruptive influence of *Ubu roi*; while the mimetic or representational trend came to the fore in Renaissance theories of comedy and in the practice of a playwright like Corneille into whose "peinture de la conversation des honnêtes gens" anything which aroused laughter was a most unwelcome intrusion. It was of course a mark of Molière's individual genius that he combined the mimetic and the ludic in a virtually original, single art-form, and nothing illustrates better the relationship between these two elements (and the inadequacy of the critical vocabulary of English in this respect) than the complaint Molière is able to put into the mouth of one of his opponents in the *Critique de l'Ecole des femmes* whereby a certain scene in *L'Ecole des femmes* itself is "trop comique" to deserve a place in a "comédie".

It is this creative fusion of the mimetic and the ludic, of the survival of the long-standing farce tradition and the literary vehicle provided by a polished five-act verse-form, which seems to have escaped Edith Kern. She makes a connection (which is certainly not always made) between the figure of Tartuffe and the gluttonous, lecherous monk of mediaeval farce and *fabliau*, but she considerably over-eggs her cake when she tries to annex this play (and even *Le Misanthrope* as well) unequivocally to the "absolute" or ludic tradition.

> For the trouble Molière encountered should not be explained entirely - as it has frequently been - on the basis of personal rivalries and animosities; it must be seen also as a clash between imagination nourished by a tradition of the absolute comic and a growing desire of dignitaries of church and state to suppress this comic and replace it with the significative ... Only in this century have we slowly come to recognize that this failure of the past resulted in neglect of those works of literature that partake of the carnivalesque.[30]

It is true that *Tartuffe*, for example, was suppressed for a time by the machinations of "dignitaries of church and state", but surely not because the play partook "of the carnivalesque". One can say quite categorically that it was not the ludic content of *Tartuffe* – the trickster tricked by Elmire, with Orgon hidden under the table – which brought down the anathema of the Church, but what Kern would call a "significative" element (and what Thibaudet would, I feel certain, identify as "comédie" rather than "comique"): that is, Molière's provocative portrayal of the harm that an unscrupulous "directeur de conscience" is capable of inflicting on a normal bourgeois family.

I have devoted some time to Kern and *The Absolute Comic* because this leads into a consideration of what must surely be one of the most distinctive works on laughter and *le comique* to have appeared since Bergson's *Le Rire*. The appearance of the word "carnivalesque" in one of my quotations from Kern will have made it clear that this critic writes under the sign of Mikhail Bakhtin, as does Thérèse Malachy in her *Molière: les métamorphoses du carnaval* of 1987. Even more than is the case with Kern, this author's single-minded pursuit of "carnivalesque" features in Molière's theatre fails to recognise that the ludic and the mimetic are important and complementary factors in Western comic drama from the Renaissance onwards, that Molière's major comedies represent a creative fusion of the two, and that to try to identify him with one at the expense of the other can only impoverish interpretation. One more example of a writer who out-Bakhtins Bakhtin himself is Howard Jacobson[31] whom I mention only because his book has recently received quite enthusiastic reviews, but who is even further removed from Bergson's notion of laughter as a corrective, civilising force. For Jacobson, the values of civilisation are there to be subverted, and laughter seems to be at the service of violence, vulgarity and obscenity.

In one important sense, of course, Bakhtin and his followers stand apart from my attempt to chart the fortunes of *Le Rire* over the last hundred years. Insofar as Bergson's views still have any currency and deserve our critical respect, it is, despite the title of his work, less for what he has to offer on the mechanics of laughter than for his contribution to the study of French comic drama. The carnivalesque provides only one strand in the social, cultural and intellectual origins of Molière's theatre, and Bakhtin himself, though hinting at the presence of this element, stops well short of the indiscriminate excesses of those who would make no distinction between carnivalesque farce and "haute comédie". As for Bergson, Bakhtin's one reference to "later theories of the philosophy of laughter, including Bergson's conception, which bring out mostly its negative functions"[32] is perhaps not unacceptable as a reflection of the difference between the joyous, life-enhancing world of Pantagruel and Panurge and that of the circumspect, self-regarding theatre-goers of Molière's Paris. Let us not forget that the author of *Le Misanthrope* found it "une étrange entreprise que celle de faire rire les honnêtes gens", even at those who, like Alceste, deviated from the social norm.

Bakhtin, as we have just seen, picks out for comment the "negative functions" of laughter. Koestler is among the most critical of Bergson's commentators, above all because, in his view, the Frenchman tries too hard to make a universally valid formula for comic laughter out of his *comique/vivant* contrast. Freud is very close in many respects, while Bergson and Freud are saluted by Charles Mauron as "les derniers grands théoriciens du rire".[33] Jean Emelina devotes a particularly favourable mention to Bergson, on the way to establishing his own "conditions nécessaires et suffisantes du comique", namely "distance", "anomalie" and "innocuité",[34] concepts which clearly owe much to the influence of *Le Rire*. Kern refers to his "extraordinary" insight into the essence of laughter and his "highly ingenious" description of the comic process,[35] Swabey describes his work as a "brilliant continuation of a French tradition stemming from Molière",[36] while Monro, whom I have not had occasion to consider, finds that his uniting of the incongruity and the superiority theories makes "a very impressive case".[37] These references are enough to show, I believe, that *Le Rire* has continued to be a force to be reckoned with even by those later theorists whose interpretation diverges from it; and hardly any of those I have considered found it possible to ignore its author.

I should like to conclude with a brief consideration of the relationship between *le comique* and *l'humour*, which is not the digression it may appear to be, since it is highly relevant to an assessment of Bergson's position. It seems always to have been a subject of general agreement that while *le comique* is properly seen as a characteristic product of the French mind, *l'humour* is equally recognisable as quintessentially English. I dealt with this topic in fairly summary fashion in 1980,[38] and it was shortly afterwards to be the subject of a masterly analysis by Paul Gifford,[39] as well as of a short study by Albert Laffay,[40] while we owe to Sam Taylor a perceptive investigation of the traditional *comique/humour* antithesis in the specific case of Voltaire.[41]

First of all, a general point: while the field of operation of the *comique* studied by Bergson is dramatic comedy, that preferred by English humorists is the novel. We may be able immediately to counter this with evidence of the opposite – Falstaff is a favourite example – but the English novel from *Tristram Shandy* to Dickens, Thackeray and beyond, is much more fertile ground, backed up by works by Anglophile French writers such as André Maurois and Pierre Daninos. Gifford relates this topic very pertinently to our consideration of Bergson's theory of *le comique*:

> Nowhere in *Le Rire* is there a hint of the distinction which English theorists of the eighteenth century had laboured to establish: the distinction between "laughing at" and "laughing with", or just simply "laughing" in gratuitous enjoyment of the comic. On the contrary, a momentary anaesthesia of the heart is posited as the precondition of all perception of the comic, "qui s'adresse à l'intelligence pure".[42]

While it would be difficult to extract an agreed definition of *l'humour* from the various attempts that have been made, one thing is agreed: "L'humour est une forme d'esprit satirique et concret, mêlée d'affection feinte ou réelle, parfois dissimulée",[43] and in this context Gifford quotes with approval the work of two French *anglicistes*, namely Louis Cazamian and Robert Escarpit.

> Cazamian developed, and Escarpit refined, the fruitful idea of humour as a paradox obtained by transposition. The germ of this idea was Bergson's law of comic invention: "on obtiendra toujours un effet comique en transposant l'expression naturelle d'une idée dans un autre ton". The humorist deliberately transposes his ideas, perceptions, feelings into a key which is at odds with the habitual, the normally appropriate, the predictable: he contrives a paradox.[44]

Without a doubt the classic example of such a paradox, much loved by analysts of *l'humour* and cited by both Gifford and Laffay, is Swift's *Modest Proposal*.

However Taylor's survey of relevant texts by Voltaire presents an effective challenge to the perhaps over-simplified view that the Channel has always provided an unbridgeable barrier between two national temperaments in the matter of what makes us laugh: the assumption

> that "cette plaisanterie, ce vrai comique, cette gaieté, cette urbanité" as Voltaire describes them, were English forms of humour, and that in France laughter was satirical, being based on ridicule, wit and raillery, and implying a degree of malice.[45]

Stressing Voltaire's ability to laugh at himself – always regarded as a litmus test of English humour – Taylor concludes:

> In the conte, Voltaire achieves a multi-dimensional effect as the author-raconteur mimics the *persona* and accent of his caricature-creations ... Emotion is constantly transmuted, filtered, distanced, but equally well the comic itself continually betrays emotion.[46]

While the lack, noted by Gifford, of any consideration of the question of "laughing at/laughing with" on Bergson's part by no means invalidates the standing of *Le Rire* as a major contribution to the study of its subject, it does help to emphasise the precise nature of this subject, namely the aesthetics of a certain type of French dramatic comedy represented above all by Molière and his successors. Humour, as defined by Gifford for example, is largely foreign to the kind of comic effects Bergson is dealing with – though it may be felt that the use of the term "French humour" as the title both of the Bristol symposium in 1996 and of the present publication, should be seen less as a provocative challenge to a well-established analytical tradition, than as evidence of the relative inadequacy of English critical terminology concerning *le comique proprement dit*.

[1] M. C. Swabey, *Comic Laughter: a Philosophical Essay* (Yale UP, 1961), p. 142.

[2] L. Cooper, *An Aristotelian Theory of Comedy* (New York, 1922), p.179.

[3] W. D. Howarth, "La Notion de la catharsis dans la comédie française classique", *Revue des Sciences Humaines*, 152 (1973), 521-539.

[4] *Loc. cit.*, p. viii.

[5] H. Bergson, *Le Rire* (Paris, 1947), p. 2. All future bracketed references are to this edition: author's emphasis throughout.

[6] See in particular W. G. Moore, *Molière: A New Criticism* (Oxford, 1949), though I note that Moore attributes the *raideur/laideur* antithesis to Thibaudet rather than to Bergson.

[7] *Leviathan*, Part I, ch. 6.

[8] *Traité des Passions*, article 178.

[9] *Réflexions critiques sur la poésie et sur la peinture*, 7th edition (Paris, 1770), vol. 1, p. 63.

[10] *Maximes et réflexions sur la comédie*, ed. C. Urbain and E. Levesque (Paris, 1930), p. 262.

[11] *Pensées*, no. 13 (Lafuma edition).

[12] *Dictionnaire philosophique*, article "Rire".

[13] *An Essay on Laughter*, ch. 2.

[14] *Critique of Judgment*, I. 1. 54.

[15] *The World as Will and Representation*, Bk. I, paragraph 15.

[16] L. Dumont, *Des Causes du rire* (Paris, 1862), pp. 48 & 62.

[17] G. Meredith, "On the Idea of Comedy", in *Complete Works*, vol. 23 (1898), p. 24.

[18] Freud, *Jokes and Their Relation to the Unconscious* (Penguin Freud Library, vol. 6, 1976), p. 256.

[19] *Le Médecin malgré lui*, Act I, Sc. 1.

[20] C. Saulnier, *Le Sens du comique: essai sur le caractère esthétique du rire* (Paris, 1940), pp. 30-1.

[21] *Ibid.*, pp. 33-4.

[22] A. Koestler, *The Act of Creation* (London, 1964), p. 38. All future bracketed references are to this edition.

[23] C. Lalo, *Esthétique du rire* (Paris, 1949), p. 5.

[24] F. Jeanson, *Signification humaine du rire* (Paris, 1950), p. 42.

[25] *Ibid.*, pp. 70-1.

[26] *Loc. cit.*, p. 82.

[27] A. Thibaudet, "Molière et la critique", *Revue de Paris* (March 1930), p. 393.

[28] *Ibid.*, "Le Rire de Molière", *Revue de Paris* (January 1922), pp. 327 & 332.

[29] *Op. cit.*, pp. 142-3.

[30] E. Kern, *The Absolute Comic* (Columbia UP, 1980), p. 16.

[31] H. Jacobson, *Seriously Funny: from the Ridiculous to the Sublime* (London, 1997).

[32] M. Bakhtin, *Rabelais and his World* (MIT Press, 1968), p. 71.

[33] C. Mauron, *Psychocritique du genre comiqe* (Paris, 1964), p. 146.

[34] J. Emelina, *Le Comique: essai d'interprétation générale* (Paris, 1991), p. 7.

[35] *Op. cit.*, p. 36.

[36] *Op. cit.*, p. 142.

[37] D. H. Monro, *Argument of Laughter* (Melbourne UP), 1951, p. 132.

[38] W. D. Howarth, "Un Etranger devant le comique français", *Le Français dans le monde* (February/March 1980), 31-5.

[39] P. Gifford, "Humour and the French Mind: towards a reciprocal definition", *Modern Language Review*, 76 (1981), 534-548.

[40] A. Laffay, *Anatomie de l'humour et du nonsense* (Paris, 1970).
[41] S. S. B. Taylor, "Voltaire's humour", *SVEC*, 179 (1979), 101-116.
[42] *Art. cit.*, p. 541.
[43] A. Mavrocordato, quoted in Gifford, 1981, p. 542.
[44] *Art. cit.*, p. 542.
[45] *Art. cit.*, pp. 102-3.
[46] *Ibid.*, p. 114.

7. Bad Jokes and Beckett
Walter Redfern

What I judge a bad joke might send you rolling in the aisles, and an excellent one leave you stone-cold, whereupon, like the music-hall straight man, you might respond with "I don't wish to know that." The whole business of seeing the joke is a minefield, and, of late for some, a gold-mine. Yet unarguably there are pointed, barbed jokes, and toothless ones. There are jokes pure and simple-minded, and jokes with ulterior motives, designs on us. Like poetry, jokes reveal language at its most self-aware, marvelling at its own clever navel. I am thinking here of modern-day stand-up comedians – or, in Beckett's case, supine or crawling comedians – who, in order to shatter the illusion of spontaneous wittiness, refer blatantly to their scripts and rehearsals, and thus gag about joke-making.

In a letter to Axel Kaun of 1937, Beckett spoke of "somehow finding a method by which we can represent this mocking attitude towards the word, through words" (*Dis*, 172). Attitude: if action in Beckett's often lunar landscapes generally seems pointless and self-defeating, the mind of his people spins on, the voices never cave in and verbal attitudes are struck. His figments are people with attitude. With some stylishness they rearrange the remnants of meaningfulness, the loose connexions, milling around in their retentive minds. Verbally, if seldom any more physically, they practise brinkmanship: as all jokers do; knowing how easy it is to come a cropper, they live on the edge. Beckett was famously taken with the "shape of ideas". Jokes, like poems, need to be crafted, craftily, and placed adroitly.

Surprisingly, in his study of Proust, Beckett does not see fit to make anything of Proust's highly-developed sense of humour, as evidenced for example in the figure of the ineffable but continuously effing Dr Cottard. Via Cottard, Proust displays his familiarity with that common occurrence in all social interaction, the failed, or mistimed, joke. Cottard hoards up what he fondly imagines are the gems he has overheard, and reproduces them, generally on the wrong cue.[1] In his desperate urge to pre-plan his life, he plants his usually atrocious, purloined puns in infertile spots. He fails to see the tricky difference between telling jokes (or anecdotes) and making jokes. As a receiver of humour Cottard invariably wears a knowing smile or smirk, just in case what others say turns out to have been a witticism. He does not want to be taken, as some Proustian characters do, from behind.

As existential etiolation is the constant mode in Beckett's universe, tired jokes might be thought entirely appropriate to it. A last resort, of course, is to make a joke out of a joke fallen flat: a meta-joke (like the series of pocket-sized joke-books called *Mini Ha Ha*). Beckett's humour is very often strained (and in a letter to MacGreevy he confessed he was dreading reading Proust at stool). Like all of us some of the time with jingles, Beckett cannot get bad jokes out of his head: so he repeats in *Watt* the "stout porter" joke that I will shortly deconstruct. After all, it is perversely logical that a writer boasting that he specialised in failure should home in on failed jokes. For Bergson (whose *Le Rire*, hyped by sociologists and literary critics with no sense of or for humour, focuses essentially on clichés and existential stereotypes, without ever acknowledging its own mandarin automatisms) humour was a kill-joy gendarme, policing citizens' behaviour. For Beckett, while humour often seems all that is left by way of reaction to frustration or pain, it is not much cop. Above all, he sees life as a bad joke, to be responded to, with justifiable unkindness, in kind. As Molloy says, "My life, my life, now I speak of it as something over, now as of a joke which still goes on" (*Moll*, 47). Any such retaliation, what Dostoyevsky called "joking through clenched teeth",[2] recalls the Absurdist tactic of Camus's *Caligula*: tit-for-tat, diamond-cut-diamond. Perhaps, as a concept, absurdity inevitably houses comic potentialities?

Time for an instance of a bad joke, from *Murphy*, whose hero, as his name suggests, is a potato, a couch-potato:

> "Why did the barmaid champagne?" he said. "Do you give it up?"
> "Yes," said Celia.
> "Because the stout porter bitter," said Murphy.

Beckett plugs on, relentlessly:

> This was a joke that did not amuse Celia. [...] That did not matter. So far from being adapted to her, it was not addressed to her. It amused Murphy, that was all that mattered. He always found it funny, more the most funny, clonic [...] He staggered about on the floor [...] overcome by the toxins of this simple little joke [...] The fit was so much more like one of epilepsy than of laughter that Celia felt alarm [...] The fit was over, gloom took its place. (*Mur*, 139-40)[3]

This was one of the "Gilmigrim jokes, so called from the Lilliputian wine" (*Mur*, 140: Beckett's, or a printer's, gremlin for Glimigrim; either way, the humour is glum). First point: this is unshared, selfish laughter (Murphy, after all, is a "seedy solipsist": *Mur*, 82). Secondly it is a bad joke, since it contradicts itself unfruitfully: if the barmaid was bitten, she would not need to sham pain, that is to simulate suffering. (Beckett elsewhere gainsays himself by claiming that Wylie, unlike Murphy, "preferred the poorest joke to none": *Mur*, 119.) Thirdly, laughter here is equated with physico-mental illness, a bout ("clonic" means spasmic, the opposite of a tonic muscular contraction). There is not much tonic in Beckettian laughter. Murphy's Law, also known as Sod's Law, *contre-finalité* (Sartre), or Resistentialism (Paul Jennings), had not yet been named in 1938, but its wry acknowledgement of the backfiring customary in human affairs, especially in its modified version ("If anything *can't* go wrong, it will"), suits Murphy to a T.

For the sake of equity, a somewhat better example relayed by Beckett to MacGreevy: "Do you know the story of the chaste centipede, who said to her suitor, crossing her thousand legs: 'No, a thousand times no'?"[4] This allusion to an old music-hall ditty is almost a good joke if we subtract the first, over-anxious "thousand", and forgive the entomological inaccuracy on centipede/millipede that we all commit. Comparably approximate (but the best kind of pun is so often the paronym, or near-pun) is this joke from *Murphy*: "Cooper never sat, his acathisia [morbid fear of sitting] was deep-seated and of long standing" (*Mur*, 119:[5] the French rendering is knock-kneed – "était profonde et de longue durée" – which is no joke at all).

With its abstruse references – "the socio-cultural equivalent of insider trading"[6] – some of Beckett's humour is more godawfully pedantic than any of us professional pedants persist in perpetrating: Molloy, leaning at an acute angle against a wall, talks of a "hypotenusal posture" (*Moll*, 9). There is, of course, an old tradition in the English (and for all I know Irish) music-hall, with its magniloquent masters of ceremony, of using long, posh words for small, common-or-garden things. In *Dream of Fair to Middling Women* there is a refrain of a "private joke": I got so little from this text that I felt it was all something of a private joke. " 'I shall write a book', he mused [...], 'a book where the phrase is self-consciously smart and slick'." (*DFMW*, 138) That sliding between recondite and idiomatic (also active in Céline and Queneau) may indeed be even more of an Irish than an English thing, given the higher respect in Ireland for articulacy.

Even though I am from Liverpool, which many Liverpudlians blasphemously christen the capital of Ireland, I have no wish to pontificate (highly suspect activity, anyway, for a 24-carat atheist) on Irishness. I cannot, for all that, resist pedantry, telling you more than you may want to know. If life is a bad joke – that is: we've heard it all before; it doesn't work; it's no laughing matter; it's a waste of breath and time – then, as the *Whoroscope* notebook informs us "Life is a Joe Miller". The hero of *Murphy* thinks he knows in advance Celia's retort: "There will be nothing to distract me from you." (*Mur*, 65) "Nothing", here, presumably bears the age-old positive charge that Renaissance paradoxers, Lewis Carroll (the king exclaiming at Alice's ability to "see Nobody") and Sartre lay upon it. The French monk Radulphus Glaber, after discovering the great Nemo in a number of Biblical, Evangelical and liturgical texts, composed a *Historia de nemine*. The phrase in the Scriptures, "nemo deum vidit", became "Nemo saw God". "Thus, every-thing impossible, inadmissible, is, on the contrary, permitted for Nemo."[7] The Beckett text goes on: "This was the kind of Joe Miller that Murphy simply could not bear to hear revived." (*Mur*, 65)

A Joe Miller is a synonym for a stale joke, a chestnut. A certain John Mottley (a suspiciously apt name, though he did author several plays, and the lives of Peter the Great and Catherine), compiled in 1739 a book of facetiae, which without permission he entitled *Joe Miller's jests: or the wit's vade-mecum* (the narrator of *The Unnamable* calls his stories "facetiae": *Unn*, 27): it was a childhood favourite of George Eliot. Joseph Miller (1684-1738) was a Drury Lane actor who could neither read nor write; his wife recited his parts to him. Miller was quite adept at Irish brogue. The actual "funny" stories in *Joe Miller's jests* are mostly dire, dividing regularly between stupidity jokes, where people make laughing-stocks of themselves, and cheekiness or insult jokes, where they turn others into butts. It is as though eighteenth-century joke-sters had surfeited on Thomas Hobbes and his superiority theory of humour. In the 1846 edition, the anonymous prefacer claims that the attribution was by antiphrasis, since the actual Joe Miller "was himself, when living, a jest for dulness [...] When others told jokes Joe main-tained imperturbable gravity."[8] The jokes, then, are credited to a sort of human vacuity, which would appeal to Beckett. The prefacer also claims that few have read the jokes they allude to so knowingly and slightingly. This is a valid point, for the unknown provenance of most jokes going the rounds is, to coin an Irish Bull, well attested.

Let us turn, like desperate sinners, to God. I am miles from being the first to remark that *cosmic* and *comic* are but one letter apart.[9] The tailor-joke in *Endgame* and that gives its name to *Le Monde et le pantalon* is naturally commandeered by Jewish experts on humour as one of their own.[10] It features a customer complaining over a long period about the mess his tailor is making of a pair of trousers, and the inordinate time he is taking over completing them. Eventually he cites God's feat of creating the cosmos in only six days. The tailor's response: "But look at the world, and look at my trousers." (*CDW*, 102-3) This story enacts chutzpah, that is brass-necked cheek, since the tailor not only compares himself to his own advantage with the Almighty, but also perseveres in boosting his own botched goods, his unspeakable bespoke strides. For his part, the narrator of *The Unnamable* speaks of having been given the low-down on God (*Unn*, 13).[11] All the same, I am not sure Beckett ever achieved the provocative serenity of Luis Buñuel: "Grâce à Dieu, je suis toujours athée!"[12] Robert Frost's sarcastic prayer: "Forgive, O lord, my little joke on Thee/And I'll forgive Thy great big one on me"[13] – and who can tell what little or great big joke Beckett plays on us readers? – is not quite matched by the less belligerent Winnie in *Happy Days*. After a play on fornication/formication, not spelt out but shared with Willie, Winnie says: "How can one better magnify the Almighty than by sniggering with him at his little jokes, particularly the poorer ones?" (*CDW*, 150) God is not a fellow of infinite jest, however, but more a jesting infinity mocking humankind. Remember Proverbs 1. 25-6: "[Because] ye have set at naught all my counsel, and would none of my reproof/I also will laugh at your calamity."

This is God the heavy father, the chastising schoolmaster, or the unrequited lover. For Baudelaire, laughter was the direct result of humanity's fallen, schizophrenic state, so that in the original confrontation at least God's creatures beat him to the draw. But He who laughs last laughs longest, and God has all eternity to play with. Less gloomily, but somehow very Beckettian, is the centenarian Abraham who, on learning that his ninety-year-old spouse Sara was pregnant, "fell upon his face and laughed" (Genesis, 17. 17). Sara also laughed, but "within herself" (18. 12), but she has to deny having laughed: the males rule the roost. God, we could say, has a funny sense of humour. As Murphy asks, a tad enigmatically, "What but an imperfect sense of humour could have made such a mess of chaos" (*Mur*, 65). When Molloy chats with Father Ambrose, they find themselves in some agreement on humour, divine and other. After an analogy between a hen sitting "with her arse in the dust, from morning to night", they laugh *seriatim*, and then the priest expatiates:

> What a joy it is to laugh from time to time. Is it not? I said. It is peculiar to man, he said. So I have heard, I said [...] Animals never laugh, he said. It takes us to

find that funny, I said [A truism, if only humans laugh]. Christ never laughs
either, he said, so far as I know [...] Can you wonder? I said. (*Moll*, 138)

The tailor joke, by implication, means that God was a worse
botcher even than the sempster. Or, of course, that perfection is always
out of reach, existing only in some Platonic form, like the narrator's hat
in *The Expelled*: "Come, son, we are going to buy your hat, as though it
had preexisted from time immemorial in a preestablished place" (*Exp*,
34). Molloy, for one, deems himself a bungler. His dangling, proto-
typically asymmetrical testicles might testify, he thinks, that he has
"made a balls of his life" (*Moll*, 47).

At the outset, I spoke of attitudes. *Watt* distinguishes between
various attitudes towards, or in, laughter:

> The bitter laugh laughs at that which is not good, it is the ethical laugh. The
> hollow laugh laughs at that which is not true, it is the intellectual laugh [...] But
> the mirthless laugh is the dianoetic laugh [= intellectual, so why the distinction?].
> It is the laugh of laughs, the *risus purus*, the laugh laughing at the laugh, the
> saluting of the highest joke, in a word, the laugh that laughs - silence please - at
> that which is unhappy. (*Watt*, 47)

I take it that the last-named involves laughing on the other side of
your face (in French *le rire jaune*); you are both triumphant and beaten.
Cancer is no joke, but "you have to laugh". Only the Homeric gods are
capable of "asbestos gelos" (inextinguishable laughter).[14] Only one of
them could claim: "I'm all right, Jack. I'm fireproof." Mere humans cope
as best they can. Lousse in *Molloy*, for example:

> She laughed. It was perhaps her way of crying. Or perhaps I was mistaken and
> she was really crying, with the noise of laughter. Tears and laughter, they are so
> much Gaelic to me. (*Moll*, 48-9)[15]

Are Beckett's jokes in some limbo area, still waiting to be
definitively labelled as bad or good? Murphy has a go:

> Not the least remarkable of Murphy's innumerable classifications [and Beckett is
> fully alert, like Rabelais, to the inherently comic nature of lists, that is the
> nearness of taxonomy to taxidermy] of experience was that into jokes that had
> once been good jokes and jokes that had never been good jokes [...] In the
> beginning was the pun. And so on. (*Mur*, 65)

The pun, then, is the foundation of all things. Did Beckett think that
"Fiat Lux" was the motto of Lever Brothers? And that Goethe's dying
words "More light!" were a request not for additional *Aufklärung*, but
for opened shutters? (Apparently it was the latter.) God may have given
Creation a verbal fillip, but "Let there be light" sounds pretty univocal.
Ackerley picks up on "And so on":

And so on, until the end, when 'excellent gas, superfine chaos' brings Murphy's body to its ultimate stasis, its final quiet. The pun implied in Murphy's death (*gas* creating *chaos*) may or may not be a good joke, but in Murphy's progress from young aspirant to old suspirant the puns reveal more than Beckett's imperfect sense of humour.[16]

I myself kick against the prick of associating imperfection with punning, as if it were only for mental defectives. Later, Ackerley restores the balance:

As a figure of language, the pun combines the extremes of both the rational and the irrational. Its insistence on the syzygy of ideas normally distinct offers to our rational understanding a challenge not dissimilar to that of Cartesian dualism: on the one hand, the yoked components are the 'same'; on the other, they are 'different' [...] Janus-like, the pun faces both creation and chaos.[17]

In several of Beckett's works the refrain of all things running, or limping, or hanging, together indicates the ideal territory for the punner, who is dedicated to overlap: mixing it. And, of course, anybody who, like Beckett, believes that less is more, will be attracted to the bargain-offer pun: two (meanings) for the price of one (word).

"My work", Beckett told Alan Schneider in a letter, "is a matter of fundamental sounds (no joke intended) made as fully as possible" (*Dis*, 109). While I might agree with Robert Desnos's wry plea, "Pitié pour l'amant des homonymes",[18] no wordplayer should wriggle out of responsibility as in that bracket. Puns should be proudly acknowledged, their paternity shouldered. Why this sheepishness about punning? Or is it feigned, by many deliberate or accidental double-meaners? If so, this is indeed having your cake and eating it, like the coprophiliac. (This tack-on is hi-jacked from Christopher Ricks on Jean Genet. Ricks ludically accused me of plagiarising this pun in my book *Puns*. He was right, except that I thought I was plagiarising Dan Jacobson.) I take comfort in Emerson's essay "Plato or the Philosopher":

Every book is a quotation; and every house is a quotation out of all forests, and mines, and stone quarries; and every man is a quotation from all his ancestors.[19]

However original Beckett fancied himself to be in writing of powerlessness, even he would have admitted to having, like all and sundry, a magpie mind. Robert Burton used the term apothecary for the plagiarist who was forever mixing and remixing given elements into different compounds. In the Addenda to *Watt*, Beckett slips in a joky quote about quotes, of great ancestry: "Pereant qui ante nos nostra dixerunt" (Aelius Donatus), which I would translate as: "May all those who scooped our script rot in hell." This is the Pataphysical concept of "anticipatory plagiarism", or harking forwards.

W. H. Auden wrote:

> Be subtle, various, ornamental, clever,
> And do not listen to those critics ever
> Whose crude provincial gullets crave in books
> Plain cooking made still plainer by plain cooks,
> As though the Muse preferred her half-wit sons;
> Good poets have a weakness for bad puns.[20]

We need look for corroboration of the last line no further than Shakespeare. But could the converse not also be true, bad poets having a forte for good puns? A pun disconcerts. It interrupts the euphoria (or inertia) of a text, like Stendhal's political pistol-shot in a concert. It thus draws attention to itself, and consorts happily with self-conscious writing. From *First Love*: "Personally I have no bones to pick with graveyards. I take the air there willingly [...] when take the air I must." (*First*, 4) Here, the pun (or puns – is there a secondary one on "musty air"?) acts as a would-be buffer-state against *de rigueur* gravity, as so often in the poems of Thomas Hood. In *Malone Dies* Malone comments while watching a mule being interred: "The end of life is always vivifying", no doubt with a horse-laugh (*Mal*, 195). Puns can be of course, and often are in Beckett, obtuse. "The hardy laurel" (*Watt*, 253) is merely echoic, repeating famous names, but not drawing them into any interesting new relationship with the shrub. When Edgar Allan Poe maintained that "the goodness of your true pun is in the direct ratio of its intolerability",[21] he did not specify whether "intolerability" meant awfulness, or terrifying pointedness. Much more to the point than that hardy laurel is the play on the magic plant moly with which Lousse/Circe tries to "mollify" Molloy. Here, the paronomasia espouses the badgering attempt to bewitch (*Moll*, 63, 72).[22]

Epithets mechanically applied to the pun – grinding, atrocious, excruciating (think of the verbal Chinese torture of *Finnegans Wake*) – depict it as a kind of purgatory, Beckett's place of predilection. Just before an account of Murphy's ululations at the instant of birth Beckett mentions "such maieutic saws as 'How can he be clean that is born' [...] Murphy required for his pity no other butt than himself" (*Mur*, 71). This tries to sound like aggressive self-pity, the kind that kicks yourself, lovingly, up the arse. At the asylum Murphy "laboured more diligently than ever at his little dungeon in Spain" (*Mur*, 180). Beckett loves thus playing new tunes on old musical saws, idioms, clichés. He might well have agreed with Stravinsky, who knew of what he spoke: "The danger lies not in the borrowing of clichés. The danger lies in fabricating them and in bestowing on them the force of law."[23] Stereotype was originally a printer's term. In clichés we run true to type. We hear ancestral voices overlaying ours. Like William Empson, Beckett could have intoned: "And I a twister love what I abhor."[24] Beckett everywhere resists what linguisticians call lexical institutionalisation, that is the process whereby words are put in strait-jackets, douched, given electro-shock treatment, and generally made to behave themselves. As well as being a form of madness *in* language, puns and other verbal twists such as revitalised fixed syntagms resemble anti-psychiatry in that they loosen the straps of that straitjacket. In *Murphy* "a person of his own steak and kidney" restores the physical sense of "kidney" by the insertion of that unmistakable meat (*Mur*, 192).

To telescope two ideas – one about odds-and-ends, and the other about homogeneity – I once coined the interlingual phrase "chop sui generis". That is an example of playing between languages: the maca-ronic tradition. I believe Beckett chose French against English for similar reasons to those of Jean Arp in selecting French against German: "Je me suis décidé à rédiger directement en français parce que maîtrisant moins cette langue, je m'y dépaysais davantage."[25] Beckett too wanted to escape the facile momentum (or inertia), the bandwagon, the contempt-ible cosiness of his mother tongue, its lullabying rhythms and unfree associations. Writing in French assisted him in his quest for lessness. He became a whispering barker offering amazing reductions: not great expectations, but picayune ones. The notorious Cartesian severance of mind from body was no doubt another magnet which drew Beckett to more scrawny French. The narrator of *The Unnamable* begets a splendid neologism, the "wordy-gurdy", which thins down in French to the mere "la chasse aux mots" (*Unn*, 157; French version, 230). Once ensconced uncomfortably in a second language, Beckett could not resist the foreign speaker's instinctive catheterisation (or piss-take) of a tongue not maternally his or hers. Even linguistic botching can be a spur. As *Worstward Ho* puts it: "Fail better." (*Worst*, 101) In *Malone meurt*, Beckett describes thus a woman's arm-movements: "Elle les écartait de ses flancs, je dirais brandissais si j'ignorais encore mieux le génie de votre langue." (45; this sentence is inevitably omitted from the English version, though it would end something like this: "If I were more expertly ignorant of the genius of your language.")

The macaronic mode is a gleeful acceptance that languages are not, and cannot be kept, in a state of apartheid each from the other. They overlap and contaminate each other, and in a non-pejorative, beneficial sense. Whether he is composing, or decomposing, in English or French, Beckett writes in a kind of homeless language. As George Craig has said: "The signs are that he is exploring a verbal no-man's-land where neither French nor English holds sway."[26] French is Beckett's host-language, but of course a house is not a home. Self-evidently French is less second-nature to him than English, but he was always suspicious of what was second-nature. Maybe all this is best typified by the pun, implicit in much of his work, on asylum/asile. As Murphy puts it: "Asylum [...] is better than exile." (*Mur*, 73) His creatures find that any haven is yet another madhouse, and that goes also for the brain skulking in the skull. Beckett said in a letter to Axel Kaun (written in German):

> From time to time I have the consolation, as now, of sinning willy-nilly against a foreign language, as I should love to do with full knowledge and intent against my own - and as I shall do - Deo juvante. (*Dis*, 173)

He plays across and skits both languages in this sentence from Molloy. Taking the set expression "je ne sais pas à quel saint me vouer", he reshuffles it to: "Connaître le saint, tout est là, n'importe quel con peut s'y vouer." (*Mol*, 33-4) The English counterpart is feeble: "Yes, the whole thing is to know what saint to implore, any fool can implore him." (35) His vestigial creatures are at their wit's end (the meaning of that French idiom), and the exile's eye and ear analyse, that is break down, the impasse. But what about instances where the two languages exhibit an *entente cordiale*? In *Mercier and Camier* the riddle "What would we do without women? Explore other channels" (188), becomes in French, "Nous prendrions un autre pli" (118): we would acquire a new habit, but "le pli" also refers to the folds of the groin.[27] In *Molloy*, the hero's legs are, in French, "raides comme la justice" (81) but in English "stiff as a life-sentence" (83). Here, idioms *are* puns, as in "high as a kite", or "réglé comme du papier à musique".

The joke can also lie in a transfer of sense, a different, subversive association, as in metaphor. In *The Calmative* a comedian is reported as

> telling a funny story about a fiasco [...] He used the word snail or slug [...] The women seemed more entertained than their escorts [...] Perhaps they had in mind the reigning penis sitting (who knows) by their side and from that sweet shore launched their cries of joy towards the comic vast (*CSP*, 37):

a nice case of a women's revenge-match facilitated, however unwittingly, by a man, who was no doubt, like many comics, trying to be disarming, which is to say disempowering.

There are gentle forms of irony, such as Ariosto's, which Beckett interpreted in these words: "The face remains grave, but the mind has smiled. The profound *risolino* that does not destroy." (*Dis*, 89) This is deadpan, poker-face. The old conundrum as to whether humour or wit undermine or preserve that which they target is perhaps most conveniently solved (or shelved) by saying that they do both. So many wise-cracks seemingly damage what they set up. But, once mentioned, even under attack, can anything be altogether blotted out? Words can counter words, but not abolish them. Of the many forms of irony, so-called Romantic irony, or self-undercutting, is the one Beckett practises most, as here in *Molloy*: "One is what one is, partly at least." (*Moll*, 72) In this respect I recall that self-cancelling motto favoured by Montherlant (and scavenged by Camus): "Aedificabo et destruam" (I will build and I will knock down); the words attributed to Aristotle: "Ho plasas ephanisen" (The [poet] fabricated and abolished it); the Surrealist compound-word *littératurer* (write/delete); and Buñuel declaring that he could joyfully burn every metre of his film-footage. Like the Hindu deity Siva, who alternates between the destructive and reproductive principles, symbolised by the deflowering and fecundating lingam, writers are creators/destroyers.

Now, if we use the old criterion of someone "protesting too much", we can see that underlined, dogged anti-sentimentality can engender just another form of mawkishness. How many writers, how many of us glossers, stand condemned by Kierkegaard's animadversion, "His soul lacked the elasticity of irony. He had not the strength to take irony's vow of silence"?[28] Some writers, of course, out of honesty have opted for what they hoped would appear a meaningful silence.

A variety of bad jokes is the dirty joke, for the senses of "not worth making" and "not worthy of making" tend to run together. For instance, "Condom est arrosé par la Baïse" (*Moll*, 193) is one literally converted in the English version, but minus the *tréma*, which makes it a better, if typographically inexact, joke, albeit translingual. Sex, there, is "un jeu de con" (76): a mug's game (or a stupid cunt's game?). Some people weary, of course, of such subvocal harassment. The nudge-nudge makes the mind's ribs ache, and the wink-wink becomes a neurotic tic. Orwell thought the dirty joke, at its best, "a sort of mental rebellion."[29] Chesterton upped the paradoxical ante: "When you have got hold of a vulgar joke, you may be certain that you have got hold of a subtle and spiritual idea":[30] a piously hopeful idea. Malcolm Muggeridge comes nearer the truth and the knuckle when he claims that "good taste and humour are a contradiction in terms, like a chaste whore."[31]

And what of gestures, rude or otherwise: kinetic puns and jokes, verbal pratfalls, the whole caboodle of "stage business"? In *Godot*, the clownish or music-hall antics of protracted attempted mastery over things (like Winnie with her parasol), including the body felt as alien presence or opponent, are recycled traditional devices to make us laugh, uneasily. *Gag*, a word of similarly dubious or mixed parentage as pun or *blague*, embraces silence, retching, and telling (or enacting) jokes. *Gags* are also actors' interpolations into scripts, as so often with Beckett's narrators.

I could cheekily annex Malone's words: "I shall not finish this inventory either, a little bird tells me so, the paraclete perhaps, psitta-ceously named." (*Mal*, 250: this enigmatic reference is perhaps to Flaubert's story, *Un coeur simple*, where Holy Ghost and parrot are melded by the simple-minded servant Félicité. Whether this criss-cross exalts parrots or degrades the Holy Spirit can be left to the theologians. Flaubert once took a cutting from a local paper about a man who worshipped his parrot, even after it died (like Félicité). He came to believe he was a parrot, perched in trees, flapped his arms, and squawked.) More simply, of course, the quote from *Malone Dies* may just be a phonic collision of "paraclete" with parakeet. The root-meaning of "gag" is "strangle" (so good jokes get us by the throat), which is what some of Beckett's protagonists, or agonists, would no doubt like to do to uncooperative parrots. Beckett would certainly have known that the boozing idiom "étrangler un perroquet" means to drink a mixture of pastis and mint-syrup. In *Molloy* Lousse's parrot squawks: "Putain de conasse de merde de chiaison", which it presumably picked up from a previous French owner, but also "Fuck!", which it may have found all by itself (65). When Lousse tries to teach it, in the English version, the stereotypical "Pretty Polly", it ponders, but then repeats the above beak-ful: "Fuck the son of a bitch." (49-50) In folk-tales all over the world, parrots (often stand-ins for obstreperous children, who have comparable dirty habits – like Dorothy Parker's bird Onan, so called because he was forever spilling his seed) talk pointedly and rudely, the implication being that the bird has mulled over the situation, and is now commenting on it. In *Malone Dies*, Jackson's parrot, taught to recite the philosophical tag "Nihil in intellectu etc." manages these first three words but balks at the following ones. The net result is to install emptiness at the heart of the human mind: there is nothing in the intellect. This resembles the intervention of the antisocial parrot Laverdure in Queneau's *Zazie dans le Métro* who indicts *homo loquens* and human psittacism somewhat tautologically: "Tu causes, tu causes, c'est tout ce que tu sais faire."[32] Whereas Jackson feels he would be cramped in his parrot's cage, Laverdure and his master exchange positions – the bird, traumatised by a flying soup-tureen, carrying the cage where now perches the master – at the surrealistic climax of Queneau's novel.

If he does not mechanically parrot Céline, Beckett is certainly at times a bird of the feather. He called *Voyage au bout de la nuit* "the greatest novel in English or French."[33] Both writers face up to death on the instalment-plan (*Mort à crédit*) with gallows-humour. Their protagonists experience an ageless fear and guilt for an unspecified sin; they expect the worst in "cette farce atroce de durer."[34] Murphy and Bardamu seek asylum in a loony-bin. Both writers find point and solace in choreography. Beckett matches the "métro émotif"[35] of Céline's diarrhetoric. Both writers strike the mucker-pose, by going slumming in speech. In each fictional world the body is disgusting and veracious. In their corners of existence, like trapped rats, the heroes (even of the anti-Semitic Céline) take refuge in a quasi-Jewish humour: lamentations, piling it on thick. Céline and Beckett meet in limbo.

Have I been talking, as my title might suggest, of Beckett's own imperfect sense of humour? "Bad" is an ambiguous word. Think of current slang, where bad equals good, and Charles Lamb's paradox whereby "the worst puns are the best".[36] A faulty sense of humour is naturally the worst thing an English, or perhaps an Irish, person can attribute to another, almost as bad as his not having a heart. In breaking down some of Beckett's jokes, I have not sought to be a party-pooper (or wake-pooper, more fittingly). I would imagine that, by analogy with Constantine Fitzgibbon's dystopia *When the Kissing Had to Stop*, Beckett's later work could be described as "When the joking had to stop". In his essay on Proust Beckett wrote: "The whisky [Jameson's, of course] bears a grudge against the decanter." (*Proust*, 10) That which, or they who, are about to be consumed, envy and cannot forgive what will survive them. No doubt language bears a grudge against silence. But, whatever or whomsoever else I may want to eff, I do not want, as Watt says, "to eff the ineffable" (*Watt*, 61).

This chapter is superficially "a doctrine of scattered occasions";[37] or *disjecta membra*. Montesquieu provides a model: "Pour bien écrire il faut sauter les idées intermédiaires."[38] Why overvalue finition? Rabelais, Pascal, Melville and Gide, all for their very different reasons, scorned it. Finition/finitude: if by chance anyone could say the last word on any subject, it would truly be time to die (as in "famous last words", a phrase nowadays always used ironically). As Molloy suggests: "Perhaps there's no whole before you're dead." (*Moll*, 35) Is there a grave pun on whole/hole there? Beckett's prose often seems on the point of pegging out for good.

A French counterpart to "Freudian slip" is *acte manqué*. Such slips are often, as it transpires, sure-footed: *actes manqués* can succeed. In its literal sense we see a plethora of *actes manqués*, or fiascos, in Beckett's world. On inadvertent puns, like the possible whole/hole above, Bearn has noted:

> The fact that we don't normally notice this [i.e. that all possible significances of a word are always in play whenever it is being used] is no more remarkable than the fact that we don't normally notice the size of people's ears. Inadvertent puns draw our attention to what was there all along.

He goes on to cite Austin's remark that every utterance can be used either seriously or unseriously, and concludes that "if inadvertent puns are possible, then there is no sentence that has ever been completely understood by anyone. No wonder that punsters should be punished." To turn the screws even further:

> Most of the expressive power of our linguistic action is outside our control. Surprising as this result is, I suppose it is no surprise to discover that if you begin with inadvertent significance, you will end by denying that anyone is master of the language they speak.[39]

There is clearly, or muddily, something delirious with the logic here: words seem to have taken over, to fulfil the prophecy of this text. Nobody could actually live with this awareness to the forefront of the mind; each of us would need to watch each other's every word like a sceptical hawk. We would all be confidence-tricksters of the word. Beckett is saner: "There is no use indicting words, they are no shoddier than what they peddle." (*Mal*, 195)

There has been a huge amount of research, especially by sociologists, psychologists and psychiatrists, on the therapeutic effects of humour ("Ve haff vays of making you laff!"). Adler used jokes as therapy, "to clarify his error to the neurotic."[40] No doubt, and we should be grateful for it, humour can help in alleviating distress and pain. But we often talk of comic relief, as if humour acted as an automatic remedy for constipation or indigestion. Humour can also rub our faces in misery, reopen old wounds, scratch at scabs. Estragon is glad to find anything that will give him the sense of being alive. In this context, joking is akin to toothache.

Probably my favourite proverb or cliché is "many a true word is spoken in jest". Humour is serious, and revelatory. As Legman said, "Your favourite joke is your psychological signature. The 'only' joke you know how to tell is you".[41] How can I fade out except with these words from *The Unnamable*: "Ah mother of God, the things one has to listen to, perhaps it's tears of mirth. Well, no matter, let's drive on now to the end of the joke, we must be nearly there" (*Unn*, 102)?

I offer my profound gratitude to Mary Bryden, for advice and generous support.

I should like to thank Edward Beckett and the Board of Trinity College Dublin for permission to re-cite the centipede joke from Beckett's letter to Tom MacGreevy (TCD MS 10402/72).

Abbreviations

CSP:	*Collected Shorter Prose*. Calder, 1988.
CDW:	*Complete Dramatic Works*. Faber, 1990.
DFMW:	*Dream of Fair to Middling Women*. Calder, 1996.
Dis:	*Disjecta*. ed. R. Cohn. Calder, 1983.
Exp:	*The Expelled and other Novellas*. Penguin, 1980.
First:	*First Love*. Penguin, 1995.
Mal:	*Malone Dies*, in *Molloy, Malone Dies, The Unnamable*. Calder, 1959. (*Malone meurt*. Union Générale d'Editions, 1951.)
Merc:	*Mercier and Camier*. Picador, 1988. (Minuit, 1970.)
Moll:	*Molloy*. New York: Grove, 1970. (Union Générale d'Editions, 1963.)
Mur:	*Murphy*. New York: Grove, 1957.
Proust:	*Proust*. New York: Grove, 1931.
Unn:	*The Unnamable*. New York: Grove, 1970.
Watt:	*Watt*. Calder, 1963.
Worst:	*Worstward Ho*, in *Nohow On*. Calder, 1992.

[Place of publication is London or Paris unless otherwise stated]

[1] The incomparable Gershon Legman describes the opposite of the miscued joke as the equivalent of a "three-cushion carom in billiards": *No Laughing Matter* (London, 1981), p. 859.

[2] F. Dostoyevsky, *Notes from Underground*, tr. A. MacAndrew (New York, 1961), p. 115.

[3] In the French version most of this passage is jettisoned, no doubt because deemed untranslatable.

[4] q.v. *infra*, p. 171.

[5] The *OED* quotes *Murphy* at the entry for "acathisia".

[6] J. Campbell, "Allusions and Illusions", *French Studies Bulletin*, 53 (1994), p. 19.

[7] M. Bakhtin: *Rabelais and his World* (MIT Press, 1968), p. 413.

[8] *Op. cit.*, (London, 1846), n. p.

[9] And the same in Greek, Latin, French, Spanish, Italian, and German. Michel Tournier makes great sport with this verbal near-incest, and calls the offspring "white laughter", which he locates in Thomas Mann, as well as practising it brazenly himself.

[10] Letters to me from D. Katz, Oxford Institute for Yiddish Studies, and J. Cohen, All Souls, Oxford, 24/1/96 and 17/12/96.

[11] In the French version, "ils m'ont affranchi sur Dieu", an even greater liberating effect is conveyed: q.v. *L'Innommable* (Paris, 1953), p. 21.

[12] Buñuel, interviewed by Jean de Baroncelli in *Le Monde*, 16 December 1959, p.13, in answer to the question whether *Nazarin* represented a return to Christianity.

[13] R. Frost (Untitled), in *The Poetry of Robert Frost*, ed. E. C. Lathem (London, 1971), p. 428.

[14] *Iliad*, 1, 599.

[15] A twist on "Greek". Queneau invented the useful blend "pleurire".

[16] C. J. Ackerley, "'In the beginning was the pun': Samuel Beckett's *Murphy*", *AUMLA*, 55 (1981), p. 16.

[17] *Ibid.*, p. 19.

[18] R. Desnos, *Corps et biens* (Paris, 1930), p. 40.

[19] R. W. Emerson, *Collected Works*, vol. 1 (London, 1866), p. 290.

[20] W. H. Auden, "The Truest Poetry is the Most Feigning", *Collected Poems*, ed. E. Mendelson (London, 1994), p. 619.

[21] E. A. Poe, "Preface to Marginalia", in *Collected Works of Edgar Allan Poe*, ed. T. O. Mabbutt (Harvard UP, 1978-9), p. 1116.

[22] In Homer it is Odysseus who uses the moly to resist Circe's spells.

[23] I. Stravinsky, *The Poetics of Music* (OUP, 1947), p. 79.

[24] W. Empson, "The Beautiful Train", *Collected Poems* (London, 1977), p. 64.

[25] J. Arp, quoted in L. Peeters, *La Roulette aux mots* (Paris, 1975), p. 163.

[26] G. Craig, "The Voice of childhood and great age", *TLS*, 27/8/1982, p. 921.

[27] Even an author's self-translation can often be improved upon (a verb which also means to exaggerate...). "Sur le demi-qui-vive" in *Oh les beaux jours* breeds "on the semi-alert", whereas "keeping your weather-eye half-open" might have been better. Or not.

[28] S. Kierkegaard, *Repetition* (OUP, 1942), p. 27.

[29] G. Orwell, "The Art of Donald McGill", in *Collected Essays*, vol. 2 (London, 1970), p. 193.

[30] G. K. Chesterton, "Cockneys and their Jokes", in *All Things Considered* (London, 1908), p. 12.

[31] M. Muggeridge, *The Times*, 14/9/1953.

[32] R. Queneau, *Zazie dans le Métro* (Paris, 1959), *passim*.

[33] Quoted in D. Bair, *Samuel Beckett* (London, 1978), p. 275.

[34] *Voyage au bout de la nuit* (Paris, 1952), p. 335.

[35] L. - F. Céline, *Entretiens avec le professeur Y* (Paris, 1955), p. 102.

[36] One of Lamb's "Popular Fallacies", q.v. *The Essays of Elia*, (London, 1840), p. 353.

[37] The title of J. P. Stern's study of Lichtenberg.

[38] Montesquieu, "Mes Pensées", in *Œuvres complètes* (Paris, 1949), vol. 1., p. 1220.

[39] G. C. F. Bearn, "The Possibility of Puns: A Defense of Derrida", *Philosophy and Literature*, 19.2 (1995), pp. 331, 333 and 334.

[40] *The Individual Psychology of Alfred Adler*, eds. H. & R. Ansbacher (London, 1958), p. 252.

[41] G. Legman, *No Laughing Matter*, p. 16.

8. "Comparaison n'est pas raison": humour and simile in San-Antonio
Keith Foley

> Dard, c'est la joute amoureuse d'un poète avec
> les mots qui transmuent nos maux en fontaine
> de Jouvence d'où jaillissent, irrésistibles, des
> trouvailles diamantées, des surprises lubriques
>
> Bernard Haller

San-Antonio is both the pseudonym of Frédéric Dard and the name of his most famous literary creation. Between 1948 and 1955 Dard adopted a plethora of pseudonyms: Kaput, l'Ange Noir, F. D. Ricard, Max or Maxwell Beeting, Frederick Antony, Verne Goody, Cornel Milk and Frédéric Charles. The nom de plume San-Antonio appears for the first time in 1949 and could equally have been San Fernando or Dallas, as Dard himself explains:

> C'était la vogue des romans noirs, comme ceux de Peter Cheyney, et il me fallait un nom qui sonne américain. Alors j'ai étalé une carte des Etats-Unis sur ma table, j'ai fermé les yeux et j'ai posé le doigt au hasard. Et quand j'ai regardé, c'était San-Antonio. (*ELP*: 197)

Hereafter, the name of Dard will be used to refer to the author of the San-Antonio series, and that of San-Antonio to the eponymous hero, a crack *commissaire* of the Police Judiciaire, a consummate solver of crimes and seducer of women, a *fin limier* and *fin limeur*.

Dard's forte is the *roman policier*, a genre in which he is enormously prolific and successful. Dard is the principal Stakhanovite of the Fleuve Noir; rumour has it that a fire bucket lies beside his desk in case of ball-point meltdown. The inside cover of *T'assieds pas sur le compte-gouttes* (1996) lists 170 San-Antonio titles. The San-Antonio production-line yields on average four novels or a thousand pages a year; the phenomenal print-runs are a publisher's idea of paradise. The story-lines of this "littérature de gare revue et corrigée" vary from fairly straightforward detective story plots to incredibly convoluted and *rocambolesque* adventures, which take San-Antonio to the "quatre coins de l'Hexagone et du globe", and, in one of the novels, even into circumterrestrial orbit. This is a life-style to which our hero is eminently and temperamentally suited: "J'adore les voyages, c'est dans ma nature et mon horoscope" (*Rate*: 150). Seven or eight adventures down the line, the reader – this reader at least – finds it difficult to remember precise details of individual novels. One suspects, however, that that is the way Dard intends it to be, or at least that "il s'en ponce les pilates". The plot is merely a trampoline for our author to display his verbal gymnastics; for this Erno Rubik of the French language, text is largely pretext. Dard is what one might call a linguistically endodermic writer, getting below the skin of language, dissecting it, seeing what makes it tick, manipulating it for his own and his readers' delectation, and jolting the latter out of their linguistic passivity "bouquin faisant".

The Fleuve Noir for Dard is like the Severn Bore: all rush and no meander. The vertiginous speed at which the San-Antonio novels roll off the conveyor-belt means that the quality of the writing is patchy. Coruscating prose there is, and in abundance, but it would be an exaggeration to claim that each page is uniformly brilliant, each rift equally loaded with ore. Dard himself makes this point, perhaps a little too modestly:

> Cela me semble être de la littérature assez facile, assez lâchée, assez bâclée avec quelques éclairs et quelques fulgurances de l'esprit. Il faut bien écumer les San-Antonio, avant d'avoir le bon bouillon, il faut bien les filtrer.[1]

Because Dard fires off salvo upon salvo of verbal whiz-bangs of every conceivable variety, however, the problem in writing about his verbal humour lies in circumscribing an area of investigation.

He is, for example, a compulsive neologiser. The cover of the *Dictionnaire San-Antonio* (hereafter *DSA*) quotes Dard: "J'ai fait ma carrière avec un vocabulaire de 300 mots; tous les autres, je les ai inventés." The editors of this tome of 630 pages, which valiantly sets out to catalogue the x-300 neologisms in which the San-Antonio series is written, declare themselves unequal to the task. Dard's lexicographers are indeed rolling a greased stone of Sisyphus, as their preface makes clear:

> En dépit de toute notre attention, les relectures successives des romans ont révélé toujours de nouvelles "trouvailles", étrangement "oubliées" lors des lectures précédentes. Comme si l'oeuvre comportait plusieurs strates sédimentaires, et que notre travail de collecte se serait davantage apparenté à une fouille archéologique qu'à un examen littéraire. (*DSA*: 8).

This essay will therefore concentrate primarily upon filtering out one particular ingredient of the "bon bouillon", namely Dard's similes.

This choice is in part justified by the author's comments:

Je crois qu'ayant un goût forcené de la comparaison, c'est pour moi un véritable exercice, c'est une colle que je me pose. Quand j'écris et que j'arrive à: "Il était tremblant comme...", je me dis: "Là, il va falloir que tu trouves quelque chose qui fasse rire." Je me creuse la cervelle, je cherche... C'est une espèce de défi que je me lance. Il faut que je trouve quelque chose de drôle.[2]

For Dard, the word "simile" is an anagram of "I smile". When he does lapse into a time-honoured comparison, or proffers one through the mouth of one of his characters, he is quick to facetiously acknowledge his lack of originality: "Elle erre comme une âme en peine, lieucommunise Pinaude" ("Bertaga" in *DSA*). Although my principal focus will be upon Dard's similes and assimilated expressions of comparison and degree, certain other aspects of Dard's verbal invention (malapropisms, reconfigured clichés, etc.) which frequently form part of the fabric of his comparisons will also be considered in some detail.

Dard's similes are both innovative and inventive. He paints vivid word pictures for any and every situation or emotion, as in his descriptions of carefulness, implacable determination and surprise: "Je deviens plus prudent qu'un gars chargé de déminer une région" (*Pattes*: 55); "Berthoche s'avance sur lui comme un chasse-neige dans la tourmente" (*Moi*: 89); "Son menton pend comme la rallonge d'une table dont on a mal assuré la tirette" (*Eléphant*: 139). Incredulity and horror are present in equal measure in this account of the brother-in-law "tinkling" the ivories on what one must assume is a *piano à queue*: "On se regarde comme vous regardez votre soeur lorsque votre beau-frère se met brusquement à uriner dans le piano." (*Vacances*: 244) Dard is of course not alone in his use of colourful comparisons. Indeed, the telling simile forms part of the fabric of any vivid description, from cricket commentary to futuristic television sci-fi script: "a delivery that jumped like a goosed ballerina"; "thicker than the offspring of the village idiot and a TV weather girl."[3]

What distinguishes Dard in this context is firstly the volume and variety of his similes, and secondly his eschewing of the trite and the hackneyed. Whether he has read Saussure on the inherent conventionality of the signifier is open to conjecture. What is certain beyond a peradventure, however, is that he is very well aware of the "arbitraire du signe". Here he is talking about an embarrassed young man blushing to the roots of his hair:

Il devient instantanément cramoisi! Tu sais, la sublime image du gars encrustacé? Rouge comme: une écrevisse, un homard, une langouste. Et puis du gars fleuri? Rouge comme: une pivoine, un coquelicot. (*Con*: 88)

Virtually the entire panoply of comparators of *rouge* in standard French
is deployed in what closely resembles a hybrid between a sea-food menu
and a horticultural catalogue. The only surprise is that the words *au
choix* are not appended and that he fails to add the story "du gars qui se
met à poil dans son jardin pour faire rougir ses tomates". A similar
inventory is provided for the verb *bleuir*, although in this case the
comparators are a shade more original: "Il bleuit, pis qu'une platée
d'épinards frais. Qu'une pomme pas mûre. Qu'une émeraude. Qu'une
gueule d'académicien." (*Os*: 83)

Dard would appear to consider stock similes, and other lexically
fixed formulae for that matter, to be rather like a construction of Lego
bricks, in being capable of being taken apart and creatively reassembled.
Talking of the French equivalent of Saga Tours he comments upon a few
traditional stereotypes:

> Dans les voyages organisés, les vieux messieurs sont toujours infirmes ou gâteux
> alors que les vieilles se portent comme le pont Alexandre III.

The startled reader is referred to a footnote, which explains: "Je suis
pour une refonte des expressions toutes faites. C'est pourquoi je me
refuse à me référer au Pont-Neuf." (*Gala*: 594) Similarly, upon discovering that a woman (his mother) whom he had hitherto considered as being
of the strictest sexual morality was in fact rather more *horizontale* than
upstanding, he comments: "Je la croyais droite comme un 'I', mais
c'était un 'Y'". (*Vacances*: 362) Dard's similes are often amplified in
some way, although rarely in an overtly literary manner. Very occasionally he introduces a "literary" simile to show, one imagines, that he can
operate in this register should the spirit so move him:

> [une voiture] dont les chromes étincellent comme le couteau d'une guillotine
> dans l'embrasement de l'aurore; (*Gala*: 83)

> Un grand concours de peuple se presse sur le port. Ces gens sont crispés et
> silencieux. On dirait les habitants de l'île de Sein guettant le retour des morutiers.
> (*Rate*: 238)

Even in these instances there is a bathetic effect occasioned by the presence of a banal (*chromes*) or banaustic (*morutiers*) reference. Generally
speaking, the precious, self-consciously crafted literary simile is as rare
as a strip of mint Penny Blacks. Dard constantly derides the *beau
langage* and the pretensions of those he terms the *académiteux* (*Doigt*:
177), a class of writers who, in his estimation and in his rewriting of
péter plus haut que son cul, "poètent plus haut que leur luth" ("Poéter"
in *DSA*). Disparaging references to the Quai Conti are in fact so numer-

ous that one suspects that Dard doth protest too much. Might this iconoclast of the academic style harbour a secret desire to have one of the famous *fauteuils* dusted off for him?

The following pages attempt to describe the stylistic mechanisms by which Dard seeks to enhance the impact of his similes and assimilated expressions of comparison and degree. An initial example will serve to illustrate the premise that Dard always burns on gas mark 9. "Comme une vache qui regarde passer un train" is something of a commonplace. Dard transmutes what has become a banal expression, retaining *vache*, including the verbal phrase *échangeons des regards* to hark back to *regarder*, substitutes *TGV* for *train* and considerably extends the image, in the process imbuing the cattle with human attributes: "Nous échangeons des regards de vaches surprises par le retard du T.G.V. sur les plateaux bourguignons." (*Allez*: 85) No longer content to chew the cud and passively watch the trains go by, our bovine friends now ruminate on the timetable, wear anoraks and carry notebooks and flasks of coffee: sad cows, in fact, rather than mad cows.

One of the most common amplificatory techniques adopted by Dard consists in adding a relative clause to the head noun in the second part of a comparison. The relative clause frequently has a verb in the conditional mood to signal the hypothetical, if not objectively impossible nature of what follows, and invite a willing suspension of disbelief on the part of the reader: "Sa langue de ruminant pend par-dessus sa lèvre inférieure comme une otarie qui tenterait de se défenestrer" (*AZ*: 96); "Vous sucrez les fraises comme un centenaire qui se serait servi toute sa vie d'un marteau pneumatique" (*AZ*: 21). An individual blushing is not simply portrayed as being *rouge comme un homard* but

> Mon mec rougit comme un valeureux homard qui plongerait dans une marmite d'eau bouillante pour sauver une langouste en train de se noyer. (*Morgue*: 197)

The relative clause allows Dard to present an extravagant accumulation of detail. The improbable story of crustacean gallantry achieves its comic effect through the anthropomorphisation of its protagonists, the semantic isotopy of the clause being fractured by the juxtaposition of nouns properly designating the participating denizens of the deep (*homard, langouste*) and terms normally associated with human activities and attributes (*valeureux, plonger, sauver, se noyer*).

An obvious manifestation of Dard's amplificatory technique is the addition of a number, or other quantifier, in the second half of the simile. Given that a man may be *fort comme un taureau*, if he is "fort comme douze taureaux" (*Girafe*: 46) he is clearly in the Charles Atlas category, and likely to be serenely immune from having sand kicked in his face on the holiday beach. A large number of similes in which a cardinal number, or equivalent term, is inserted in a standard simile could be quoted. Let three suffice: "Lorsque je la laisse choir [following an amorous bout], elle est aussi flasque qu'une douzaine de limandes" (*Pattes*: 95); "Elle est jalmince comme douze tigresses" (*Girafe*: 26); "Condor est miraud comme deux taupes" (*Allez*: 241). Although this is perhaps the most basic of emphatic devices, even here standard simile is perhaps not the most appropriate description, for in cases such as these Dard tends to substitute an argotic synonym for the usual adjective or verb, hence *jalmince* for *jalouse* and *miraud* for *myope*.

The number used in comparisons of this kind is usually arbitrary, as in the following "limp", "bloody" and "pleasant" offerings:

Elle s'en va toute contente en claudiquant comme cent quatre-vingt-douze canards (*Joconde*: 437);

Il tend la bretelle à cinquante centimètres de sa valeureuse poitrine et la bretelle casse à la hauteur de la boucle. Il morfle celle-ci en plein pif et se met à saigner comme quinze gorets vautrés sur des lames de rasoir (*Votez*: 530);

Un gros dog allemand, sympa comme seize chaudes-pisses privées d'antibiotiques, erre sourdement par la propriété, cherchant l'emplacement où il défèquera plus tard. (*Doigt*: 33)

The only exception seems to be when the number has an extralinguistic cultural reference: "Il se recule, apeuré, comme si cent un dalmatiens lui montraient leurs crocs." (*Bosphore*: 18)

Where a set expression already includes a number, Dard either ensures that three-figure inflation sets in: "Moi, je suis comme quatre ronds de flan" (*Joconde*: 428); or, if he does retain the time-honoured number, he embroiders upon it like a hyperactive denizen of a Howarth rectory: "J'en reste comme les deux ronds de flan que vous n'avez pas bouffés le jour de votre crise de foie." (*Moi*: 72)[4] The number thirty-six, so common in standard French idioms (e.g. *voir trente-six chandelles, tous les trente-six du mois*), is also well represented in Dard's similes:

une riche héritière moche comme trente-six derrières de singe collés sur un bâton (*Sirop*: 32);

Furax, il file un shoot mammouthien dans le flanc du distributeur, lequel, sous l'impact, devient d'une folle prodigalité et se met à pisser comme trente-six vaches à la fois ("Emballage" in *DSA*).

A variation on the theme of adding a number comes when he uses a term indicating a great quantity or collection of the comparator as in the use of *tonneau*, *tribu* and *course* in the following: "Un type jeune, mince comme un toréador, et plus brun qu'un tonneau de goudron paraît. C'est Alonzo, le serveur" (*Sirop*: 45); "Alors, l'Ernest saute sur l'occase comme une tribu de morpions sur un pubis négligé" (*Sirop*: 45); "La noye s'est écoulée, lente comme une course d'escargots." (*Tueur*: 405) Metonymy is also employed to the same effect, as when *congrès politique* is used instead of a specific number of politicians:

> Sur la petite place jouxtant le commissariat, la pétanque fait rage. Bérurier vocifère comme un congrès politique en affirmant que Pistouflet est un arnaqueur. (*Sirop*: 211)

Moving from political congress to the sexual variety, the following metonymic simile brings *la petite mort* face to face with the grim reaper in person: "Elle râle comme un champ de bataille." (*Doigt*: 178) The determiner *tout* is often used in such comparisons: "Je suis plus baba que toute la devanture d'un pâtissier" (*Sirop*: 33); "Je me suis assis dans le bahut en bâillant comme toute une salle de conférence." (*Tueur*: 414) *Tout* is particularly productive when associated with the name of a country or area noted for a particular product or characteristic, a terminally tired and emotional individual being described as "beurré comme toute la Normandie" (*Moi*: 38) and a moderately attractive woman as "pas belle, pas laide, neutre comme toute la Suède" (*Joconde*: 477).

The pun is a well-whetted instrument in our author's toolbox. Dard considers punning to be a jubilatory celebration of the potential of his mother tongue:

> Il ne faut pas avoir honte de ses calembours car ils constituent une espèce d'hommage rendu à sa langue qui permet de telles distorsions. (*Lire*: 127)

He often tacks a pun on to a standard simile, almost as though in expiation for having had recourse to the well-trodden path of everyday idiom. Of a fabulously rich industrialist, our *calembourreau* observes: "On entre chez Bita comme dans un moulin. D'ailleurs n'est-ce pas une usine à blé." (*Sirop*: 179) He brings the same technique of the punning coda to similes of his own invention. In the same novel, a male secretary is depicted as being "bronzé comme une bouteille de Fernet-Branca", which is, as far as it goes, an apt enough description of a sun-tanned Adonis. Dard, however, affected at least as much by paronomania as Catherine the Great by nymphomania, uses the comparison as a spring-

board for a pun: "Le secrétaire est bronzé comme une bouteille de
Fernet-Branca; on dirait un secrétaire d'acajou." (*Sirop*: 86)

Many if not most French words exhibit multiple meaning, and the
language "s'en porte très bien". In Saussurean terms, *langue* sets up
potentially confusing polysemy while *parole* disambiguates it, which is
to say that language disambiguates via the context in which the word is
used. Polysemic and homophonic puns on the other hand depend for
their effect on a focusing of these parallel but distinct meanings upon a
single point. Puns, then, are converging lenses. Many standard similes
are based upon this semantic coalescence: *fin comme du gros sel, high
as a kite*, etc.

It goes without saying that Dard exploits these possibilities to
good effect. *Retourné* is used both in the sense of "emotionally upset"
and "physically overturned":

> Oui, il pleure, comme un petit môme, à gros sanglots, avec des hoquets, des
> reniflements, des coups de langue à droite et à gauche pour boire ses larmes et
> gober sa morve. J'en suis retourné comme une voiture de course un jour de
> verglas. (*Joconde*: 410)

Similarly, *rayonner* is employed in both its literal and figurative senses
of "to beam": "Elle [une femme heureuse] rayonne comme un miroir
soleil sur un mur tendu de velours noir." (*Moi*: 98) The polysemy of
tendu ("tense" and "outstretched") in the following simile produces a
double comparison allowing a sideswipe at the cupidity of the clergy:
"Depuis le départ de la jeune blonde, l'atmosphère s'est tendue comme la
main d'un mendiant à la sortie de la grand-messe (ou comme celle d'un
curé pendant)." (*Gala*: 531) Dard frequently uses the nouns *pastis, eau*
or a synonym thereof, plus the verb *se troubler*, to convey a feeling of
flustered consternation, and particularly in the context of sexual arousal:
"Elle se trouble comme un verre de pastis sous la pluie" (*Gala*: 260); "Je
la trouble comme la flotte trouble le pastis." (*Sirop*: 123)

As most of the gallery of San-Antonio's confederates and advers-
aries are "entre deux pastis" at least some of the time, in Dard's similes
metaphorical adjectives describing those who have over-partaken of the
dive bouteille are particularly susceptible to polysemic exploitation.
These "ivrognes invertébrés" (*Standinge*: 254) are variously characterised as being "blindé comme un porte-avions" (*Eléphant*: 149), "blindé
comme un char d'assaut" (*Morgue*: 169), "bourré comme le métro aux
heures de pointe" (*Gala*: 609), or "plus chargé qu'un canon de D.C.A.
pendant une alerte." (*Con*: 243) Moving from celebration to cerebration,

San-Antonio is proud of his mental agility and places his light squarely on top of the nearest bushel:

> J'ai l'avantage spectaculaire de posséder un cerveau en comparaison duquel celui de Blaise Pascal aurait ressemblé à de la mayonnaise tournée. (*Compte-gouttes*: 250)

Eating humble pie, accompanied by mayonnaise of any kind, is clearly not good for our hero's digestion.

San-Antonio frequently comments upon the rapidity and intensity of his thought-processes in similes which reveal at least a foundation knowledge of optics: "Je réfléchis comme un miroir à trois faces" (*Poulet*: 180); "Je réfléchis comme un miroir qu'on vexerait s'il n'était concave." (*Eléphant*: 180) Perhaps he is right to vaunt his mental prowess, for as Descartes' wife, the nurse, said when dressing a wound, "Je panse, donc j'essuie", and as the old *contrepèterie* has it, the difference between man and dog is that "l'homme réfléchit".

A particularly fine polysemically determined comparison alluding to a prisoner on death row is based on the literal and figurative meanings of *survolté* and *mettre au courant*, the excitement-level being stepped up with the voltage:

> En ce moment, les gars, j'sais pas si vous vous êtes rendu compte, mais je suis aussi survolté que le zig de Sing-Sing à qui on dit: "Asseyez-vous, on va vous mettre au courant!" (*Poulet*: 186)

Word-play based upon the literal and figurative senses of the adjective also characterises: "Son regard est aussi glacé qu'un wagon frigorifique" (*Sirop*: 19); "Ecoutez, mon vieux, fais-je d'un ton tellement tranchant qu'il me coupe les lèvres" (*Girafe*: 60),[5] while in the following image the same semantic trait (angularity) is at issue, although the collocates to which the adjective *anguleux* is applied are highly disparate: "C'est un type brun et maigre, anguleux comme une cathédrale gothique." (*Poulet*: 142)

In addition to exploiting the existing polysemy of a lexical item, Dard frequently semantically remotivates a word for his own purposes, thereby endowing it with two meanings, these being its dictionary meaning and one that, *se non è vero, è molto ben trovato*. A beautiful potential but unresponsive sexual conquest, for example, is described as "ce merveilleux produit de contrebande" (*Doigt*: 164).[6] The type of word-form particularly affected by his semantic tinkering is the parasynthetic derivative. Parasynthesis is the formation of a word by the simultaneous adjunction of both a prefix and a suffix to a base where no form exists with the base attached to a prefix or suffix alone, e.g. *dépigeonnisation*, based upon *pigeon*, where neither *dépigeonne* nor *pigeonnisation* are attested.[7] The parasynthetic *décontenancé* means "disconcerted", "crestfallen", "having lost one's composure", being derived from *contenance* in the sense of "bearing" or "attitude". *Contenance*, of course, also has the sense of "that which is contained" and "capacity". This being so, our author feels free to treat *décontenancé* in the same way as he treats genuinely polysemic terms: "Me voici plus décontenancé qu'un bidon de lait sans fond." (*Moi*: 72)[8] A further case of artificially attributed referentiality concerns a perplexed bovine, a "bewildebeast". Describing a somewhat shell-shocked individual Dard writes: "Il est étonné comme un boeuf qui serait remboursé" (*Joconde*: 476). The poor beast's stupefaction is attributable not to any advantageous financial restitution but to the return of what one might euphemistically refer to as its "bullhood", *boeuf* in animal husbandry technically designating a steer or castrated male. In the present state of veterinary surgery, the hypothetical conditional is particularly justified here.

Dard patently regards this reinterpretation as something of a *trouvaille*, as he sees fit to employ it elsewhere: "une voix fluette d'eunuque qu'on n'a pas remboursé." (*Poulet*: 166) "Shaken but not stirred", a famous fictional husband figures in: "Il restait aussi inébranlable que le mari de lady Chatterley" (*Lire*: 127), in which *inébranlable* is reanalysed in terms of *branler* rather than *ébranler*. (It may be noted in parenthesis that San-Antonio is an anagram of "O! an onanist".) Another specimen *de la même farine* concerns a dusky miller's ablutions: "Il se rembrunit comme un meunier nègre qui vient de faire sa toilette" (*Girafe*: 98); while: "Je me sentais aussi déprimé qu'un cachet d'aspirine dans un verre d'eau chaude" (*Pattes*: 15) involves the remotivation of the adjective *déprimé* by analogy with the substantive *comprimé*.

A compelling case could be made for Dard's novels being preceded by a warning sign similar to those seen at level crossings: "Attention, une connerie peut en cacher une autre!" This would be appropriate in the case of: "Je le bigle droit dans les cocards et je constate que ses yeux se dérobent comme une strip-teaseuse." (*Votez*: 620) As though the idiosyncratic remotivation of *se dérober* in terms of ecdysis were not enough, our "asidophone" detective adds: "Tiens, tiens! me dis-je en aparté, car je parle couramment cette langue." A consummate "blague-ard", Dard never lets an opportunity slip to cram in yet another pun, for as he once said in anticlerical mode: "Il faut battre le frère pendant qu'il est chauve." (*Lire*: 127) In his more indulgent moods he feels the need to come to our rescue with a helpful gloss on his quips, as when he describes a disappointed *quidam* – a *quimonsieur* as it happens – as being "Désappointé comme un employé en chômage" (*Moi*: 36); the footnote elucidates: "Etant en chômage, il n'est plus appointé." Dard is often affected (afflicted) by an irresistible urge to provide philological commentaries on his neologisms, to parodically justify himself in case we should find ourselves at neologgerheads with him. A ship sailing in the Pacific carrying an atom bomb will serve to illustrate this *cacoethes explicandi*: "Le commandant Kelbelburn donna l'ordre de débarquer la bombe atomique et de l'encorailler." (*Rate*: 265) A mock-serious self-exegetic footnote asserts with something of the authority of the dictionary committee of the *Immortels*:

> Le verbe enterrer ne pouvait convenir, un atoll se composant exclusivement de corail; d'où le néologisme "encorailler" que nous approuvons sans réserves.

A subset of Dard's invented polysemy consists of punning allusions to the names of real people. In Dard's scheme of things the existence of people whose names are homophonous with inflections of the verbs *verdir* "to go green" and *piaffer* "to be impatient" ineluctably leads him to draw several conclusions. Firstly, it is manifestly obvious to him that Giuseppe Verdi was more than a little green around the gills: "Elle verdit comme le compositeur du même nom." (*Gala*: 617)[9] Secondly, the little sparrow was a rather impatient bird: "Je piaffe autant qu'Edith" (*Poulet*: 232); which possibly explains why she was always saying "Allez, venez!" A geographical variation on this onomastic device is: "Question majeure comme le lac du même nom" (*OC*, *passim*). Although these examples are mildly amusing, they lack a point. The homophony of *miro* (short-sighted) and the name of Joan Miró, however, gives rise to a particularly telling *boutade*, in that visual acuity is, for traditionalists at least, a *sine qua non* of painting. On a good day the Catalan surrealist was apparently lucky if he could see the brush in front of his face, which disability, Dard tacitly suggests, might explain some of his paintings: "Il perd ses lunettes... Le v'là plus miro que le peintre du même nom." (*Vacances*: 290)

In a similar vein, if San-Antonio proffers a compliment, he is either "galant comme un général en retraite" (*Sirop*: 196), or, more likely, "galant comme le Vert" (*Morgue*: 208), an obvious disjunction of Henri IV's sobriquet *le vert galant*.[10] Dard describes an elderly lab rat (the appropriately named Professor E. Prouvette) using both of his left feet to dance the tango[11] with a ravishing young lady, the beautiful

Antigone: "La petite Antigone est maintenant dans les bras du Professor E. Prouvette, lequel danse comme un plat d'Anouilh." (*Joconde*: 395) The serendipitous paronymity of *de nouilles* and *d'Anouilh* is sufficient to elicit the name of the author of *Antigone*. Indeed such literary allusions are usually engendered by fortuitous similarity of sound, although occasionally it is possible to glimpse what Dard feels about the work of a given author, as in this description of a detumescent penis:

> Il se dresse, la biroute au vent, dodelinante comme une tête de tortue de mer à laquelle on lit un texte de M. Robbe-Grillet. ("Têtes" in *DSA*)

Literary allusions abound in Dard's similes and form part of what he calls his "marotte du clin d'oeil", which he explains in these terms:

> Me sachant lu par nombre d'intellectuels, j'éprouve de temps en temps le besoin d'établir une complicité, de leur montrer que je ne les oublie pas, qu'on est quand même un peu entre nous, aussi! C'est une façon de garder le contact.[12]

These allusions often do not redound to the greater glory of the individual named: "une carpette dont la trame est aussi grosse que celle d'une pièce de Labiche." (*Morgue*: 98) Meanwhile allusions to well-known lines and incidents abound. References to Pascal, Hugo, Verlaine and Tirso de Molina *et al.* provide a typical sample: "La façon dont elle a culbuté mes deux gorilles en dit long comme le nez de Cléopâtre sur ses capacités" (*Rate*: 243); "C'est beau, hein? fais-je en découvrant l'horizon d'un geste aussi auguste que celui du semeur" (*Sirop*: 157); "Marie-Louise éclate en sanglots longs, exactement comme les violons de l'automne" (*Princesse*: 118); "Il se dresse, beau Sana, comme la statue du Commandeur." (*Doigt*: 69) God, rumour has it, hates ingratitude, and Dard, mindful of the injunction *Il ne faut jamais dire: Fontaine, je ne boirai pas de ton eau*, alludes to the great *homme affable* himself: "J'ouvre un bec large comme celui du corbeau qui paumait son camembert pour pousser sa tyrolienne au renard." (*Girafe*: 65)[13]

Although literary figures hold pride of place in Dard's similes, people from all "airts and pairts" are pressed into service. This description of fetid post-prandial breath depends upon the metaphorical association between *ail* and lesbianism in French (cf. *marchande d'ail*, *vendre de l'ail*, etc.), and the name of Suzy Solidor, lesbian singer of the 1930s: "Le digne flic pue l'ail comme un qui aurait becté Suzy Solidor avec l'ailloli." (*Sirop*: 81) One would have to travel a long way to find a better image of violation than: "Dégâts considérables. Ça se voyait comme un chancre mou sur le visage de Sophia Loren." (*AZ*: 19) Historical figures loom relatively large, as in this use of the name of the assassin of Henri

IV to evoke feelings of horror and disbelief: "Il a un haut-le-corps et me regarde exactement comme si j'étais la réincarnation de Ravaillac." (*Pattes*: 101) The ludicrous nature of the proposition contained in the vehicle of the comparison provides the bathetic key to: "Je fais claquer mes doigts comme quelqu'un qui vient de se rappeler le prénom de Louis XIV." (*Poulet*: 213) San-Antonio laments the apparent death in action of his *fidus Achates* Bérurier, with a reference to Roland's sword: "Oui, lui, le roc, le mammouth, l'invincible. Lui dont le lard est mieux trempé que l'acier de Durandal, le voilà qui gît sur la moquette de Nini." (*Moi*: 63) Napoleon's characteristic stance is commented upon:

> Napoléon gardait la main dans son gilet parce qu'il souffrait de l'estomac. Rendons grâces à Dieu qu'il n'ait pas eu de maladie vénérienne.

The polysemy of *état*, *sacrer* and *à plat* lies at the heart of: "Elle est dans tous ses états, comme Charles Quint" (*Sirop*: 120); "Je sacre comme Jeanne d'Arc à Reims" (*Morgue*: 123); "Ma mémoire reste aussi à plat que l'électroencéphalogramme de Louis XVI" (*Allez*: 33), an ECG presumably best examined *à tête reposée*.

But "l'histoire se corse" ("chef-lieu Ajaccio", adds Dard *passim*), as there are also seats on the tumbril reserved for twentieth-century public figures. Anatomical distinguishing features form the basis of most of these comparisons. Perhaps taking his cue from Winston Churchill who, in the language of Vaugelas and the style of La Palisse, is reputed to have reflected, "Quand je regarde mon derrière, je vois qu'il est divisé en deux grandes parties", San-Antonio announces his astonishment with: "Je fis des yeux gros comme le cul du chancelier Kohl." (*Dégustez*: 116) With a liberal dash of Windsor sauce Dard has recourse to another famous fundament to provide a colour comparison: "Je coupe! L'écran redevient d'un blanc laiteux, comme le cul de la reine d'Angleterre" (*Allez*: 26): the *anus horribilis* revisited?

Antithetical similes form part of the ironist's arsenal in the standard language, "bronzé comme un cachet d'aspirine", "adroit comme un cochon de sa queue", "fin comme du gros sel" springing immediately to mind. With their juxtaposition of two contradictory elements they have an almost oxymoronic quality. Dard also frequently uses similes in which the adjective is used in a sense opposite to that of its normal use. Some of his antiphrastic contributions have a surrealistic flavour, as in this description of San-Antonio dancing with a partner somewhat less gifted than Ginger Rogers: "Je me sens aussi à l'aise, flanqué de cette cavalière, qu'un scaphandrier à cheval sur un pur-sang." (*Girafe*: 84)

Others rely upon word-play for their humorous impact, as in the following punning triple reference to officers of the law: "Son regard est aussi aimable que celui d'un gardien de la paix visionnant un film sur la traite des vaches à peau lisse." (*Trinquer*: 283) Still others are reworkings of standard comparisons, the usual simile providing the starting point for the transition from *koine* to coinage. "Comme un éléphant dans un magasin de porcelaine", for example, no doubt provides the model for the verbally innovative:

> Les regards qui se posent sur moi sont aussi bienveillants que ceux qu'un marchand de porcelaines accorde à un monôme d'étudiants déboulant dans sa boutique. (*Moi*: 19)

To provide terms of comparison for a high proportion of these similes delivered with reverse swing, Dard delves into his contradictionary for expressions relating to disease, physical decay and death: "La porte du labo s'ouvre et trois messieurs aussi sympathiques qu'une épidémie de peste bubonique font irruption" (*Gala*: 623); "L'interpellé lui file un zoeil aussi sympa qu'un crachat de phtisique galopant" (*Os*: 40); "Le lieu est aussi marrant qu'un dispensaire centrafricain pendant une épidémie de choléra baveux" (*Compte-gouttes*: 288); "Il est aussi sympathique qu'une plaque d'eczéma" (*Sirop*: 147); "Je le trouve au bord d'une piscaille de six mètres sur trois, ragoûtant comme la résultante d'une diarrhée intempestive" (*Compte-gouttes*: 233); "[...] deux méchantes ogresses aux cheveux tirés. Aussi sympas que la mort des forêts" (*Dégustez*: 148); "un drôle de déjeté, beau comme un caveau de famille" (*Sirop*: 20); "un regard aussi frais que des reliefs de poissons dans une poubelle" (*Eléphant*: 95); "Pinaud, à poil, se pointe, beau comme la carcasse d'un poulet de pays sous-développé." (*Allez*: 129) This is clearly a universal tendency: *Coronation Street*'s Jack Duckworth, for example, was heard to say recently, "That's about as funny as a trip to the chest clinic", moreover, in common with Baudelaire and government abattoir inspectors, Dard seems to have an obsession with the spleen: "En me voyant entrer, elle a l'air aussi joyce que si on l'opérait de la rate sans l'endormir." (*Sirop*: 213) Indeed, one of his novels bears the intriguing title of *La rate au court-bouillon*, a dish probably best avoided in these days of BSE. Béru, needless to say, mixes up his *torchon-rat* with his *serviette-rate* in: "Il fonçait comme un dératisé." (*Bouge*: 124)

It might be allowed that there has been a modicum of ludicrous exaggeration in the extracts quoted so far. The following comparisons rely almost totally for their comic force on hyperbole. The etymological root of this word is the Greek *hyperballein*, "to throw beyond"; that which is hyperbolic is thus thrown beyond the usual mark, or over-pitched, and a typical San-Antonio novel contains a fair quota of such full tosses, beamers and bean-balls. A stunningly beautiful woman is portrayed in these terms: "A côté d'elle, la plus fabuleuse vedette d'Hollywood ressemblerait à une exploreuse de poubelles." (*Rate*: 228) In another "mighty fallen" comparison, San-Antonio shows a neat turn of phrase to comment upon his own electrifying turn of speed: "Je sprinte derrière le gars... Et quand je sprinte, Mimoum ressemble à un cul-de-jatte qui aurait des engelures." (*Sirop*: 131) San-Antonio uses a similar formula to speak of his swimming prowess: "Je saute dans la tisane et je produis mon crawl à côté duquel celui de Mosconi ressemble aux exercices de rééducation d'un hémiplégique." (*Sirop*: 22) When the telephone rings at an inopportune moment, San-Antonio complains: "Le biniou se met à carillonner comme la corne de brume d'un port breton un jour de grosse tempête." (*Joconde*: 395) A particularly outlandish simile involves a shipping magnate and San-Antonio's "supérieur rachitique" (*Béru dixit, passim*): "L'armateur bondit sur le Dirlo comme un jaguar sur le dos d'un phacochère" (*Vacances*: 190). This simile is "outlandish" in several senses for, as Dard explains in a footnote: "Ce qui représente un foutu bond, vu que le phacochère [warthog] vit en Afrique et le jaguar en Amérique du Sud."

When Dard is on hyperbolic steroids, the overblown comparison may be engineered by an extravagant accumulation of detail. A simple case is provided by: "C'était quoi? demande Véra d'une voix plus blanche que le Nord Canada un soir de Noël patronné par Omo" (*Bouge*: 117), in which the figurative use of *blanc* is reinforced by successive references to *blanc* in its literal sense. A heaper of Pelion upon Ossa, Dard is the literary equivalent of that annoying person who, if you say to him "I've got a white cat", always claims to have a whiter one. A more extreme illustration is provided by the guinea-fowl or, to be more specific, the female of the species, the guinea-hen. It is in the nature of the guinea-hen to cluck. When Mistress Guinea-Fowl has a cold she clucks even more. When she has a cold and Mr Guinea-Fowl suggests what might be euphemistically termed a quick drumstick over, she goes cluck-ing mad: "La vioque glousse comme une pintade enrhumée à laquelle monsieur pintade proposerait une partie de plumes retroussées" (*Gones*: 46); the alliteration of the voiceless bilabial plosives is no doubt intended to render onomatopoeically the squawking of the flattered fowl. Meanwhile the reverse of the coin of hyperbole is litotes, as in this description of a woman of more than ample proportions: "une madame à peine plus grosse qu'une vache sur le point de vêler." (*Gala*: 520)

Thus far Dard's similes have been analysable in terms of the meaning of the words used, however *tiré par les cheveux* the perceived resemblance between the entities compared may be. Less commonly he will also indulge in comparisons even more *capillotracté*, in which such meaning as there is is to be inferred from the phonic substance of the syntagmatic chain at least as much as from the sense of the individual constituent words. A series of phonetic approximations reinforce the comparison and Dard here demonstrates a childlike enjoyment in the concatenation of strings of similar sounds, his similes being ludic rather than lucid. The verb *se gondoler* with its two senses of to warp and to laugh, the second meaning presumably being derived from the first (cf. *se tordre de rire – curled up*), is used in just such a comparison: "Il se gondole comme un Vénitien qui mangerait des biscuits Gondolo sous de la tôle ondulée." (*Gala*: 551) Here a crescendo of sounds (nothing is diminuendo in the world of San-Antonio) is intended to convey an impression of terminal corrugation. By its form *se gondoler* evokes Venice and its gondolas together with the (real? invented?) brand name *Gondolo*, while corrugated iron is warped in shape, and its denomination *tôle ondulée* also presents a serendipitous sonority which concludes the sound chain of liquids and rounded nasal vowels. A similar example is based on the stock simile "souffler comme un phoque", that is to puff and blow, or to blow like a grampus: "Béru souffle comme un phoque qui viendrait de gagner le gros lot à l'otarie nationale." (*Morgue*: 26) The presence of *phoque* elicits *otarie*, which in turn attracts the paronymic play between *l'otarie nationale* and *loterie nationale*, with, for good assonantial measure, a verbal echo and semantic ricochet in *le gros lot*.

San-Antonio has a larger than life henchman, a redoubtable butcher of villains and the French language, one Alexandre-Benoît Bérurier, alias Béru, Le Gros, Le Mastard, le Frère-Jean-des-Entonnoirs-de-la-Police, l'Homme qui baise plus vite que son ombre, plus a myriad other *noms de guerre*. The reader quickly realises that this man-mountain is none other than Sheridan's Mrs Malaprop[14] reincarnated "en chair et en graisse" and draped in the tricolor.

Béru is an extremely corpulent individual, whose snout is seldom out of the trough and in whose conversation the topic of food is something of a recurring decimal. On one occasion his Gargantuan appetite leads him to start talking, apparently inexplicably, about Indians and Incas:

Il va bientôt êt' l'heur de la jaffe, Antoine. Je pense qu'on d'vrait retourner à l'auberge, moi et Violette, on t'ramènererait [sic] un indien. - Un indien?!?! - J'veux dire un inca ("Bal" in *DSA*).

Our trencherman's *en-cas* would feed a family of four normally constituted people for a week, or Helmut Kohl for two days.

Instances of Béru's ludicrous misuse of words are legion, or *lésion*, as he would probably say. In Béru's barbarous idiolect Ravel composed "le beau vélo" (*Morgue*: 18), motorists go down "rues agaçantes" (*Standinge*: 285), rabbis perform "circonscriptions" (*Standinge*: 105), top chefs deploy their "dons enculinaires" (*Con*: 49) when inviting their guests to "prendre la crème à Hyères" (*Béru*: 213), office workers dream of holiday seas "couleur d'hémorroïde" ("Gala" in *DSA*), compatible souls "s'entendent comme lardons en poire" (*Cochons*: 85), faddy eaters are "algébriques aux sardines" (*Morgue*: 154), hypochondriacs run to their doctors for "quétcheups" (*Béru*: 25) concerned about their "tactique hardie" ("Mange" in *DSA*) and worried about their "tête-en-os" ("Queue" in *DSA*), family historians delve into their "arbres gynécologiques" ("Plaisir" in *DSA*), burglars, even of the non-smoking persuasion, leave their "empreintes de gitanes" (*Cochons*: 68) at the scene of their crime, heavy sleepers are found "dans les bras de l'orfèvre" (*Votez*: 594), orators "balancent des harengs à la foule" (*Cochons*: 136) in a resonant "voix de centaure" (*Eléphant*: 96) and at a high level of "jézabels" (*Doigt*: 188), fornicators are caught "en flagrant du lit" (*Standinge*: 107), utter "des cris d'or vrai" (*Sirop*: 121) and catch "des maladies vénitiennes" (*Standinge*: 240), scapegoats are "têtes de truc" (*Eléphant*: 52) or, in the case of senior policemen, "boucs commissaires." (*Eléphant*: 52) In short, wayward words are Bérurier's "violon d'inde" (*Standinge*: 246) and "lycée de Versailles" (*Morgue*: 97). Alexandre-Benoît Bérurier could go fifteen rounds with the French language and leave it bruised and bleeding.[15]

Similar lexical improprieties also find their way into Béru's similes: "Le frangin à Marysca s'est pointé, fier comme bar-tabac" (*Gones*: 132); "fier comme Barre-Chaban" ("Fête" in *DSA*). Béru is not alone in not having read La Calprenède's *Cléopâtre* and has reinterpreted the name of the hero Artaban, whose vanity was proverbial, in terms commercial and political with which he is more familiar. As with so much else in the *style san-antonien*, Béruspeak enables Dard to keep his readers *en état d'alerte* like Henry VIII "avec ses six reines" (*Lire*: 127). He implicitly challenges his readers to decode his paronymic perversions and establishes a complicitous superiority with them once the lexical solecism has been corrected.

Dard is also in the business of taking *syntagmes figés* (congealed phrases) and loosening them up a little, as here when San-Antonio alludes to his own strikingly handsome appearance: "Je me débats comme un beau diable, comme un très beau diable." (*Moi*: 57) He takes the gallicism *en dire long sur* and expands it with a tail almost as long as an England batting order: "Iachev a un sourire qui veut en dire long comme l'article de fond du Figaro" (*Morgue*: 133).[16] He rings the changes on the terms of this basic comparison with the fervour of a demented Quasimodo:

> Vendre le Mer d'Alors! [a boat] répète le Vieux en me coulant un regard qui en dit long comme un pensionnat de serpents en promenade; (*Vacances*: 237)

> Montrez la permission à ce vaillant jeune homme, grand-père! ordonné-je à Sam Gratte en ponctuant d'une oeillade qui lui en apprend long comme la voie du transsibérien sur mes intentions; (*Eléphant*: 233)

> On go to bed? - Elle n'est pas contre, mais elle a un regard à mon larfeuille qui en dit long comme une rame de métro sur son désintéressement. (*Pattes*: 50)

More typically, Dard takes the constituent elements of a set phrase and rearranges them like furniture in a room. He inverts the first two terms of the proverb *Coeur qui soupire n'a pas ce qu'il désire* to produce: "Elle soupire comme un coeur qui n'a pas ce qu'il désire." (*Morgue*: 95)[17] Similarly he reverses the terms of the idiom *se jeter sur qch/qn comme la vérole sur le bas clergé (espagnol/breton)* (to descend on something/somebody like a swarm of locusts), generating: "Je me jette sur l'article comme le clergé sur l'Ave Rol." (*Girafe*: 50)[18] He also fills semantic templates with terms of his own choosing. The most fecund of such matrices is perhaps the Rhett Butleresque expression *Je m'en moque comme de la ma première chemise/comme de ma première culotte*. With the occasional exception (e.g. "Je m'en moque comme de l'an 40") the term of comparison in these depreciative similes is usually an item of clothing. Other authors vary the discarded item of clothing: e.g. "comme de ma première babouche/comme de ma première paire de socquettes/comme de mon premier babygro", etc.[19] San-Antonio opts for a warm *pelisse*, which will preserve him from the chill north wind, if not from what one might call the clap trap. Speaking of a stolen diamond, he exclaims: "Je m'en moque comme de ma première chaude pelisse." (*Gones*: 127)[20]

Dard pursues the theme of clothing, or rather the strategic lack of it, in: "Barbara s'en soucie comme de son premier décolleté au-dessous du nombril." (*Doigt*: 165) He also makes free with set expressions other than similes, often modifying the idiom by replacing one of its canonical terms with a word deemed better fitted to the circumstances of the plot. One is reminded of the classic story of the customer who takes a torn pair of trousers into a tailor's shop in ancient Athens: "Euripides!" exclaims the tailor; "Eumenides!" replies the customer. The arts of writing as practised by Dard, and of tailoring as generally practised, are sister disciplines in that terms such as "fitting", "cutting" and "expanding" apply equally to both: the San-Antonio series is the Saville Row of bespoke idioms. Referring to a one-eyed man, San-Antonio says in just such a fashion: "Hier je l'ai interviewé entre trois yeux."[21] In another bespoke idiom the expression *bâiller à s'en décrocher la mâchoire* (to yawn one's head off) is tampered with when San-Antonio rings up the hotel switchboard operator in the middle of the night: "Elle me dit: 'Alla' au lieu de 'Allô' parce qu'elle bâille à s'en décrocher le standard." (*Votez*: 562) To follow another car is "emboîter le pneu à quelqu'un" (*Sirop*: 156), while to follow suit when somebody laughs is "emboîter le rire à quelqu'un." (*Sirop*: 75) Explaining his lack of knowledge of matters halieutic, San-Antonio confesses: "Je ne m'y connais pas des masses en poisson, moi. Sorti du brochet, de la truite et du goujon, je donne ma langue au poisson-chat!" (*Rate*: 172) Of an inveterate hypochondriac, he observes:

> Ce qui le botterait, ce serait que sa rate se mette à distiller du mercure, par exemple, ou bien son foie de l'ambre, comme l'intestin des cachalots. Bref, il voudrait être un cas, un vrai, intéressant jusqu'à la mort et ensuite inventorié de fondement en comble pour le salut de l'humanité inquiète. (*Standinge*: 125)

Relating a difference of opinion between two diners who cannot agree on the choice of a bottle, he writes: "A la fin, ils décident de faire cave à part. Ils se regardent en tastevins de faïence!" (*Vacances*: 146) Murky water is described by the substitution of *encre* for its homophone in the verbal locution *jeter l'ancre*: "L'eau est noirâtre comme si cent seiches venaient de jeter l'encre." (*Bouge*: 120) Of a private detective with ideas above his station San-Antonio opines: "L'adultère n'est pas son bidet de bataille. Il essaie de mijoter de la vraie policerie, lui." (*Vacances*: 230)[22] Doctored idioms such as the above can clearly only work if the element substituted in the *expression consacrée* – and here we are probably talking about desecrated idioms – is in some way applicable to the new situation alluded to. The opposition between *mâchoire/standard*, *pas/pneu/rire*, *chat/poisson-chat*, *fond/fondement*, *bande/cave*, *ancre/encre*, *chien/tastevin*, *cheval/bidet* fulfil this criterion. The case of *cheval/bidet de travail* is particularly effective in that *bidet* designates both a horse and the instrument of personal hygiene which stands in a metonymic relation of spatiotemporal contiguity with the act of adultery.

Weather expressions often provide Dard with images to distort into what one might tautologically name idiosyncratic idioms, *Il fait un temps à ne pas mettre un chien dehors* being subjacent to "Il fait un soleil à ne pas mettre une motte de beurre dehors" (*AZ*: 55). A particularly fine neo-meteorological idiom is based upon the expression *Il fait un vent à décorner un boeuf.* In weather apparently roaring in from the forties, Bérurier walks into a bar and remarks conversationally: "Il fait un vent à décorner un gendarme." (*Votez*: 566) One of the company, a certain Morbleut and *gendarme de son état*, objects:

> Dites donc, je n'apprécie pas beaucoup ce genre de plaisanterie! [la boutade lui monte au nez, perhaps] Mme Morbleut a toujours eu une vie privée irréprochable. (*ibid.*)

The cuckold as the butt of sarcasm is of course plurimillennial as a literary topos: elsewhere in a bespoke idiom Dard refers to: "L'époux! The mari! Mister Cocu, en cornes et en os!" (*Compte-gouttes*: 131)[23] The same type of lexical legerdemain occasionally operates at the level of the individual word: "Elle se remblondit (vu qu'elle est blonde elle ne peut pas se rembrunir, hein?)." (*Rate*: 146) With a half Nelson here and a Chinese burn there, Dard is a past-master at pulling an idiom out of shape; a poker he'll transform into a corkscrew, a yard of pump water into a cascade of ringlets.

But "revenons à nos poulets". The similes examined thus far are based upon adjectives or verbs. A further type of simile consists in bringing together two unrelated concepts expressed by nouns and explicitly establishing a link between them. Dylan Thomas says somewhere that "comparing one thing with another is like comparing Milton to Stilton". Dard, as might be imagined, is an exponent of the art of comparing Emile Zola to Gorgonzola, D'Alembert to Camembert, Diderot to Livarot, Georges Perec to Pont-l'Evêque and La Bruyère to Gruyère.[24] These love-is-like-a-butterfly comparisons are invariably sententious in tone, and give the impression of distilling the fruits of the author's reflection as though they were eternal verities. Dard has epigrammatic *mots d'auteur* on most aspects of life, which he looses off from his well-oiled maxim-gun: "La vérité, c'est comme un bouton de col, on finit toujours par mettre la main dessus, à condition de ne pas s'énerver" (*Joconde*: 497); "La peine, c'est comme la fidélité, le temps de l'apprécier et elle a foutu le camp" (*Joconde*: 484); "Rien de telle que les larmes pour vous décontracter. Les larmes, c'est comme les crevettes grises: plus elles sont salées, meilleures elles sont pour la santé." The subtleties of the English language are also memorably and scatologically commented upon: "L'anglais c'est comme le cassoulet toulousain: ça vous échappe." (*Polka*: 414)

Whatever Dard's feelings may be about the English language, it is certain that he has conducted a protracted love affair with French in all of its registers and guises. In spite of the sophistication of some of his linguistic flights of fancy, it is often the simplest and most puerile lines that appeal most. In one story San-Antonio finds himself constrained to haul a boat along a towpath and observes: "Je me mets à hâler – Comment hâlez-vous?" He has an etymologist's fascination for sound and sense (some would say the unsound and the nonsensical), and he takes pleasure in confronting the literal and figurative meanings of a word or phrase. Take the expression *il n'y a pas le feu* (there's no hurry). In one episode people are trapped inside a burning building. In her panic a woman shouts "Au feu!" five or six times and starts to jostle San-Antonio during her attempt to escape. Annoyed, San-Antonio retorts: "Oh, ta gueule! On sait qu'il y a le feu. Bouscule pas, y a pas le feu." (*Doigt*: 182) In argot the term *congre* is sometimes used as a false euphemism for *con*. There is an episode in which our hero dons wet-suit, flippers and oxygen bottle, and, in Jacques Cousteau's immortal words, "plunges into the murky depths" in the furtherance of his investigations. No sooner is he *à palme-d'oeuvre* than he is chased by an adversary armed with a harpoon gun. San-Antonio, who has an eye for aqueous humour, observes:

> J'ai déjà essuyé des balles, mais la perspective d'être traversé par un harpon me rend tout chagrin. C'est jamais marrant d'être pris pour un congre. (*Rate*: 212)

Some of the techniques Dard uses to turn the stock simile into the *bon bouillon* have been briefly reviewed, yet we have, as the unscrupulous bowler protested, only scratched the surface. By picking away at the linguistic semes of one aspect of Dard's humour, one runs the risk of doing our author less than justice. There is more to Beethoven than the Fifth Symphony and there are more sides to Dard's verbal humour than a 50 pence piece. Puns,[25] *à-peu-près*,[26] malapropisms, bespoke idioms, catachresis,[27] spoonerisms, riddles, the deliberate juxtaposition of collocates from widely differing semantic fields,[28] *tuyaux de pipes*,[29] pseudo-neo-classical compounds,[30] syllabic metanalysis[31] and assorted other *sananoniaiseries* flow from the pen of this *obsédé textuel* as steady as ticks from a clock. Dard has been variously compared to Céline, Queneau, Rabelais, Prévert, Vian and Cohen, but as a juggler of linguistic forms he is essentially *sui generis*. For those as yet unacquainted with Dard and his crack detective, perhaps the best thing to do is to pick up a San-Antonio from a station bookstall. *Sans crier Dard*, of course.

Abbreviations:

The following are all novels signed San-Antonio by Frédéric Dard and published by Fleuve Noir. The letters OC plus Roman numeral indicate the volume of the *Oeuvres complètes* where the novel has been referred to in this form.

Allez: *Allez donc faire ça plus loin*, 1993.
AZ: *De A jusqu'à Z...*, 1961.
Bal: *Au bal des rombières*, 1990.
Bertaga: *Viva Bertaga!*, 1968.
Béru: *Béru-Béru*, 1970,
Bosphore: *Bosphore et fais reluire*, 1991.
Bouge: *Bouge ton pied que je voie la mer*, 1982.
Clefs: *Les Clefs du pouvoir sont dans la boîte à gants*, 1981.
Cochons: *Les Cochons sont lâches*, 1991.
Compte-gouttes: *T'assieds pas sur le compte-gouttes*, 1996.
Con: *Les Con*, 1973.
Dégustez: *Dégustez, gourmandes!*, 1985.
Doigt: *Mets ton doigt où j'ai mon doigt*, 1974.
Eléphant: *Un Eléphant, ça trompe*, 1968.
Emballage: *Emballage cadeau*, 1971.
Fête: *La Fête des paires*, 1986.
Gala: *Le Gala des emplumés*, 1963 (OC, V).
Girafe: *En peignant la girafe*, 1963 (OC, II).
Gones: *San-Antonio chez les "gones"*, 1962 (OC, V).
Joconde: *Passez-moi la Joconde*, 1954 (OC, I).
Mange: *Mange et tais-toi*, 1966.
Moi: *Moi, vous me connaissez?*, 1971.
Morgue: *Entre la vie et la morgue*, 1959.
Os: *Un Os dans la noce*, 1974.
Pattes: *Bas les pattes!*, 1954.
Plaisir: *Tout le plaisir est pour moi*, 1959.
Polka: *San-Antonio polka*, 1963 (OC, V).
Poulet: *Du Poulet au menu*, 1958 (OC, V).

Princesse: *Aux Frais de la princesse*, 1993.
Queue: *Si "Queue d'âne" m'était conté*, 1976.
Rate: *La Rate au court-bouillon*, 1965 (OC, I).
Sirop: *Du Sirop pour les guêpes*, 1960.
Standinge: *Le Standinge selon Bérurier,* 1995.
Tête: *Têtes et sacs de noeuds*, 1991.
Trinquer: *Tu vas trinquer, San-Antonio*, 1958.
Tueur: *Un tueur kaput*, 1982.
Vacances: *Les Vacances de Bérurier*, 1969.
Votez: *Votez Bérurier*, 1964 (OC, I).

Other works cited:

DSA: *Dictionnaire San-Antonio*, Paris, 1993.
ELP: *Ecrire, lire et en parler: Dix années de littérature mondiale en 55 interviews publiés dans LIRE et présentés par Bernard Pivot*, Paris, 1985.
Lire: "10 monstrueux calembours de San-Antonio," in *Lire*, N° 120, September 1985, 127-8.

---

[1] *ELP*, p. 198.
[2] *Ibid.*, p. 201.
[3] Respectively John Barker, *Summer Spectacular* (London, 1965), p. 34, and *Red Dwarf*, BBC2, 3 October 1997.
[4] Dard frequently implicates his readers in his narratives, typically taking them to task for some inadequacy or stupidity: "Par moments, l'homme a besoin de faire comme la tomate, c'est-à-dire de se concentrer (si vous trouvez ce calembour mauvais, c'est que vous êtes moins idiots que je ne le pensais)." (*Sirop*: 129)
[5] Writing of the one-day series between England and Australia in the summer of 1997, Martin Johnson shows that he too has been in the knife-box: "England's fielding in this series has been sharp enough to cut your finger on" (*Daily Telegraph*, 26 May 1997).
[6] The same human iceberg is further described as being "moins joyce à embroquer qu'une chèvre des Pyrénées" (*Doigt*: 164). The opposite extreme is represented by a woman "qui fait roussir la paille des chaises quand elle s'assied" (*Joconde*: 492), while another sends the sexual thermometer off the end of the scale with her "tempérament de lampe à souder" (*Moi*: 46). The *lampe à souder* is Dard's preferred vehicle for the figuratively hot in any context; cf. "Il me pétrit les mains avec une chaleur plus intense que celle qui se dégage d'une lampe à souder." (*AZ*: 210)
[7] Dard also exercises his lexicogenetic verve to produce parasynthetic forms without seeking to create multiple meaning: e.g. *décalifourcher une moto* (*Clefs*: 312) - to get off a motor bike; *les encouronnés* (*Rate*: 183) - crowned heads; *éburner un homme comme des olives à farcir* (*Moi*: 14) - to enucleate a man's balls like olives for stuffing.
[8] Some would claim this is a case of *humour bidon*: je ricane.

[9] One wonders whether Dard has heard the story of the man who goes into the music shop. Customer to sales-girl: "Avez-vous 'le Trouvère'?" Sales-girl: "Non, monsieur, je n'ai rien de Verdi."

[10] Dard clearly likes ripping words limb from limb. Cf. the reversal of irreversible binomials in: "A mesure et au fur, y'a le Dirlo qui bée et le caustique M. Himker qui blêmit" (Os: 100); the tmetic interpolation of: "Je m'approche de la tenancière du camp (de concentration) ping" (Vacances: 68); and the scission of the "nose-horn" in: "Avouez que c'est rosse, comme disent les rhinos, hein?" (Rate: 163)

[11] The verb used is tangoter. Cf. "sambater" in DSA.

[12] ELP, p. 201.

[13] A mouth-watering prospect would be an argotic reworking of La Fontaine's fables by Dard, starting perhaps with L'Amygdale et la fourmi.

[14] There can be no doubt that Béru and Mrs Malaprop sing from the same spread-sheet. Although comparisons between literary creations are often as odorous as between one's own children and those of close friends, one could say of Bérurier and Mrs Malaprop, as Dard remarks elsewhere of a pair of dopplegängers: "A croire qu'ils sont issus, soit de la même paire, soit du même maire." (Rate: 177)

[15] Béru's barbarisms should perhaps not be subjected to the strictest of censure, however, given that lexical misapprehensions often become enshrined in the standard language. Without departing from standard French comparators for fier, it could be mentioned that alongside fier comme un coq or un paon, fowls that visibly and literally strut their stuff, the rather surprising fier comme un pou also occurs. Pou, in this expression, is commonly considered as meaning louse (from Vulgar Latin *peduculus), whereas it is more likely to represent the Vulgar Latin pullius (cock). Dard, for his part, embroiders on this image: "Ça plastronne comme un pou dans la chevelure d'une Suédoise." (Moi: 190)

[16] Dard routinely affects disdain for the broadsheets of the French press. Cf. "Son regard est morne comme la première page du Monde" (Poulet: 144). The insult is compounded in a footnote: "Je ne puis parler des autres, n'ayant jamais osé ouvrir cet honorable journal."

[17] I am unaware of an English equivalent of this proverb but I am grateful to the late Mrs Margaret Campbell, Professeur ès dictons écossais, for providing a Scots equivalent in "Gantin's wantin", the verb to gant meaning, literally, to gape or yawn, and, figuratively, to sigh.

[18] The meaning of "Rol" in this context is unclear, if indeed it has one.

[19] For the last expression I am indebted to Mrs Michèle Dickson.

[20] This simile is taken from San-Antonio chez les "gones", a novel set in Lyon, where the word gone means kid or youngster. As "chaude pelisse" is patently a corruption of chaude-pisse, perhaps Dard might have considered the alternative title San-Antonio chez les gonnocoques. For a similar play upon words, cf. "Le pied [de la femme] racle le sol comme celui d'un fox-terrier affolé par une chaude piste" (Vacances: 73).

[21] Indeed, Dard seems to take a mathematician's interest in the numerical implications of including one-eyed people in his calculations, describing the effect of a beautiful woman walking along a beach in these terms: "Douze cents paires d'yeux, plus un oeil (un borgne se faisait bronzer dans le secteur) se sont braqués sur la passante." (Sirop: 15)

[22] Strictly speaking cheval de bataille is a metaphorical extension of a compound noun rather than an idiom. The same substitutive principle nonetheless applies. The

lexicogenetic matrix $n + n$ is particularly productive of bespoke compounds. Cf. "Je la voyais un brin barbue, la dame, avec des grains de mocheté plus gros que des framboises, et de même couleur" (*Compte-gouttes*: 65); "L'Hindou déclina son nom de famine" (*Lire*: 127); "Il avait collaboré pour se faire de l'argent de Boche." (*Lire*: 127)

[23] Cf. "Il souffle un vent à décorner tous les maris restés à Paris pendant le mois d'août" (*Os*: 146), and the chiasmic aphorism: "Le mariage est soit une corne d'abondance, soit une abondance de cornes." (*Lire*: 127)

[24] Or indeed Tomme to Prudhomme, a thinker who never drank Earl Grey because "proper tea is theft."

[25] Many of Dard's puns are of the professional variety: "Je décide de tirer la chose au clerc, comme dit un notaire de mes relations" (*Sirop*: 134); "L'indifférence dont elle a fait montre, comme dit mon ami l'horloger du coin, n'a fait qu'accroître mon désir de la mieux connaître" (*Sirop*: 22). It is often a case of "les calembours se suivent et ne se ressemblent pas": "Le barlu [bateau] file bon train, si tu me permets cette image plus hardie que Laurel." (*Os*: 224)

[26] E.g. "Les archanges qui se grattent le trou du luth." (*Rate*: 146)

[27] E.g. "Je bigloche le cliché à m'en faire pleurer les glandes salivaires." (*Moi*: 98)

[28] E.g. "C'est une voie tranquille, bourgeoise, urinaire (étant sombre et déserte, elle remplace les édicules publics en voie, urinaire, de disparition." (*Doigt*: 169)

[29] From the schoolboy tag extension: "Comment vas-tu(yau de pipe)?" Cf. "Ross, le dévoué serviteur du Vioque, son zélé, son omniprésent (de Noël)" (*Vacances*: 337). The word *lapsus* is invariably followed by the parenthesised (-*la-moi*) and *aubépine* by (*de cheval*).

[30] E.g. "Le Gros hoche la tête d'une manière évaso-négative" (*Vacances*: 96); "Il secoue sa tronche de gorille et devient aussi rouge que sa limace homardo-thermidorienne." (*Sirop*: 94)

[31] E.g. "Récitons un pater et un navet maria." (*Vacances*: 191)

9. Humour and Gender in French New Wave Cinema
Caroline M. Cooper

Within the field of film studies there are various clearly marked contexts for discussion of the French New Wave: in association with the development of French cinema; in connection with French history and culture (France in the 1950s and '60s, the Algerian War, political and intellectual trends); by reference to trends in world cinema (textual and theoretical relations to Hollywood and to European art cinema). It is also studied – as it has usually been marketed – as a cinema of *auteurs*, that is of directors with distinct creative styles.

The early films of directors such as Truffaut, Chabrol and Godard have maintained a constant popularity among art-house audiences,[1] having an image of light-heartedness which stems partly from the way they are advertised (on British television, anyway) by shots of Paris and/or of attractive young men and women flirting to the accompaniment of "French" accordion music, chansons or jazz. Sexuality and fun seem to be on offer; *l'amour* is in the air. Intertwined with this ostensibly "easy viewing" are intellectual pleasures which demand active participation from the spectator, especially in recognising cinematic allusions, quotations from Hollywood, literary and artistic references, etc. Yet this active viewing never feels (except perhaps with the later work of Godard) political. The intertextuality of the films is as witty and surprising as, sometimes, their editing and their (often slender) narratives. Audiences laugh.

Truffaut's *Tirez sur le pianiste* (1960) and *Jules et Jim* (1962); Chabrol's *Les Bonnes Femmes* (1960); Godard's *A bout de souffle* (1959) and *Pierrot le fou* (1965): these products of the New Wave are still popular and clearly considered representative, since they are staple diet for retrospectives. But is there any justification for labelling them as comedies? Is audience laughter definitive? What is film comedy? The central concern of this chapter is an exploration of where precisely these films should be located in relation to various theoretical discourses, particularly those relating to cinematic comedy, to melodrama, and – since romantic relationships form the core of many of their narratives – more generally to humour and gender in everyday social life.

However "art cinema" seems a more appropriate context than "comedy" through which to identify some of their stylistic quirkiness. Art cinema became strong just after World War Two in various

European countries as they engaged in complex ideological struggles to resist American cultural imperialism, so as to maintain their distinct national identities. In the cinema industry the manifestation of these struggles lay in competition with Hollywood and in fighting for a corner in the extremely profitable market of film production. Various marketing niches were sought, leading to state-subsidised self-consciously national European films. These were marked visually by shots of such icons as Big Ben, the Eiffel Tower, Swedish lakes, or thematically by preocc-upation with such supposedly national characteristics as, for example, the British class-system or Scandinavian angst. They were sold as "art" in that they were usually identified by the director's name, thus setting up a "creator" – in contrast to the seemingly authorless products of classic Hollywood which were for the most part advertised by genre or by star. By proclaiming an "artist" or "auteur" – and it was Truffaut who in "A Certain Tendency of the French Cinema" (1954) led the way in arguing theoretically for this[2] – the films became intellectually respect-able and could be screened to self-selected audiences in so-called art-house cinemas.

In many ways the New Wave is typical of these European move-ments. In connection with nationhood its films correspond so neatly to international images of Frenchness – images to which it has of course itself contributed – that one critic has commented that they could be said to correspond to a tourist's view of France: summer in the countryside, the Mediterranean, above all the street life of Paris.[3] Its textual prop-erties also have much in common with other European art films. Related to, say, Antonioni are the often perplexing narratives, with loose causal chains, discontinuities of time and place, and open, ambiguous endings: and in many ways the work of Resnais is most similar to that of Antonioni, although the image of *L'Année dernière à Marienbad* or *Hiroshima mon amour* as "difficult and heavy" films marks them as very different from those to be discussed in this paper. Related to, say, Bergman is the fundamental existential anxiety of the protagonists, in that New Wave characters, however diverting their stories, seem socially marginalised, personally dissociated from their surroundings, disaffected pleasure-seekers or intellectuals without family ties or political affil-iations. Lacking the purposeful orientation of characters in goal-oriented Hollywood, they drift through life, their actions seemingly motiveless and arbitrary.

The mise-en-scène is correspondingly casual-looking: unglossy, location-shot, with the occasional accidental intrusion of passers-by. The casting of unknowns and new natural types produces an unaffected acting style, and the encouragement of improvisation leads sometimes to extraordinarily inconsequential snatches of dialogue. The documentary feel is augmented by the cinematography: natural lighting and mobile lightweight cameras give freedom of angles, offering the sense of spontaneity associated with television. Sweeping panning and tracking-shots follow the characters through their locations – Parisian cafés or sunlit fields. Extreme long takes and freeze frames combine with discontinuous editing, especially in Godard who quickly changes key from jokey conversation to murder – or the reverse. Such shifts in tone are startling to a spectator accustomed to the seamless appearance of the average Hollywood product and, considered in terms of humour theory, they produce the pleasurable surprise of the incongruous.

Many of these apparent irregularities may be ascribed to the French directors' rejection of the cohesiveness of 1950s French *cinéma de qualité* which consisted largely in faithful renderings of novels. For Truffaut, Chabrol and Godard all started their careers as film critics and theorists who conceived the cinema not as a neutral form through which something else could be transmitted via illusions of reality, but rather as a specific aesthetic system, a language in itself. Influenced by Bazin, co-founder of the Paris film journal *Cahiers du Cinéma*, they used its pages to attack the most artistically respected French film-makers of the day, accusing them of being essentially literary men rather than true *cinéastes*, producing nothing more than worthy adaptations of fiction. Over and against these they championed Hollywood genre cinema, with which they were deeply engaged. Especially Rivette, Godard and Truffaut spent much time in the early 1950s at the Paris Cinémathèque viewing retrospectives of the work of Hawks, Preminger, Fuller, Minnelli, Ray and Hitchcock. Inspired by these directors, they followed Truffaut's call in his ground-breaking essay of 1954 for a "politique des auteurs". New French directors (they themselves in fact) were to create films which would be fresh, natural, cinematic rather than literary, visual rather than verbal, and bearing clear marks of authorship. Above all, film would present itself as text, that is as a language in its own right. In narratological terms films were to be not *histoire*, masquerading as recordings of reality and effacing their traces of enunciation, but *discours*, with a sense of createdness and address to audience.

If ideas of address relate to the politics of representation, they also relate to comedy, for there is a somewhat unlikely connection between Brechtian theories of active readership and film comedy, in that the latter also refuses to be contained by the demands of realism. Having its origins in the theatre, comedy has (like the musical) moments cut off from the main narrative, scenes of obvious exhibitionism when audience response seems expected and when a live performer would allow a pause for laughter. Even if we are not amused, we sense the intention. Film comedy manifests a form of address to audience, though not necessarily directly to camera, which breaks illusion, foregrounding the fictional and constructed nature of the films themselves. Is not the French New Wave, then, in spite of the intellectual aspirations of its directors, closely related to mainstream cinematic comedy?

Film comedy shares theoretical problems with literature and theatre, including questions concerning the relationships between humour, the adjective "comic" as generic indicator, and "a comedy" as narrative form. Very few films of any genre do not at some point occasion laughter and therefore pertain to the comic. However comedy – although it may be so identified in video-stores and television listings – is a complex matter. The term can cover such diverse forms as cartoons, silent slapstick, screwball, and romantic comedy; but these are so disparate as hardly to constitute a genre. Many film comedies are parodic versions of mainstream forms: the western (*Blazing Saddles*, *Cat Ballou*, *Calamity Jane*), the thriller (*Charade*, *How to Steal a Million*), the melodrama (*The Seven Year Itch*, *Philadelphia Story*). Such parodies involve the subordination of the conventions of one genre to those of another – and most types of feature film are amenable to having their conventions broken or sent up. Film comedy is not in itself a genre, but rather a term which may be applied to almost any film which tells its story in a humorous way, has a cheerful up-beat ending, and is marketed as happy, that is as offering laughter – or at least amusement.[4]

What "comic" films share is play with reversals: improbable characters, illogical sequences of events, and comic effect stemming from the abandonment of narrative logic. An extreme example is the animated short, where there is a carnivalesque defiance of the expected: events are out of control, leading to reversals of fortune, accident and coincidence, and Bakhtinian topsyturvydom (think of *Tom and Jerry*); or the characters are up to mischief, human manipulation, which in turn leads to scheming and plotting, pretence and disguise (perhaps cross-dressing as in *Some Like it Hot* or *Tootsie*). Often different characters are scheming for different things, all being variously foiled by odd events and/or each other. Usually there is a combination of both of the above – incongruous events and incongruous characters – as well as of visual and verbal humour. Always there is suspense and surprise.

Some straight genres are almost directly paired with a comic form, and one of these relationships is relevant to the French New Wave. Thematic concerns with love, romantic relationships, and women's expected place in patriarchal society are shared three-ways: by melo-drama (usually with a sad ending, a sense of "love which might have been" as in, say, *An Affair to Remember*), by musical comedy, and by romantic comedy (both usually ending with characters being in love, as in, say, *Singin' in the Rain* or *Pretty Woman*). Through their central concern with love, these genres are closely related, and it has been suggested that romantic comedy exists in the same kind of generic tension with melodrama that Frye finds between comedy and tragedy.[5] Their closures also have something in common, for the sad ending of a melodramatic weepie, for example of *Magnificent Obsession*, can seem just as contrived as the happy ending of a romantic comedy such as *Pillow Talk*.

To New Wave titles such as *Jules et Jim*, *Les Bonnes Femmes* or *Pierrot le fou*, none of this seems obviously relevant. Yet relating these films to some basic definitions of comedy reveals very starkly that they are not just out for laughs, and that their underlying tone, and certainly their endings, are also, quite crudely, too sad to class them as comedies. Their closure in death relates them more to melodrama, while their basic narratives, if recounted in straight prose, are tragic. Yet with their often blithe tone and provocative narrative structures circling round questions of romance, they have a feel which relates them to romantic comedy.

Romantic comedy is still popular: witness for example the huge success of *When Harry Met Sally* (1989), *Four Weddings and a Funeral* (1994), or, in France, *Gazon maudit* (1996). This term also embraces the one type of comedy which probably has genre status: screwball. Screw-ball is the forum not for mere play of the sexes or sexual farce (think of Feydeau), but, through the exploration and sometimes reversal of gendered stereotypes, the actual battle of the sexes. Here we see women who refuse male power, who can make a fool of Cary Grant, as do Katherine Hepburn in *Bringing up Baby* or Rosalind Russell in *His Girl Friday*. For while men who fail to control women are comic objects, women who test the boundaries of acceptable femininity are threatening to the established order and have to be suppressed.[6] Yet the ultimately conservative closure of screwballs traditionally involves the containment of the woman and the reassertion of the man – as in *The Taming of the*

Shrew – and archetypally so, for film comedy has ancient roots in the western theatrical tradition.

Gender role-reversal, like melodrama, sounds a long way from the French New Wave. But here too stereotypes are explored, though less by a comedic reversal of traditional male and female behaviour than by showing them at their most clichéd: the attempted macho-ness of Belmondo's roles in *A bout de souffle* and *Pierrot le fou*, the unpredictable femininity of Jeanne Moreau in *Jules et Jim*, the warm-hearted prostitute and the tortured artist in *Tirez sur le pianiste*, the silly shop-girls in *Les Bonnes Femmes*. All these characters are struggling in relations with the opposite sex and, given that the directors of these films were consciously seeking to set up a French cinema, it is tempting to suggest that, with France's image as a nation preoccupied with *l'amour*, sexual and romantic love would inevitably become (conveniently marketable) recurrent themes, and themes to be not mocked and then celebrated as in screwball, but, rather, explored – and exploited – fairly seriously. They are of course a fundamental human preoccupation, and as such play no less a role in everyday social discourse than they do on film. So how can the sometimes tragic, sometimes comic representations of gender relations in the New Wave be related to theories of humour?

Fundamental to normality and to our subjectivity is our sex. It is the first fact to be noted after the birth of a normal baby; equally it is thought to be the first fact we note about a person in the street. Indeed the process is so fundamental that we are not even conscious of it until confronted by the enigma of an androgynous figure. However Freud's widely accepted work on the engendering of the young child (the omni-directional sexuality of the infant, the socialising process of repression of so-called opposite sex characteristics) suggests that gender behaviour is an aspect of life from which we have a strong need for release, and one where repression operates most crushingly. If we are to accept the basic premise of his theory of humour – that laughter is a psychological release of repressed urges of an aggressive or sexual nature which are thereby rendered harmless – it is logical that issues of sex, sexuality and engendered social behaviour form a preoccupation which is central to much everyday humorous exchange, as well as to comedy as a genre in either literature, the theatre or cinema.

Of course a distinction needs to be made between humour as it occurs in everyday discourse, and humour when it is presented (usually commercially) as entertainment or comedy. The critical literature is distinct: research on the former is contributed by social psychologists and anthropologists; on the latter by literary and media scholars. Yet it is obvious that, especially as far as gender relations go, there is a strong interrelationship between the two zones. Sexual banter plays a role in social life which is just as prominent as the place, in formal comedy, of humour stemming from relations between the sexes. Another inter-relationship is that between humour about sexual relations (jokes about sex, often told in single-sex groups) and humorous interchange between the sexes (men and women laughers).

Traditionally joking has been regarded as masculine. Women have been regarded as respondents to − or butts of − male joking. Freud argues that sexual humour reveals insecurities of male sexual identity, defusing threats to the sexual order which men sense to be represented by women. Thus, although he offers no section specifically related to gender and humour, Freud clearly sees joking as serving the male ego. He appears to assume that women are always the butts, and never the instigators, of humour. Dirty jokes ("smut") are "originally directed towards women and may be equated with attempts at seduction".[7] He also suggests that women have different senses of humour; for example, repression "makes it impossible for women, and to a lesser degree for men as well, to enjoy undisguised obscenity".[8] Such observations are clearly bound, like all his thinking, by his own cultural context. In 1966 David Zippin developed Freud's theories to argue from a psychoanalytic perspective that joking behaviour and its meaning vary with the sex of the jokester and the sex of the person confronted with the joke.[9]

Such psychoanalytic theories await careful reinterpretation from a 1990s perspective. But it is clear that a similar conception has been current in the western developed world among behaviourists and social psychologists: women have until very recently been conceived of as responding to jokes rather than making them. Numerous pieces of research in the 1970s and '80s, involving recorded conversations or groups of students being presented with jokes to develop, claimed to confirm this.[10] Meanwhile the anthropologist Mahadev Apte explores sex-related differences in the nature, dissemination, use and appreciation of humour across cultures, asking to what extent these differences are related to societal attitudes toward sex-role models and to normative behavioural patterns concerning women. He concludes that women's humour reflects existing inequalities between the sexes not so much in its substance, as in the constraints imposed on its occurrence. These constraints relate to those which emphasize male superiority and female passivity, while certain social factors such as marriage, advanced age, and the greater freedom enjoyed by women in groups, reduce the differences between men's and women's humour. In so-called developing societies women's relative freedom to engage in humour in the public domain is related to their position in the life cycle: "as they advance through it, the restrictions are relaxed, and women publicly engage in humor to greater degrees, eventually competing with men."[11]

Instigating humour seems in some way to be regarded as incompatible with femininity. It is as if joking were a form of mating display to which the nubile female should respond but which she ought not seek to rival. She should be generally smiling and charming, and laugh – but not raucously.[12] It is perhaps with this expectation of a pleasant manner – which has little to do with humour or real laughter – that feminists have taken issue, for it positions women as receptive, passive, inarticulate and sometimes foolish. Feminist humour, upturning traditional gender relations, is the opposite of the conventionally feminine. It is perhaps the latter quality, the traditional gentle, smiling demeanour, which some perceive to have died with the recent women's movement.[13] There is a popular view among those, women as well as men, who found (find?) them threatening, that feminists lack humour – a view which corresponds to an ancient tradition whereby powerful and/or unattractive women have been branded as humourless monsters or cackling witches.[14]

Feminism, or rather new sexual-political awareness, has even spoiled the fun for some critics. Wayne Booth, for example, claims that feminist criticism has affected his appreciation of Rabelais to the extent that he can no longer laugh at his work as he used to, partly because

> the specific ideology on which Rabelais's laughter depends is ... still a dominant ideology of our culture: women are fair game; they are sillier than men, as nine out of ten television comedies proclaim.[15]

Others have suggested that women as well as men find it funnier to see a woman than a man disparaged.[16]

Clearly humour is related to power. This was Bergson's main thesis, with his view of the social role of humour as essentially corrective and containing, functioning to shame people into conforming to their expected social roles. However he was unconcerned with questions of gender, and was interested in literary and theatrical satire rather than in everyday humorous discourse. Taking a different approach, sociologists such as Jerry Palmer investigate ways in which power comes into play in questions of humour and gender. Wisely sceptical of generalisations about the role of humour in human life, Palmer cautiously accepts the evidence of research that men and women do have dissimilar senses of humour as far as jokes about sex and aggression are concerned, and concludes that this difference may be related to questions of social power:

> Perhaps the traditional division of attributes between masculinity and femininity makes the attribute of a sense of humour on the part of a woman a threat to masculinity in its traditional form. ... It seems that male attempts to monopolise the right to be funny are a part of male power in the public domain.[17]

Psychologists have set up experiments to explore whether it is the *type* of joke used in research that has tended to amuse female subjects less than male, and current thinking seems to be that women tend to laugh more than men in everyday social situations but less than men at set-piece jokes[18] – perhaps they are unconsciously resisting the self-assertion which the latter tend to demonstrate.

Susan Purdie believes, similarly to Palmer, that "joking, precisely because it offers immediate individual psychic pleasure, is very likely to be at the service of entrenched social power".[19] Social joking involves a discursive exchange whose distinctive operation constitutes jokers as masters of discourse, that is as those able to break and to keep the basic rule of language, and consequently in controlling possession of full human subjectivity. In jokes "women do not occupy the 'Irish' position of inept speakers, but function ... almost exclusively as objects of male sexuality. 'Woman' conventionally signifies ... 'not a person'."[20] Patriarchy's appropriation of joking is illustrated also by jokes about feminised men – who are always gay – the "near neighbour" from whom patriarchal man must "other" himself being homosexual man: lesbianism is largely absent from popular joking. Purdie insists that women and all subjected groups need to lay claim to joking, since it seizes ideological power and constructs and confirms socio-economic power. The rise of the female stand-up comedian, if it lasts, must be both a sign and an agent of change. Even if her jokes are conservative, a woman is at least present as the originator of joking discourse.[21]

It is only in the last ten years or so that women's humour has entered public consciousness as a concept – though it is noticeable that, as far as female comedians go, their routines are often self-deprecating, focusing on, say, their unattractiveness. The sociologist Michael Mulkay attacks the popular misconception whereby women have a less developed sense of humour than men, but concedes that the view may have arisen partly because women tend to contribute less to humorous discourse in the presence of men. Why is this so? He suggests a variety of reasons: men tend to regulate the production of discourse in general; women may well be amused by different things from men; they are not amused by men's jokes, but do not wish to introduce specifically female humour into social situations dominated by men; there are stronger taboos on women telling sexual jokes; sexual joking is not always deemed proper, and might be seen as the wrong sort of invitation; women's signals of humorous intent may be less clear than men's and may therefore get less social recognition in mixed groups; finally, much male humour expresses men's sexual domination of women and women would not wish to participate in a discourse which involves them in self-denigration. Women's joking tends, therefore, to happen amongst themselves.[22]

How do such theories of gender and humour in social discourse relate to the presentation of romance in cinema? Is the inversion of traditional sexual roles automatically funny? Which sex is the more disparaged, and in what manner? To what extent is sexuality a key factor in that disparagement? And how does humour arise from love stories? The relationship between gender and humour in social discourse and gender factors as a *source* of humour in film has yet to be explored. And how could such questions relate to the New Wave? If its films are funny, to what extent is it on questions of gender that the humour is dependent? Or does it have its source in the narrative more generally? Or again in formal properties of the films?

Truffaut is regarded by many as the most human of these French directors: his narratives are always in some way touching, his cinematography not so experimental (his fierce attack on traditional French cinema notwithstanding) as to alienate audiences. His films tend to focus centrally on relationships between human beings, that is on love in some form: male/female couples, the importance and difficulty of male friendship. However he is generally regarded as having a pessimistic view of the human condition and of human capability. He stated that his

> characters are on the edge of society. I want them to testify to human fragility because I don't like toughness, I don't like very strong people, or people whose weaknesses don't show.[23]

Often the films are about characters creating their identity as if this were a fragile and uncertain matter.[24] Consider the famous closing still of his first full-length feature film *Les Quatre Cents Coups* which sets the tone not just for the rather melancholy Antoine Doinel cycle but for much of his later work. Yet, largely because of their cinematic playfulness, their experimentation with genres and with the legacy of 1940s and 1950s

Hollywood, the potential melancholy of the films is overlaid by a certain volatile buoyancy. Roy Armes quotes him as having considered his films as circus shows: "I'd never show two elephant acts running. After the elephant comes the conjuror";[25] further suggesting that for changes of mood to work successfully, depth must be avoided, which may explain a certain superficiality, and hence why his best work is in comedy.[26]

Female characters are the determining force in the two films chosen for the present discussion: the two women in the life of the Aznavour character Charlie/Edouard in *Tirez sur le pianiste*, and the *femme fatale* Catherine who triangulates the friendship between the two men in *Jules et Jim*. It is the women who control the relationships – and therefore the narrative – and these women are experienced by the male protagonists as seductive, unpredictable, somewhat threatening, and bearers, largely, of problems and unhappiness. They are certainly not the limp admirers of male joking suggested in early humour research, but rather archetypes of woman as the unfathomable other.

Tirez sur le pianiste is almost as much *about* genre as in one. The film falls into two halves: the Edouard story – told in flashback and almost pure melodrama – and the Charlie story – a vaguely constructed parody of a Hollywood gangster-and-his-moll story. Truffaut commented:

> I know that the result seems ill-assorted and the film seems to contain four or five films, but that's what I wanted. Above all I was looking for *the explosion of a genre* (the detective) *by mixing genres* (comedy, drama, melodrama, the psychological film, the thriller, the love film, etc.).[27]

It is, perhaps, in the incongruity of this mixing, rather than in anything to do with gender relations, that the humour of this film lies.

The first startling incongruity follows on from the opening credits when we see a man (Chico, brother to the protagonist) running in *film noir* style through dark streets from a pursuing car. He bangs, slapstick-style, into a lamp-post (it is only later that we meet the two implausible gangsters from whom he is fleeing), and thereby into a totally different and comic discourse: that of domesticity, which brings both marital bliss and strife. For he is helped up from the pavement by a solid citizen of a man who is carrying a large bunch of flowers home to his wife of eleven years' standing. The ensuing conversation between strangers is a man-to-man confession: how the husband first met his wife, the challenge of her virginity, how he found himself buying a ring, almost wandering into marriage, feeling trapped, then wanting to get rid of her, and only falling in love with her after their first child was born. Chico contributes a remark about how he wouldn't mind being married too, yet when he suggests to the husband that perhaps he had wanted his freedom back, the latter's responding shrug of the shoulder and rather grudging "oui" does not sound at all convinced. Thus the self-contained little episode establishes a theme of the film as the relationship between marriage and love, and prepares us for the conflicting desires of the central male character Edouard/Charlie as between commitment (domesticity, stability) and liberty – with woman as the central problem. The spectator gets intrigued by their unexpected conversation, only to be surprised again when, the husband having turned off on his way home, Chico runs back into the *film noir*. This incidental character never appears again, and Chico's final words to him are "Bonne chance!" To the spectator it is the fugitive Chico who looks in need of luck: is this film a gangsterish *film noir*, or a domestic comedy?

Shortly afterwards, in the bar where Charlie plays, the dancing is presented not as loving or enjoyable but as a war of the sexes. Chico comments casually to his dancing partner, whom he has just met for the first time, "This evening I have decided to get married; you are the first one I have asked." Quite unfazed, her perfectly logical reply is, "You haven't asked if I'm free." The spectator may be amused by this socially and cinematically unconventional dialogue, but it seems to be perfectly normal to the characters. A second woman (we later learn that she is the prostitute Clarisse) lures a dumpy little man out of his seat towards her on the dance floor only to push him back down – and then repeats the gesture. A third woman has a short and bespectacled partner transfixed by what is to him her nearly eye-level bosom. When she asks, "Are my breasts really all that interesting?", he tells her not to worry: "I am a doctor." Her sceptical and bored shrug reveals her *ennui* at male pretentiousness and hypocrisy, and at years of what today would be called sexual harassment.

In the case of all three couples it is the man who is the petitioner/wooer, the woman who has the power to reject. The women are as conventionally attractive as the men are unattractive – though the unshakeable confidence and vanity of the latter are suggested by two ugly and bespectacled wall-flower men who agree, as they sit partnerless with their cigarettes, that there is not much talent around. Whose talent?? The theme of sexual antagonism has been set before we even know what Chico is running from, or that the Aznavour pianist is to be the central character.

Plyne, the bar owner, brings Charlie to the point of considering whether he is afraid of women, as seems to be suggested soon after by his nervous and tongue-tied shyness when the waitress Léna asks him to walk her home. The camera tellingly shows extreme close-ups of Charlie's hands as he tries to pluck up courage to touch her. Yet when, shortly afterwards, Clarisse comes to his bed, he is suddenly in role as the cool French lover, bare-chested, smoking, joking, as he pulls the sheet up over her breasts, "In the cinema, it's like this" – a multi-layered reference to the narrative medium, to the act of cinema viewing, to sexual titillation and to a lack of censorship which would be unthinkable in classic Hollywood cinema.

Bundled into a car by the friendly and incompetent gangsters, Charlie is drawn into an out-of-context-seeming conversation with them: subjects include problems with women, the nuisance of having to talk to them before and after sex, and knickers. For the second time in the film men bond in a discussion about the problem of women. Misogynistic though this is, Léna seems to find it amusing, and joins in as their laughter becomes infectious. The generic juxtaposition of gangster genre against comedy-of-the-sexes is further confused by a shift to melodrama in the central flashback section in which, still "Edouard", the Aznavour character was a classical pianist married to Thérésa. The tone is solemn and sad, but still the theme is the unpredictability, potential treachery and power of women, for it is by sleeping with an impresario that she secured professional advancement for Edouard. Léna also seeks to control him, for the minute their relationship is established, she says she hopes to turn Charlie back into "Edouard" – as if ordering him out to buy her a pair of stockings were the way to set about doing this. Humour is based on sexual difference: snatches of banter suggest that men and women can never understand each other; both the women who love Edouard/Charlie end up dead. The ultimate tone is, moreover, bitter. Men seem almost to be better off without women, either alone or in male company.

Truffaut's other best-known New Wave film, *Jules et Jim*, shares with *Tirez sur le pianiste* a preoccupation with the challenge to men of women, or indeed of Woman, for the Jeanne Moreau character, Catherine – epitomised by the enigmatic smile of the statue the two friends visit while journeying on the Adriatic – is presented as a symbol of female sexuality, freedom and unconventionality: as Jules says, "She is a force of nature ... a real woman, and it is this woman we love and whom all men desire". Her famous song is about a *femme fatale*, yet when she first appears in the film (significantly only *after* the Jules/Jim friendship has been firmly established) she has been on screen for just a few moments as her be-skirted female self before we see her cross-dressed as "Thomas" in her successful attempt to pass as male. The ensuing three-person race across the bridge, though playful (and marked as such by circus-style music), has an undertone of concern about the workings of gender. Indeed the whole film seems to be exploring questions of gender, and particularly the nature of femininity (for masculinity appears to be taken as the unproblematic norm), even down to a conversation about the grammatical gender of sun and moon in French and German.

Cross-dressing relates to one of the most common reversals in the comedy of dominant cinema: that of gender behaviour in its various aspects. Given that the confirmation of conventional masculinity and femininity is central to the project of Hollywood, this is hardly surprising. Some of the most popular and famous pieces turn on cross-dressing – in the case of comedy, usually male-to-female – as this disempowering (in pantomime dames, Old Mother Riley, *Some Like it Hot, Tootsie, Mrs Doubtfire, Priscilla, Queen of the Desert*, etc.) is usually perceived as humorous to the same degree that female-to-male cross-dressing seems threatening or provocatively sexual (in Shakespeare comedies, pantomime principal boys, *Queen Christina, Morocco, Victor/Victoria*). These plays and films offer a momentary glimpse of the potential fluidity of gender options, while simultaneously – as in Bakhtin's reading of medieval carnival – celebrating and reinforcing the norms which are supposedly being mocked. It is some such kind of existential freedom that the Moreau character embodies in *Jules et Jim*, questioning and rejecting the roles into which woman is forced by society.

Chabrol in *Les Bonnes Femmes* seems to explore the social traps for both sexes, as he continues to do in the stylish *policiers* of his later work where he presents the bourgeoisie as materialistic, pretentious, often stupid, engaged in rituals such as those of eating which he often details with an irony comparable to that of the famous meal scenes in Buñuel. For – in parallel to the loneliness which is central in Truffaut – Chabrol declared himself to be interested in foolishness: "Foolishness is infinitely more fascinating than intelligence, infinitely more profound. Intelligence has limits whilst foolishness has none."[28] His attitude to his characters has been said to be one of "unmitigated coldness",[29] and he himself declares an almost scientific attitude to people, saying that as a child

I was interested in the people passing in the street. I watched them, from my high position, as one contemplates an anthill ... But my subjects were more appealing than insects thanks to their great diversity - different behaviours, faces, bodies, clothes, which indicated an age, a social class, a certain sort of character.[30]

All his films indicate a strong awareness of the conditioning effects of environment, showing grand passions such as jealousy, adultery and envy in ironic tension with the petty and seemingly meaningless rituals of everyday life.

Les Bonnes Femmes offers a detached, almost anthropological study of the four girls who are its main protagonists: in documentary style the camera chronicles the banality of their work in the customerless electrical-appliance shop, their seemingly foredoomed aspirations to love and success. When the girls visit the zoo, the camera pans and hovers over the animals just as hitherto it has done over the girls them-selves: all are similarly trapped creatures on display. Nor are men spared this relentless gaze. Both sexes are stereotyped almost to the point of caricature (the patronisingly flirtatious shop-owner and his morbid cashier are comic grotesques) and relations between men and women appear as a cold pairing-off quite devoid of the romantic love which Jacqueline alone seems to seek.

The tone of a lonely search for sex is set by the opening Paris evening sequence. People leave bars and hotels late at night; a voice off advertises "the most gorgeous nudes in Paris"; a club doorman offers to procure a companion for a solitary elderly man; the leather-clad biker lurks. Two very ordinary-looking men, shot in close-up to reveal their respectable overcoats bespattered with something like confetti, grimace and wink at each other while they peer at a group of girls in anticipation of chatting them up. They are similar types to the two critical observers of the dancing in *Tirez sur le pianiste* and, as in that film, the spectator watches them as they watch the girls. The dance/war of the sexes is a drab, slightly sordid and potentially tragic spectacle of silly and lonely people trying to find a mate. The two men are presented as predators, but they are not so much threatening as comically repulsive. The plump middle-aged Marcel assures Jane and Jacqueline, cruising behind them in a car with Albert as they walk home, that he is respectable, a "householder". The two men seem inexperienced, more nervous than the quite cheeky girls, and their crude chamber-pot attempt at being amusing is counterpointed by the sad and worried face of the sensitive-looking Jacqueline. Later, in the night-club, the more drunk the characters get and the more they laugh (mainly at their own jokes), the less the spectator is inclined to, their high spirits being so embarrassing, and the ensuing carnivalesque conger dance, with swirling and unfocused camera, seems but a desperate group attempt at gaiety. Meanwhile the (by intention) seriously sexy strip act with its sultry music is undermined in its attempted eroticism by cruel close-ups of the leering and drunken Marcel and Albert, now wearing clown masks with bulbous noses and moustaches – conscious echoes of the humiliation of Professor Jannings in *The Blue Angel*. The only conventionally macho male – the lurking leather-clad biker whose continuous presence becomes ever more menacing as the film progresses – turns out at the end to be a maniac and a murderer. But here, at the opening of the film, we know little more of the characters than their names. They are types, ciphers, participants in a desperate sex game. The two men find Jacqueline "a bit stuck up", but are informed by her cynical friend Jane that "she is waiting for true love". No-one else seems to believe in such a thing. A close-up of Albert's sad clown face is accompanied by frantic cha-cha-cha music from the night-club they have left; the bacchanalian revels have an unmissable bass-note of scepticism and sadness.

Another cameo scene makes a humorous dig at the mores of the petite-bourgeoisie: shop-girl Rita is taken for lunch to a restaurant to meet her future in-laws. Disconcertingly, her three co-workers are at the next table. Her nervous fiancé Henri criticises her blouse, tells her to "act as if you knew a bit about music and the arts, talk about Michelangelo for example ... ", and he is clearly terrified of his truffle-salesman father. Male pretentiousness is as ridiculous as the ignorant anxiety-to-please of an uneducated working-class young woman. Chabrol had stated that he "wanted to make a film about stupid people that was very vulgar and deeply stupid ... It was a film about fools".[31] The only men who are not caricatured are the two associated with Jacqueline: the murderous biker, whom she believes to be in love with her, and the shy, gentle delivery boy Nounours, who is in love with her, but whom she barely notices. However this is not a milieu which allows any mutual understanding or closeness between men and women. As in the films of Truffaut, romantic love is sought after – but impossible.

And in Godard? The very term "love" seems too sentimental to be associated with his work. Yet his films, like theirs, circle round relations between the sexes, and especially the nature and social positioning of women. Their very titles suggest this: *Une femme mariée*, *Une femme est une femme*, *Deux ou trois choses que je sais d'elle*, *Masculin-féminin*. As in the films of Truffaut and Chabrol there is a feeling that male-female relationships can never be close or lasting. His characters too seem to live on the fringes of bourgeois society, happening purposelessly through flimsy and sometimes incoherent narratives in a multimedia world. Yet his attitude is sharp and satirical, the tone of his films fast and crisp, his style challenging. Illusion is broken, and far more so than in the work of Chabrol or Truffaut. Fiction and documentary elements mingle in a collage construction of elliptical editing, jump-cuts and direct looks to camera. These films, in contrast to undemanding traditional cinema, require from the spectator a Brechtian active participation. Much of the pleasure in watching them comes from their intertextual references to other popular discourses such as newspapers, advertising, and comics, and Hollywood films are honoured and parodied in a complex web of cinematic references. *A bout de souffle* plays with the American gangster genre just as its Belmondo character plays with the persona of Humphrey Bogart. Jean Seberg had just starred in Preminger's *Saint Joan*, and her "American in Paris" role would be familiar to international audiences. These in-jokes offer pleasures of recognition, plus amusement at their occasional audacity. There is also a tone of sexual titillation in a critique of the smutty innuendoes of advertising.

This note is set in the opening juxtaposition where we are given a close-up of a drawing on the back of a newspaper depicting a woman in sexy lingerie plus a male voice-over: "So, I'm a son-of-a-bitch." The camera pans up to show the reader of the paper and owner of the voice, the gangster Belmondo/Michel. His rapidly-executed crime has a woman accomplice; driving his getaway car he rejects female hitch-hikers because one of them is "too ugly"; the banter with the woman friend whose purse he rifles is laced with sexual looks. Woman are for use – for practical help, for sex, for money – and sexual desire is curiously bound up with the thrills of random-seeming amateur crime. The mood is cheeky and coquettish, qualities epitomised in the press conference with the famous novelist which centres on "l'amour", and a conventionally romantic atmosphere is accentuated by the two young and attractive central characters who interact in sunny and determinedly Parisian streets. There is freedom in a certain play with gendering: witness Seberg/Patricia's androgynously short hair, and Belmondo's facial explorations as he peers into mirrors in a way that conventional film associates with female vanity. In the central scene, in Patricia's hotel room, it is unclear who is pursuing whom, who wants "just sex" and who is after "true love". The conversation is so unpredictable and illogical, their movements so frolicsome, that the first impression the scene makes is carefree. Yet their dialogue circles round themes of loneliness, death, men's and women's conflicting desires, the impossibility of knowing what another is thinking: "We look each other in the eye and it's no use." The underlying tone, the emphasis on the ultimate separateness of men and women and the impossibility of love between them are as pessimistic as in Truffaut and Chabrol. It is the stuff of melodrama.

Likewise In Godard's *Pierrot le fou* the sexes are destined to mistrust and a mutual failure of comprehension. In the opening sequences women are shown as imprisoned in and conditioned by the discourses of advertising: their talk is of girdles, deodorants, hair-sprays, suitable fabrics for lingerie. But their social engendering is paralleled by the artistic and literary pretensions of the male characters, particularly of the protagonist Ferdinand. He indeed wants to be the novelist "Ferdinand", but his lover Marianne wants him to be her "Pierrot". She is concerned with "ma ligne de chance", he with her "ligne de hanche". Ciphers for their sex, almost cartoon characters, the two are fundamentally incompatible and united only by their alienation from bourgeois society: they have no ground on which to meet except that of exile, in a Hollywood-style narrative of outlaws in retreat from society. The film ironically presents a colourful idyll of lovers-in-flight, cross-edited with songs, literary, cinematic and political allusions, precariously holding together a fragmented story.

The relationship between Ferdinand and Marianne, established during their first car ride, is of lovers as isolated figures rebounding from one unfulfilling relationship to another. Any sentimental potential in their quirky conversations about love is nipped in the bud by unconventional editing, refusal of close-ups at expected moments and inconsequential dialogue. The obscure thriller-plot in which they seem to be involved has a ridiculous side, and the occasional instances when the film moves into the genre of musical, the central couple dancing and singing of love, bring a bitter-sweet change of key. Yet these upbeat features, like the bright Mediterranean blues and reds, remain in ironic counterpoint to a basic mood of despair, and the sometimes forced gaiety is overlaid with an atmosphere of pessimistic aimlessness, a *mal de vivre* which leads to the (slapstick-style) ending in death. It is a narrative – like those of the films discussed above – which could be easily presented as a doomed love affair, and refilmed as a tragic melodrama, with Hollywood-style dialogues, conventional editing, lingering facial

close-ups at emotional moments quite easily effecting such a transformation. These ostensibly jaunty films are the obverse of romantic
tragedy, precariously removed from it.

This is not least because in them, and in many ways, men and
women perform their traditional roles. The women are archetypal male
constructs, associated with the natural and instinctive, conventionally
feminine in a manner quite unknowing of feminism. They are either
enigmatic and inconstant (see the unpredictable and unfaithful Catherine
in *Jules et Jim*, the pleasure-seeking Marianne in *Pierrot le fou*, the boy-
ishly appealing but ultimately treacherous Patricia in *A bout de souffle*),
but afflicted underneath their superficial flirtatiousness by some existential angst. Or they are unawakened, unconscious in their lives, witness
Charlie's two waitress women, Léna and Thérésa in *Tirez sur le pianiste*,
or the uneducated romantic shop-girls of *Les Bonnes Femmes*. There is a
strong sense of gynophobia, stronger perhaps in Truffaut than in Chabrol
and Godard, who both seem slightly more sympathetic to the position of
women, but the films present male characters also as trapped, conditioned by images of masculinity which are current not only on screen:
tough guy Belmondo in *A bout de souffle*, creative types such as aspiring
novelist Belmondo in *Pierrot le fou*, classical pianist Aznavour – helped
in his career but also destroyed by a woman – in *Tirez sur le pianiste*.
The two men in *Jules et Jim* are cinematically-familiar male buddies,
their close bonding preserved from intimations of homosexuality by the
positioning of the Woman-Catherine as their mutual love object. Traditional gender roles prevail. But because the films explore the medium of
cinema, it is easy to be misled into thinking that they also explore
sexuality and gendering, and that there is some celebration of free love,
an abandonment of bourgeois convention.

It is, rather, from the abandonment of cinematic convention that
this impression stems. Surprising juxtaposition of sequences, unlikely
shifts in tone – in *Tirez sur le pianiste* that from *film noir* into a world of
comic marital banter; Michel, driving through sunny countryside in *A
bout de souffle* and addressing the camera in a comic monologue, then
suddenly, and apparently quite without motive, shooting a policeman –
these are moments of incongruity which bring, even after several view-
ings, a pleasurable *frisson* of surprise. Such moments also make the
spectator aware of the constructed nature of film: we are in the realm of
discours. In spite of their revolutionary aesthetics, Truffaut, Godard and
Chabrol were not really political activists, and certainly not in the early
'60s, and their films suggest that they were in no way revolutionaries in

the realm of sexual politics. But there is in their work a sense of being confronted with something new, unconventional, questioning, which, in the existential explorations of these young men and women, is energising and life-enhancing.

So is this comedy? Is the whole experience of watching these films "integrative"– which is how Northrop Frye defines comedy, as mythically associated with springtime, coming together, the future, "the triumph of life and love over the wasteland".[32] Taking this definition, the New Wave seems to define the obverse – not mating, birth and rebirth, but the impossibility thereof: the eternal oppositeness of the sexes, their inability ever to communicate fully, the impossibility of remaining faithful, death as the only resolution to romantic relationships. The wasteland triumphs.

Kathleen Rowe suggests that "melodrama depends on a belief in the possibility of romantic comedy's happy ending".[33] These French films behave much like romantic comedies, or like quirkily-told melodramas. But they do not have that belief. It is perhaps in this paradox – in the laughter they cause in spite of their ultimately unhappy stories – that part of the appeal of these films may be located: sad subjects lightly treated. The pleasurable release of the repressed – fear of loneliness, of rejection, of death? We are back with Freud ...

---

[1] While there is general consensus about the beginning of the New Wave as being 1959, there is considerable debate about when it ended. P. Cook, in *The Cinema Book* (London, 1985), suggests 1963, D. Bordwell and K. Thompson, *Film Art: An Introduction* (London, 1990), 1964 or 5. The later films of the major directors are usually regarded as "post New Wave".

[2] q.v. Truffaut, "A Certain Tendency of the French Cinema", in B. Nichols (ed.), *Movies and Methods* (U. of California Press, 1976), pp. 224-237.

[3] Cook, *op. cit.*, p. 42.

[4] In some ways the cinematic genre to which comedy is most closely related is horror, these being the two forms which are marketed and even measured by their ability to create a bodily reaction, namely laughter or fear.

[5] q.v. K. Rowe, "Comedy, Melodrama and Gender", in *Classical Hollywood Comedy*, ed. K. Karnick and H. Jenkins (New York, 1995), p. 49. For a discussion of the relationship between romantic comedy and melodrama, see also S. Neale and F. Krutnik, *Popular Film and Television Comedy* (London, 1990), pp. 133-6.

[6] According to Rowe (*loc. cit.*, p. 46) their ranks include spinsters, dowagers, prohibitionists, mothers-in-law, librarians, suffragettes, battle-axes, career women, "women's libbers" and lesbians.

[7] Freud, *Jokes and their Relation to the Unconscious* (Penguin Freud Library, vol. 6, 1976), p. 140.

[8] *Ibid.*, p. 145.

[9] D. Zippin, "Sex Differences and the Sense of Humour", *Psychoanalytic Review*, 5.53 (1966), 209-219.

[10] See for example C. Kramarae, *Women and Men Speaking* (Rowley, Mass., 1981), or P. McGhee, "The Role of Laughter and Humor in Growing Up Female", in C. B. Kopp, *Becoming Female: Perspectives on Development* (New York, 1979), pp. 183-206.

[11] M. Apte, *Sexual Inequality in Humor and Laughter: An Anthropological Perspective* (Cornell UP, 1985), p. 81.

[12] This is advised in old etiquette books; but smiling and listening are still considered crucial today, see "How to be the most popular woman you know", *Woman's Journal*, September 1997, pp. 39-40; meanwhile some Japanese and South Asian women consider it polite to cover their mouths when they laugh so as to remain "discreet".

[13] See for example N. Weisstein, "Why Aren't We Laughing Any More?", *Ms*, 49-51 (Nov. 1973), 88-90.

[14] cf. J. Wilt, "The Laughter of Maidens, the Cackle of Matriarchs: Notes on the Collision Between Comedy and Feminism", in *Gender and Literary Voice: Women & Literature*, vol. 1 (new series), ed. J. Todd (New York, 1980), pp. 173-196. Example: "How many feminists does it take to change a light bulb?" "That's not funny."

[15] W. C. Booth, "Freedom of Interpretation: Bakhtin and the Challenge of Feminist Criticism", *Critical Inquiry*, 9 (Sept. 1982), 45-76.

[16] See for example J. R. Cantor, "What is Funny to Whom? The Role of Gender", *Journal of Communication*, 26, no. 3 (Summer 1976), 164-172.

[17] J. Palmer, *Taking Humour Seriously* (London, 1994), p. 72.

[18] A central methodological problem should here be noted in that behavioural researchers tend to make generalisations about the population at large based on research using students.

[19] S. Purdie, *Comedy: The Mastery of Discourse* (London, 1993), p. 126.

[20] *Ibid.*, p. 133.

[21] *Ibid.*, pp. 128-149.

[22] M. Mulkay, *On Humour* (Cambridge, 1988), p. 125.

[23] Quoted in J. Monaco, *The New Wave: Truffaut, Godard, Chabrol, Rohmer, Rivette* (Oxford UP, 1976), p. 42.

[24] q.v. A. Insdorf, *François Truffaut* (Boston, 1978), p. 29.

[25] R. Armes, *French Cinema* (London, 1985), p. 65.

[26] cf. *ibid.*, pp. 67-8.

[27] Quoted in Monaco, *op. cit.*, p. 41.

[28] q.v. R. Armes, *French Cinema since 1946*, vol. 2 (London, 1970), p. 54.

[29] *Ibid.*, p. 52.

[30] Quoted in A. Williams, *Republic of Images: A History of French Film-making* (Harvard UP, 1992), p. 343.

[31] Armes, 1970, p. 54.

[32] N. Frye, *Anatomy of Criticism* (Princeton UP, 1957), p. 182.

[33] Rowe, *loc. cit.*, p. 49.

Bibliography

Ackerley, C. J., "'In the beginning was the pun': Samuel Beckett's *Murphy*", *AUMLA*, 55 (1981).

Amerval, Eloy d', *Le Livre de la Deablerie*, ed. R. Deschaux and B. Charrier, Geneva (Droz), 1991.

Ansbacher, H. and R., eds., *The Individual Psychology of Alfred Adler*, London (Allen and Unwin), 1958.

Apte, M., *Sexual Inequality in Humor and Laughter: An Anthropological Perspective*, Cornell University Press, 1985.

Aristotle, *Poetics*, tr. W. H. Fyfe, Loeb Classical Library, 1927.

Armes, R., *French Cinema*, London (Secker and Warburg), 1985.

- *French Cinema since 1946*, London (Zwemmer), 1970.

Aubailly, J.-C., *Le Théâtre médiéval profane et comique*, Paris (Larousse), 1975.

Auden, W. H., *Collected Poems*, ed. E. Mendelson, London (Faber), 1994.

Austin, J. C., *American Humor in France*, Iowa State University Press, 1978.

Bair, D., *Samuel Beckett*, London (Cape), 1978.

Bakhtin, *Rabelais and his World*, tr. H. Iswolsky, MIT Press, 1968.

Baudin H., et. al., "Humor in France", in *National Styles of Humor*, ed. A. Ziv, New York (Greenwood), 1988.

Bearn, G. C. F., "The Possibility of Puns: A Defense of Derrida", *Philosophy and Literature*, 19.2 (1995).

Beattie, J., "An Essay on Laughter", in *Essays*, ed. B. Fabian, New York (Olms), 1975.

Beevor, A., and A. Cooper, *Paris after the Liberation*, New York (Doubleday), 1994.

Benhamou, P., "L'Humour de Georges Brassens", *Thalia* 3.1 (1980), 17-20.

Bergson, H., *Le Rire*, Paris (PUF), 1947.

Blamires, A., ed., *Woman Defamed and Woman Defended*, Oxford (Clarendon Press), 1992.

Blum, A., "La Caricature politique en France pendant la guerre de 1870-1871", *Revue des Etudes napoléoniennes*, 8 (1919), 301-311.

Booth, W. C., "Freedom of Interpretation: Bakhtin and the Challenge of Feminist Criticism", *Critical Inquiry*, 9 (Sept. 1982), 45-76.

Bordwell D., and K. Thompson, *Film Art: An Introduction*, London (McGraw Hill), 1990.

Bossuet, J.-B., *Maximes et réflexions sur la comédie*, ed. C. Urbain and E. Levesque, Paris (Grasset), 1930.

Boucher, J., *La Vie et faits notables de Henry de Valois*, Paris, 1589.

Breton, A., *Anthologie de l'humour noir*, Paris (Poche), 1972.

Brewer, D., "Notes toward a theory of medieval comedy", in *Medieval Comic Tales*, Cambridge (Brewer), 1973.

Bruncaux, N., *Vie de M. le Baron de Ratapoil, sénateur*, London and Geneva, 1871.

Cahaigne, J., *La Couronne impériale, satire. A Louis-Napoléon-Werhuel, dit Bonaparte*, Jersey, 1853.

Cameron, K., "Henri III - a maligned or malignant king?", in *Aspects of the Satirical Iconography of Henri de Valois*, University of Exeter Press, 1978.

- ed., *Humour and History*, Oxford (Intellect), 1993.

- "La Polémique, la mort de Marie Stuart et l'assassinat de Henri III", in *Henri III et son temps*, ed. R. Sauzet, Paris (Vrin), 1992.

- "L'Illustration au service de la propagande contre Henri III", in *Le livre et l'image en France au XVIe siècle* (Paris, 1989), *Cahiers V.-L. Saulnier* 6, Paris (Presses de l'Ecole Normale Supérieure), 1989, pp. 89-104.

- "Suetonius, Henri de Valois and the Art of Political Biography", *International Journal of the Classical Tradition*, 2 (1995), 284-298.

Campbell, J., "Allusions and Illusions", *French Studies Bulletin*, 53 (1994).

Camus, A., *Le Mythe de Sisyphe*, Paris (Gallimard), 1942.

Cantor, J. R., "What is Funny to Whom? The Role of Gender", *Journal of Communication*, 26, no. 3 (Summer 1976), 164-172.

Céline, L.-F., *Entretiens avec le professeur Y*, Paris (Gallimard), 1955.

Chabanne, T., ed., *Les Salons caricaturaux*, Paris (Réunions des Musées Nationaux), 1990.

Chesterton, G. K., *All Things Considered*, London (Methuen), 1908.

Cook, P., *The Cinema Book*, London (BFI), 1985.

Cooper, L., *An Aristotelian Theory of Comedy*, New York (Harcourt Brace), 1922.

Coquillart, G., *Œuvres*, ed. M. J. Freeman, Geneva (Droz), 1975.

Craig, G., "The Voice of childhood and great age", *TLS*, 27/8/1982.

Dauphiné, J., "Le Jeu de la transgression dans *Les XV joies de mariage*", in *Amour, mariage et transgressions au moyen âge*, ed. D. Buschinger and A. Crépin, Goppingen (Kummerle), 1984, pp. 471-9.

Delany, S., "Anatomy of the resisting reader: some implications of resistance to sexual wordplay in medieval literature", *Exemplaria. A Journal of Theory in Medieval and Renaissance Studies*, 4 (1992), 7-34.

Desnos, R., *Corps et biens*, Paris (Gallimard),1930.

Dostoyevsky, F., *Notes from Underground*, tr. A. MacAndrew, New York (New American Library), 1961.

Du Bos, J.-B., *Réflexions critiques sur la poésie et sur la peinture*, 7th edition, Paris, 1770.

Dufournet, J., "La Génération de Louis XI: quelques aspects", *Le Moyen Age*, 98 (1992), 227-250.

 - *Recherches sur le Testament de François Villon*, 2e édition, 2 vol., Paris (SEDES), 1971-1973.

Dumont, L., *Des causes du rire*, Paris, 1862.

Elias, N., *The Court Society*, Oxford (Blackwell), 1983.

Emelina, J., *Le Comique: essai d'interprétation générale*, Paris (SEDES), 1991.

Emerson, R. W., *Collected Works*, vol. 1, London, 1866.

Empson, W., *Collected Poems*, London (Hogarth), 1977.

Etiemble, R., *Parlez-vous franglais*, Paris (Gallimard), 1964.

Fabre, F., "La Fontaine s'amuse", *Thalia* 4.1 (1981), 33-39.

Faranjus, S.,"Allocution d'ouverture", published in *Humoresques*, vol. 1, Nice (Z'Editions), 1990, 16-22.

Fierro, A., *Histoire et dictionnaire de Paris*, Paris (Laffont), 1996.

Fox, J., *The Poetry of Fifteenth-Century France*, 2 vol., London (Grant and Cutler), 1994.

Freeman, M., "Aspects du théâtre comique français des XVe et XVIe siècles: la sottie, le monologue dramatique et le sermon joyeux", in *Le Théâtre au Moyen Age*, Montreal (Aurore/Univers), 1981, pp. 279-298.

 - "La Satire affectueuse dans les *Droitz nouveaulx* de Guillaume Coquillart", in *Réforme Humanisme Renaissance*, 11 (1980), 92-99.

Freud, S., *Jokes and Their Relation to the Unconscious*, tr. J. Strachey, Penguin Freud Library, vol. 6, 1976.

Frye, N., *Anatomy of Criticism*, Princeton University Press, 1957.

Gaines, J. F., "Social Structures in Molière's Theater", Ohio State University Press, 1984.

Garbaty, T. J., "Chaucer and Comedy", in Ruggiers, 1977, pp. 173-190.

Gauna, M., *The Rabelaisian Mythologies*, London (Associated University Presses), 1996.

Gifford, P., "Humour and the French mind", *Modern Language Review*, 76 (1981), 534-548.

Girard, R., *Le Bouc émissaire*, Paris (Grasset), 1982.

Grand-Carteret, J., *L'Histoire - la vie - les moeurs et la curiosité par l'image, le pamphlet et le document (1450-1900)*, Paris (Bibliothèque de la Curisoité et des Beaux-Arts), 1927-28.

Gray, F,. *La Bruyère: amateur de caractères*, Paris (Nizet), 1986.

Guiraud, P., *Les Jeux de mots*, Paris (PUF), 1976.

Halkin, H., Introduction to Sholem Aleichem's *Tevye the Dairyman*, New York (Schocken), 1987.

Haswell, J., *The Man of His Time. The Story of the Life of Napoleon III. By James M. Haswell. The Same Story as told by Popular Caricaturists of the last thirty years*, London, 1871.

Henkle, R. B., "Beckett and the Comedy of Bourgeois Experience", *Thalia* 3.1 (1980), 35-39.

Hornik, H., "Three Interpretations of the French Renaissance", in *French Humanism 1460-1600*, ed. W. L. Gundersheimer, London (Macmillan), 1969, pp. 19-47.

Howarth, W. D., "La Notion de la catharsis dans la comédie française classique", *Revue des Sciences Humaines*, 152 (1973), 521-539.

 - "Un Etranger devant le comique français", *Le Français dans le monde* (February/March 1980), 31-5.

Huizinga, J., *The Waning of the Middle Ages: A Study of the Forms of Life, Thought and Art in France and the Netherlands in the XIVth and XVth Centuries*, tr. F. Hopman, London (Arnold), 1924.

Hunt, T., *Villon's Last Will. Language and Authority in the Testament*, Oxford (Clarendon), 1996.

Insdorf, A., *François Truffaut*, Boston (Twayne), 1978.

Jacobson, H., *Seriously Funny: from the Ridiculous to the Sublime*, London (Viking), 1997.

Jeanson, F., *Signification humaine du rire*, Paris (Seuil), 1950.

Johnson, L. W., *Poets as Players: Theme and Variation in Late Medieval French Poetry*, Stanford University Press, 1990.

Juvenal, *Satires*, tr. G. G. Ramsay, Loeb Classical Library, 1940.

Kant, I., *Critique of Judgment*, tr. J. C. Meredith, Oxford (Clarendon Press), 1952.

Kasprzyk, N., "Les XV joies d'un mariage", in *Mélanges offerts à Jean Frappier*, Geneva (Droz), 1970, pp. 499-508.

Kern, E., *The Absolute Comic*, Columbia University Press, 1980.

Kierkegaard, S., *Repetition*, tr. W. Lowrie, Oxford University Press, 1942.

Kirsch, D., *La Bruyère ou le style cruel*, Presses de l'Université de Montréal, 1977.

Koestler, A., *The Act of Creation*, London (Hutchinson), 1964.

Kramarae, C., *Women and Men Speaking*, Rowley, Mass. (Newbury House), 1981.

Kunzle, D., *The Early Comic Strip*, University of California Press, 1973.

La Bruyère, J. de, *Œuvres complètes*, ed. J. Benda, Paris (Pléiade), 1951.

Laffay, A., *Anatomie de l'humour et du nonsense*, Paris (Masson), 1970.

Lalo, C., *Esthétique du rire*, Paris (Flammarion), 1949.

Lamb, C., *The Essays of Elia*, London, 1849.

Lambert, S., *The Franco-Prussian War and the Commune in Caricature 1870-71*, London (Victoria and Albert Museum), 1971.

Lathem, E. C., ed., *The Poetry of Robert Frost*, London (Cape), 1972.

Lawrence, F. L., *Molière: the Comedy of Unreason*, Tulane University Press, 1968.

Le Goff, J., "Rire au Moyen Age", *Cahiers du Centre de recherches historiques*, 3 (1989), 1-14.

Legman, G., *No Laughing Matter*, London (Cape), 1981.

McGhee, P., "The Role of Laughter and Humor in Growing Up Female", in C. B. Kopp, *Becoming Female: Perspectives on Development*, New York (Plenum Press), 1979, pp. 183-206.

Mabbott, T. O., ed., *Collected Works of Edgar Allan Poe*, Harvard University Press, 1978-9.

Magen, H., *Histoire du Second Empire*, Paris, 1878.

- *Les Nuits et le Mariage de César, par L. Stelli*, Jersey, 1853.

- *Prostitutions, Débauches et crimes de la famille Buonaparte*, London, 1871.

- *Les Tyrans et le Tyrannicide jugés par l'histoire*, London, 1858.

Mauron, C., *Psychocritique du genre comiqe*, Paris (Corti), 1964.

Mazaheri, H., *La Satire démystificatrice de La Bruyère*, New York (Lang), 1995.

McBride, R., *The Sceptical Vision of Molière*, London (Macmillan), 1977.

Ménard, P., "Le Rire et le sourire au moyen âge dans la littérature et dans les arts. Essai de problématique", in *Le Rire au Moyen Age*, textes recueillis par T. Bouché et H. Charpentier, Presses Universitaires de Bordeaux, 1990, pp. 7-30.

- *Le Rire et le sourire dans le roman courtois en France au moyen âge*, Geneva (Droz), 1969.

Meredith, G., "On the Idea of Comedy", in *Complete Works*, vol. 23, London, 1898.

Mermier, G., "La Ruse féminine et la fonction morale des *Quinze Joies de Mariage*", *Romance Notes*, 15 (1973-4), 455-503.

Michelet, J., *La Renaissance, Histoire de France*, vol. 9, Paris, 1899.

Miller, H., *The Books in My Life*, London (Owen), 1961.

- *Flash Back*, Paris (Stock), 1976.

- *Tropic of Capricorn*, Paris (Obelisk Press), 1939.

Moi, T., *Sexual/Textual Politics: Feminist Literary Theory*, London (Methuen), 1985.

Monaco, J., *The New Wave: Truffaut, Godard, Chabrol, Rohmer, Rivette*, Oxford University Press, 1976.

Monro, D. H., *Argument of Laughter*, Melbourne University Press, 1951.

Montesquieu, C. de, *Œuvres complètes*, Paris (Pléiade), 1949.

Moore, W. G., *Molière: A New Criticism*, Oxford (Clarendon), 1949.

Mulkay, M., *On Humour*, Cambridge (Polity), 1988.

Murphy, S., *Rimbaud et la ménagerie impériale*, Presses Universitaires de Lyon, 1991.

Neale, S., and F. Krutnik, *Popular Film and Television Comedy*, London (Routledge), 1990.

D'Orléans, H., duc d'Aumale, *A Napoléon III. Qu'avez-vous fait de la France? Complément à la lettre du 15 mars 1861*, London, 1867.

Orwell, G., *Collected Essays*, vol. 2, Harmondsworth (Penguin), 1970.

- *Nineteen Eighty-Four*, Oxford (Clarendon), 1984.

Pagnol, M., *Notes sur le rire*, Paris (Pastorelly),1982.

Palmer, J., *Taking Humour Seriously*, London (Routledge), 1994.

Parkin, J., *Humour Theorists of the Twentieth Century*, Lewiston (Mellen), 1997.

Passeron, R., *Daumier*, Oxford (Phaidon), 1981.

Peeters, L., *La Roulette aux mots*, Paris (Pensée Universelle), 1975.

Plessis, A., *The Rise and Fall of the Second Empire, 1862-1871*, tr. J. Mandelbaum, Cambridge University Press, 1979.

Poirion, D., "Déclin ou décadence: une confusion du sens et des valeurs", in *Apogée et déclin. Actes du Colloque de l'URA 411, Provins, 1991*, Textes réunis par C. Thomasset et M. Zink, Presses de l'Université de Paris, 1993, pp. 293-304.

Purdie, S., *Comedy: The Mastery of Discourse*, London (Harvester), 1993.

Queneau, R., *Zazie dans le Métro*, Paris (Gallimard), 1959.

Recueil général des sotties, ed. E. Picot, 3 vol., Paris (Didot), 1902-1912.

Rabelais, F., *Œuvres complètes*, ed. M. Huchon, Paris (Pléiade), 1994.

Ramier, E., *Les Mémoires de Badinguet*, Brussels, London and Leipzig, 1869.

Rowe, K., "Comedy, Melodrama and Gender", in *Classical Hollywood Comedy*, ed. K. Karnick and H. Jenkins, New York (Routledge), 1995.

Roy. B., *Une culture de l'équivoque*, Presses Universitaires de Montréal, 1992.

Ruggiers, P. G., ed., *Versions of Medieval Comedy*, University of Oklahoma Press, 1977.

Rutten, R., et. al., *Die Karikatur zwischen Republik und Zensur*, Marburg (Jonas), 1991.

Santucci, J., "Pour une interprétation nouvelle des *Quinze Joies de Mariage*", in *Le Récit bref au moyen âge*, ed. D. Buschinger, Paris (Champion), 1983, pp. 153-179.

Saulnier, C., *Le Sens du comique: essai sur le caractère esthétique du rire*, Paris (Vrin), 1940.

Schopenhauer, A., *The World as Will and Representation*, tr. E. F. J. Payne, New York (Dover), 1969.

Schrempp, G., "Our Funny Universe", *Humor*, 8.3 (1995), 219-228.

Screech, M. A., *Rabelais*, London (Duckworth), 1979.

Scully D. E., and T. Scully, *Early French Cookery*, University of Michigan Press, 1995.

Siciliano, I., *François Villon et les thèmes poétiques du moyen âge*, Paris (Colin),1934.

Silex, P., *La Chronique Bonapartiste scandaleuse. Histoires véridiques, anecdotiques et galantes*, Brussels, 1871.

Sosthène-Berthellot, M. C., *Essai sur le caractère et les tendances de l'Empereur Napoléon III d'après ses écrits et ses actes*, Paris, 1858.

Soucy, A.-M., "Le Rire dans l'oeuvre de Baudelaire", *Thalia* 9.2 (1987), 32-39.

Spencer, R. H., "The Treatment of Women in the *Roman de la Rose*, the Fabliaux and the *Quinze Joies de Mariage*", *Marche Romane*, 28 (1979), 207-214.

Sprigge, T., "Schopenhauer and Bergson on Laughter", *Comparative Criticism*, 10 (1988), 39-65.

Stern, J. P., *Lichtenberg: a doctrine of scattered occasions*, Indiana University Press, 1959.

Stravinsky, I., *The Poetics of Music*, Oxford University Press, 1947.

Strumingher, S., "Die Vesuviennes: Bilder von Kriegerinnen im Jahre 1848 und ihre Bedeutung für die französische Geschichte", in Rutten, 1991, pp. 260-276.

Swabey, M. C., *Comic Laughter: a Philosophical Essay*, Yale University Press, 1961.

Taylor, S. S. B., "Voltaire's humour", *SVEC*, 179 (1979), 101-116.

Le Testament de Néro tel qu'il a été dicté le 19 janvier 1867 à son très humble et dévoué sujet Georges Sauton, Paris, 1868.

Thiry, C., "L'altérité du rire médiéval: la farce et son public", in *Der Ursprung von Literatur*, ed. G. Smolka-Koerdt et al., Munich (Fink), 1988.

Thibaudet, A., "Molière et la critique", *Revue de Paris*, March 1930.

- "Le Rire de Molière", *Revue de Paris*, January 1922.

Thompson, I., "Latin 'Elegiac Comedy' of the Twelfth Century", in Ruggiers, 1977, pp. 51-66.

Thompson, J. M., *Louis Napoleon and the Second Empire*, Columbia University Press, 1983.

Tissier, A., ed., *Recueil de farces (1450-1550)*, tome X, Geneva (Droz), 1996.

Truffaut, F., "A Certain Tendency of the French Cinema", in B. Nichols (ed.), *Movies and Methods*, University of California Press, 1976, pp. 224-237.

Vésinier, P., *L'Histoire du nouveau César*, London, 1865.

Waldstedt, G., *Des Teufels Minister, Zeitdichtung*, Oserburg, 1870.

Wathelet-Willem, J., "Note sur les *Quinze Joies de Mariage*", in *Etudes offertes à Jules Horrent*, Liège (D'Heur), 1980, pp. 517-529.

Weisstein, N., "Why Aren't We Laughing Any More?", *Ms*, 49-51 (Nov. 1973), 88-90.

Williams, A., *Republic of Images: A History of French Film-making*, Harvard University Press, 1992.

Wilt, J., "The Laughter of Maidens, the Cackle of Matriarchs: Notes on the Collision Between Comedy and Feminism", in *Gender and Literary Voice: Women & Literature*, vol. 1 (new series), ed. J. Todd, New York (Holmes and Meier), 1980.

Zippin, D., "Sex Differences and the Sense of Humour", *Psychoanalytic Review*, 5.53 (1966), 209-219.

Index